The Last Man
on the Mountain

K2 base camp, 1939. *(Courtesy of the George C. Sheldon Family)*

The Last Man on the Mountain

---

*The Death of an
American Adventurer on K2*

JENNIFER JORDAN

W. W. NORTON & COMPANY • New York London

For information about permission to reproduce
selections from this book, write to Permissions,
W. W. Norton & Company, Inc.,
500 Fifth Avenue, New York, NY 10110

For information about special discounts for bulk
purchases, please contact W. W. Norton Special Sales
at specialsales@wwnorton.com or 800-233-4830

Manufacturing by RR Donnelley, Harrisonburg
Book design by Helene Berinsky
Production manager: Anna Oler

Library of Congress Cataloging-in-Publication Data

Jordan, Jennifer, 1958–
The last man on the mountain : the death of an
American adventurer on K2 / Jennifer Jordan. — 1st ed.
p. cm.
Includes bibliographical references and index.
ISBN 978-0-393-07778-0 (hardcover)
1. Mountaineering—Pakistan—K2 (Mountain)
2. Mountaineering accidents—Pakistan—K2 (Mountain)
3. Wolfe, Dudley. 4. Mountaineers—United States—Biography.
5. K2 (Pakistan : Mountain) I. Title.
GV199.44.P18J67 2010
796.522092—dc22
[B]

2010014201

W. W. Norton & Company, Inc.
500 Fifth Avenue, New York, N.Y. 10110
www.wwnorton.com

W. W. Norton & Company Ltd.
Castle House, 75/76 Wells Street, London W1T 3QT

1 2 3 4 5 6 7 8 9 0

Charlie Houston
1913–2009
Last of the Golden Age

(I know that I can't keep dedicating my books to him,
but I will always want to.)

Contents

Preface

I have been a journalist for thirty years, but it wasn't until I began researching *The Last Man on the Mountain* that I learned that history is deeply flawed. Not necessarily wrong or deliberately misleading —I simply discovered the extent to which history is sketched by the pen of its writer. In the case of Dudley Wolfe, from his ancestors in seventeenth-century Maine to recent mentions of the infamous 1939 expedition in books and articles, I found errors, omissions, prejudices, selective arguments, and deliberate falsehoods. There was also the effect of high altitude I had to take into account. In few areas is history more skewed than in Himalayan climbing: witnesses often suffer oxygen deprivation and acute mountain sickness, adding to the fog through which history is remembered and written.

As a result, I had to deconstruct the account you are about to read to its essential pieces before reassembling it. Certain "irrefutable facts" were questioned and some interesting skeletons fell out of the closet.

Finally, I have employed a tactic used effectively by many writers, notably Sebastian Junger in his brilliant account of the *Andrea Gail*'s sinking off the Grand Banks in 1991, *The Perfect Storm*, and I did it for the same reason: it is impossible to re-create the actual dialogue of the dead with no living witnesses to the event. Therefore, in the pages that follow there are two forms of the spoken word: direct quotes, which I gathered from journals, letters, books, and witnesses, and speech given in italics, representing thoughts and conversations based on the facts I could gather, but which to my knowledge is not verbatim.

Therefore, seventy years after his death, let me introduce you to the Dudley Francis Wolfe I discovered.

Jennifer Jordan
Salt Lake City
January 2010

The Last Man
on the Mountain

The Godwin–Austen Glacier, K2, July 2002

Naked of life, naked of warmth and safety, bare to the sun and stars, beautiful in its stark snow loneliness, the Mountain waits.

—ELIZABETH KNOWLTON, *The Naked Mountain*

Dudley Wolfe's skeletal remains found in 2002. (*Jennifer Jordan / Jeff Rhoads*)

On a sunny afternoon with a breeze light enough to bring fresh air into base camp but not so stiff that I needed a parka, I found myself carefully picking my way among the uneven rocks, ice towers, crevasses, and run-off rivulets of the Godwin–Austen Glacier at the base of the world's second highest mountain, K2, in Pakistan.

A few years earlier, I had learned that only five women had reached the summit of K2, and all of them were dead. Three perished on their descent, and the two that had managed to make it off the so-called Savage Mountain alive had died soon after while attempting other 8,000-meter peaks, a legendary distinction which separates the fourteen Himalayan giants which stand above the mark from the countless peaks which sit below it. Just as hikers in the Rocky Mountains aim for all of Colorado's fifty-three "14ers," those mountains at and above 14,000 feet, high-altitude climbers aim for all fourteen of the Himalayan "8,000ers." High-altitude mountaineering is not a sport for the faint-hearted, and K2 is not a peak for weekend warriors. As of the 2009 climbing season, 297 people have reached its summit, while seventy-eight have died trying.

That summer of 2002, when I made my second trip to the mountain, while our team* climbed, I spent my mornings working on my first book, *Savage Summit*, and my afternoons walking the glacier, becoming as familiar with the rocky, shifting river of ice as I was with the Wasatch Mountains in my own backyard in Salt Lake City. The glacier offered a fascinating array of odds and ends. Because of K2's topography and climate—steep rock walls and icy slopes, avalanches and hurricane-force winds—everything

---

* Araceli Segarra of Spain, Hector Ponce de Leon and Armando Dattoli de la Vega of Mexico, and cameramen/climbers Jeff Rhoads and Jeff Cunningham of the United States.

and everyone that has ever been on the mountain eventually ends up at its base. I rarely returned to base camp from my hikes without some relic, harmless or horrific, of climbers past.

That sunny July day, while some of our team rested in their tents waiting for the mountain to shed a layer of avalanches from the latest storm, I started out on my afternoon walk. Because I had fallen into a crevasse in 2000 on our first trip to K2, my partner, high-altitude climber and cinematographer Jeff Rhoads, worried that I would disappear into another, and whenever possible accompanied me on my walks. We got further away from our tents than we ever had before, venturing down the glacier rather than our usual up it, picking our way over rock-strewn ice through the maze of ice towers. Then, about a mile off track, we turned a corner and found ourselves standing in a frozen sea of debris. While I had stumbled upon climbing rubble all summer, even the occasional desiccated body, this collection of relics was different. Unlike the bright parkas and nylon tents used by climbers since the 1970s, here was evidence from another era. Slowly we picked up fragments of canvas, leather straps, hemp rope, a rusted crampon, a tin plate and pot, even a burner plate from an old Primus stove. Then, my eyes picked something out of the rocks and rubble that I knew shouldn't be there: a bone fragment. It looked like a white pencil stub, rounded by years of exposure to the rocks and sun. I picked it up and wordlessly handed it to Jeff, fearing the worst but knowing the truth.

"Yup," he said, rather casually, "definitely human. See the calcified marrow inside?"

I hadn't seen the marrow. He handed it back and said, "Probably a piece of the ulna." I gazed at the shard in my glove and pictured the once bronzed arm from which it had come. I placed it on a piece of torn canvas, unwilling to hold it any longer.

I rejoined Jeff in picking through the old wreckage. As he went off around an icy corner, I bent to look more closely at what appeared to be a shock of long white hair. Repulsed and yet fascinated, I was considering whether to pick it up when something to the right caught my eye. There, laid out on the rocks and ice, was the very recognizable skeleton of a human being: the pelvis, two femurs, and scattered ribs.

With tears stinging my eyes, I squatted to look at the bleached bones. Even though I had come to know that high-altitude climbing is the deadliest of adventures, having the evidence in front of me was shocking. I felt sad, not only for the person at my feet but for his or her family thousands of miles of away, a family which never had the chance to say goodbye. It reminded me of a moment years before when I walked through a World War II cemetery at El Alamein in northern Egypt and saw a gravestone reading, "You are closer to my son than I will ever be. Please say a prayer for his Mother." Like that graveyard in Egypt, this one at the base of K2 echoed in silence. I cried then and I cried now at being so intimately connected to another person's loss.

Jeff's sharp whistle cut through the air. I whistled in response and stood up so he could find me. He appeared around an ice tower with a strange look on his face, and carrying something carefully in his hands. It was a weather-beaten canvas and leather mitten. On its cuff was a single name written in faded block letters: WOLFE.

Dudley Wolfe. We had found Dudley Wolfe, an American who had disappeared on K2 in 1939. After sixty-three years, K2's first fatality, and its most prolonged mystery, had finally been found.

Chapter 1

An Invitation to the Ends of the Earth

> *So, if you cannot understand that there is something in man*
> *which responds to the challenge of this mountain and goes out*
> *to meet it, that the struggle of life is itself upward and forever*
> *upward, then you won't see why we go.*
>
> —George Leigh Mallory

Dudley Wolfe at the helm of the *Highland Light*, August 1931.
(Courtesy of the Dudley F. Rochester and Dudley F. Wolfe Family)

It was 1938 and Dudley Wolfe needed an adventure.

At forty-two, he had already done more than most men do in a lifetime, from driving an ambulance on the front lines in Europe during the Great War to hunting caribou in the Canadian Rockies and racing his custom-made schooners across thousands of miles of open ocean. But now, as he entertained guests in his New York penthouse with a slide show of his latest skiing and climbing trips through Europe, he realized he needed something more.

He looked over at his wife, Alice, as she walked through the dimly lit room refilling their guests' wine glasses. She was a strong, attractive woman who, although four years his senior, had bested him on the ski slopes more times than he could count. Their marriage had been a whirlwind of travel between her hunting lodge in Austria, his summer estate in Maine, and this apartment on Fifth Avenue overlooking Central Park. And while it had been a loving and comfortable marriage, it wasn't enough to sustain him for the long term. He had been single thirty-eight years before they married and he had come to realize that he preferred being on his own. Alone, but not lonely—independent. Free to pick up and go without explanation or apology. He hated to hurt her, but it wasn't fair to either of them to stay in a marriage simply for convenience and comfort. They both deserved to have passion. For nearly a year he had tried to explain to Alice why he wanted to end the marriage, but she was still very much in love with him and with their life together. She had finally and regretfully agreed that if he would be happier alone, they would separate. The divorce would be final in a few weeks.

Dudley turned his attention back to the images of his climbs on the Matterhorn, Mont Blanc, and the Italian peaks around

Monte Rosa as they flashed on the screen at one end of the living room. He explained each picture and answered questions on how crevasses formed in glaciers, how heavy the nearly three-foot-long wood-handled ice axe was, how the steel crampons helped you climb ice walls, how the double-layer wool pants with long underwear underneath were perfectly adequate in subzero temperatures and hurricane winds, and, always, what he and Alice thought of the rumors of war in Europe.

When the last slide clicked out of its slot in the projector, the room went momentarily dark and there was a polite spray of applause. Then the lights came on and people rose from their seats, stretched, and headed to the bar for another drink, chatting about Europe and the mountains and Dudley's wonderful adventures.

Watching the small crowd of his and Alice's friends move about the room, Dudley saw that one guest had remained in his seat. Alice and he had met the man two years earlier at a cocktail party at the home of one of Alice's Upper East Side friends. Born in Dresden, Germany, Fritz Wiessner was a mountaineer who had come to the States a decade before and had amazed the American climbing community with his grace and skill on some of America's toughest cliff faces. As Dudley looked across the couch at Wiessner now, he liked what he saw. The man was competent, self-assured, educated, and built like a rock climber: short, lean, and strong. He reminded Dudley of his favorite climbing guide in the Alps—a man of purpose.

From the couch, Wiessner was taking in his surroundings. He too liked what he saw. The room was utterly white: white walls, white curtains, white floors, white leather furniture, white roses on the piano. Even the wine was white. The scene was a masterpiece of simple elegance. Then he turned to study Wolfe. The man was shy, gentle, and cheerful, and he was built like a football player with a barrel chest and thick, strong arms and legs. Quietly handsome with an infectious smile and impeccable grooming, Wolfe wore his money without embellishment. Sitting in Wolfe's lovely home high above Fifth Avenue, Fritz could see that Wolfe surrounded himself with the finest of everything: sterling silver ashtrays and candy dishes with "DFW" engraved into their bowls, starched Irish lace draping the grand piano, priceless oils by Cézanne and Renoir on the walls. Even the crystal wine glass Fritz held in his hand was exquisitely cut, hand-blown Austrian lead. Unlike other fabulously rich people Fritz had met, Wolfe didn't mention his wealth or the cost of anything. He was more refined than most, particularly most rich Americans, and Fritz appreciated that.

As other guests milled comfortably about the room, Dudley asked Fritz what he had been up to since they had last met. Fritz began with great enthusiasm to explain his latest endeavor, and Dudley listened attentively to every detail.

Wiessner was planning an expedition. Not just any expedition, but one to the top of the world—a deadly region high in the Himalayan Mountains. After man had conquered the planet's poles, its oceans, and its deserts, he had turned to its roof as the last frontier on which he could stake his claim. While the sport of mountaineering had begun in 1854 when Sir Alfred Wills ascended the Wetterhorn (12,000 feet) in southern Switzerland, no one had yet conquered any of the Himalayan giants, although several early attempts had met with death: Alfred Mummery and two Sherpas on Nanga Parbat in 1895, George Mallory and Sandy Irvine on Mount Everest in 1924, and then in 1934, again on Nanga Parbat, twenty-six members of an expedition of the Third Reich perished in an avalanche. In fact many experts had begun to doubt whether the ice, the snow, the nearly vertical rock faces, the punishing cold, and above all the scant oxygen at such an altitude, would allow man to reach the summit of the world and return alive. But the mountaineering and scientific communities were determined to show they could.

As he listened, Dudley learned that Wiessner was aiming to scale the second highest mountain in the world, known as K2, which sat on the Chinese–Indian border at the western edge of the remote Karakoram range. In the high-stakes post–World War I race to reach and claim these alpine giants, Mount Everest had been all but reserved by the British, while American climbers were looking at K2 as theirs for the conquering. For decades explorers and climbers had tried and failed to get much above K2's base camp at 16,500 feet, Wiessner said, but an American expedition which had just returned from the mountain had climbed to within 2,000 feet of the 28,250-foot summit. Learning from the 1938 team's mistakes, Wiessner assured Dudley, his own team the following summer would succeed. The challenge was great; the achievement would be extraordinary.

Dudley Wolfe listened, rapt, as Fritz described the six-month trip, the awe-inspiring mountain, its location, the 330-mile trek from Srinagar in northern India to a natural spot for base camp, and, of course, the 12,000-foot ascent from that camp to the mountain's summit.

Nearby, Alice looked at Dudley's face, then at Fritz's, not liking what she saw on either. She didn't know Fritz well but she recognized a sales pitch when she saw one. And, Dudley, whom she did know, was taking the bait, hard. She knew Dudley was strong and incredibly determined, but he was also facing his forty-third birthday in February and, while he had done a lot of climbing in the Alps, it had been on other men's ropes. Besides, K2 was twice the size of anything they had ever seen, let alone tried to climb. No one even knew if the human body could survive for weeks at altitudes which balloonists had visited for mere minutes—and in several cases those balloonists had been found dead when the balloon finally descended to earth. For heaven's sake, this K2 was 20,000 feet *higher* than her last trip in an airplane, a trip where most of the passengers became dizzy and sick from the altitude! No, she thought, this is too much for Dudley. Yes, he had seen his share of danger and death on the front lines in 1917 and 1918, but somehow this was different. This was more personal. This was closer to the bone. She edged nearer to their conversation.

Fritz's next words to Dudley confirmed her fears: "Maybe you should come on my expedition to this K2."*

The air in the room seemed to stop moving as Alice looked from Dudley to Fritz and back to Dudley again. She knew he was excited at the offer but, as was typical of him, he remained reserved and measured in his response, questioning whether he had enough experience to handle such a mountain.

I've only been climbing a few years in the Alps, Fritz. Do you think I've enough experience to tackle such a mountain? Dudley asked.

Wiessner assured Dudley he did. What was needed, Fritz told him, was strength, balance, endurance, and determination, all of which Dudley seemed to have in abundance. Wiessner, with over twenty years of experience, would lead the team to and up the mountain, assuring the route was secure and, where necessary, anchoring it with guide ropes to guarantee that all members returned safe. Dudley would have a qualified guide every step of the way.

Dudley mulled over the conversation as his attention was diverted to other guests. As soon as she politely could, Alice pulled Fritz aside.

---

* Observation by Betty Woolsey, who was in attendance.

"You shouldn't persuade Dudley to go on such a hazardous trip," she said. "He is an older man than the other members of the expedition and he would not be equal to it."*

Fritz assured her Dudley would be fine—that he, Wiessner, was an experienced guide and that Dudley would be perfectly safe climbing with him.

Alice looked at Fritz. She could see that he was just as determined to take Dudley as Dudley was to go. She knew she couldn't do anything more to protect the man she still loved, divorce or no divorce. With a heavy heart, she stepped away from Fritz and out of the conversation, promising herself not to burden Dudley with her concern again.

For the rest of the evening, Dudley walked through the party lost in thought. He was emboldened. He had loved the challenge of getting his small schooners across thousands of miles of wild ocean; just men and boat against forces beyond their control. This expedition, to a place and an altitude where men had never gone, would test him in ways he could only imagine. He would be out there, defining what it means to achieve a goal through mean survival, not as a pampered client in a gaming preserve or on his guide's rope above Zermatt. On this expedition, there wouldn't be any qualifiers to his achievement. It would be a pure feat and it would be his. His brother Clifford wouldn't look down his nose at it and Alice wouldn't consider him just another client of one of her many guide friends in St. Anton. And he would experience what centuries of explorers and pioneers had: the sheer joy found in hard-won success through physical endurance.

When the two men were again seated on the couch, Dudley looked at the diminutive yet powerful man sitting across from him.

---

* Again, an observation by Betty Woolsey in attendance.

He suspected Fritz might be a tough leader; he had seen that type of arrogant swagger at the boatyards and on the front lines. But with his quiet resolve he had always been able to manage large, loud egos.

After several more moments, he reached across to shake Wiessner's hand and sign up for the 1939 American Expedition to K2.

Chapter 2

The Gentleman Soldier and Sailor

Solitude is a silent storm that breaks down all our dead branches. Yet it sends our living roots deeper into the living heart of the living earth. Man struggles to find life outside himself, unaware that the life he is seeking is within . . .

—KAHLIL GIBRAN

In Genesis it says that it is not good for a man to be alone, but sometimes it is a great relief.

—JOHN BARRYMORE

Dudley Wolfe in his French Foreign Legion uniform, 1919. *(Courtesy of the Dudley F. Rochester and Dudley F. Wolfe Family)*

Rockport, Maine—1907

Dudley Francis Cecil Wolfe stood at the helm of his beloved fifteen-foot sloop watching the wind change course across the water of Glen Cove inside the larger Penobscot Bay. Feeling each of the wind's ripples in his fingertips as he teased the rudder in tiny flicks, he smoothly brought the boat back toward the shore where the family's hired boatkeeper waited on the dock. Dudley was eleven years old and this was his maiden sail as captain.

Some children are born with a silver spoon in their mouths; Dudley had the entire mine, thanks to his grandfather, B. F. Smith.

Benjamin Franklin Smith and his three brothers had, in little more than forty years, created an eight-figure fortune from nothing but their own prescience, persistence, and pluck. From their family farm in the hills of Berwick, Maine, the four men set out in the 1840s to make their way in the world, eventually joining the wagon train west. But unlike the dusty pioneers with whom they shared the trail, the Smith brothers had already made enough money in publishing and commissioned lithographs to start a bank in Omaha. From those profits they bought stakes in quartz, silver, and gold mines in Colorado, one of which was the prolific Briggs Pocket in the Gregory Tailings discovered in the mid-1800s. More interested in building capital than in running the mine, they sold their gold as shares on the New York Stock Exchange at the height of the market, earning several times what the gold was worth on the scales back in Colorado, and they turned that money into real estate, railroads, and the second largest stockyard in the country.

By the time the Smith brothers returned to Maine in the 1880s to build a vast summer estate overlooking Penobscot Bay, they had amassed a fortune rumored to be somewhere between twenty and thirty million dollars—more than $450 million today. But while they were proficient in business, they were less successful in producing heirs. Their grandparents had had twelve children, ten of them boys, and their parents had had six children, four of them boys, but Francis, George Warren, and David Clifford Smith had no legal heirs.* The Smith family name was therefore left to the youngest brother, B. F., to carry on. While B. F. had a son, Clifford Warren Smith, in 1868, it was his daughter, Mabel Florence Smith, who would provide him with the heirs which the family so desperately wanted.

Mabel had the strong features of her father and uncles: dark, wide-set eyes in a square face, thin lips, and a broad forehead. Too determined-looking to be considered pretty, she had an arresting self-confidence and the look of a woman who enjoyed her place in the world. In 1891, when she was twenty-six, Mabel met a dashing Englishman dressed in the fashionable four-button long coat of the times, who offered all of the charm and mystery her life in the dusty mining towns and cattle yards of Colorado and Omaha had not. His name was Dudley Wolfe.

Expertly groomed and trim, Dudley Wolfe had the effete good looks of gentility: an aquiline nose, cleft chin, neat mustache, and startlingly clear blue eyes. After disembarking from Liverpool and filling out his immigration papers in 1888 at the age of twenty-nine, he ventured off to find his fortune in the bustling, dusty, horse-and-buggy-filled streets of lower Manhattan. Once established as a

---

* Although he remained childless in his marriage, Francis Smith sent $50 a month (roughly $1,120 today) to a woman, Imogene Tappan of Concord, New Hampshire, to support a girl he called his ward, Helen Tappan, from 1884 until 1905 when she turned twenty-one. There is no record to determine whether in fact Helen was his daughter, although such ongoing support suggests she was. Also, the fact that Francis kept the receipts as well as Helen's written confirmation of the final payment, releasing him from further financial obligation, indicates he wanted an assurance against any future claims to the Smith estate which a child, even if illegitimate, might bring.

coffee and nut trader, and with a genuine enjoyment of opera and the arts, he mixed easily in the upper-class English and American societies of New York. At dinners hosted by visiting English nobility at the Waldorf, St. Denis, and Brunswick hotels, Dudley Wolfe would charm and entertain tables of rapt diners with tales of his youth in India hunting tigers and visiting the Taj Mahal. At one such gathering he met one of the richest young women in America, and on October 15, 1892, at the Grace Church in New York City, Dudley Wolfe took Mabel Florence Smith as his wife. They quickly started their family and over the next eight years had four children: Clifford Warren, Dudley Francis Cecil, Gwendolen Florence, and Grafton.

If it looked like a fairy tale, in fact that's all it was. While presenting himself as a successful coffee importer, living on an estate in the Connecticut suburb of Harrison-on-the-Sound, Dudley was actually on the brink of financial collapse, and the year after he and Mabel married, he and his partner in the import business declared bankruptcy. Nonetheless, only months after the bankruptcy, Dudley organized the Knollwood Golf Club in Elmsford, New York, with fellow founders Oliver and H. M. Harriman, William Rockefeller, and Frederick Bull, which boasted one of the nation's first full eighteen-hole courses designed by the famous Scotsman Willie Park. Dudley moved his family to the nearby town of Irvington-on-Hudson, twenty miles north of Manhattan. He and Mabel sent their four young children to the best boarding schools money and breeding could command, the boys to Hackley Hall in Tarrytown, New York, and Gwendolen to Miss Porter's in Farmington, Connecticut.

While it was a life of privilege, it was also a very staid, almost impersonal, one. The Wolfes did not meet at the dinner table and hear of each other's day in funny and boisterous detail. Mabel was not a warm, natural mother who easily wrapped them in her arms. They barely saw their father. When they did, he never spoke of his own childhood and memories; when they would ask of his parents, their grandparents, Dudley Senior would grow silent and withdraw even further. The children spent most of their young lives with servants and at the age of eight each was shipped off to his or her boarding school.

In May 1908 whatever sense of family they had came crashing down when Dudley Wolfe, Sr., died suddenly. Strangely, although he was the son-in-law of the richest man in New England and the founder of a social and sporting club, his death warranted only the smallest of notices in the general death listings of the *New York Times*. There was no public funeral or formal obituary. He left no will, because he had no money.

After her husband's death, Mabel Wolfe left New York and resettled in Connecticut, where, with her father's support, she enrolled the three boys in Pomfret Academy. While each Wolfe boy was a popular classmate and member of the football squad, none excelled academically, particularly young Dudley.

A strong, healthy child with a natural athletic ability, Dudley was far better outdoors than he was in the classroom. Struggle as he might, he could never find the joy in mastering schoolwork that he did in sailing a boat, playing football, or trudging through the woods hunting elk and moose. Like many a child of vast wealth, he lacked the need, and therefore perhaps the drive, to dedicate himself to learning algebra, Latin, or the history of ancient Rome. Instead, he spent untold hours poring over old nautical journals, absorbing every detail that he could find of shipbuilding, sail-making, and the wind and water currents of the North Atlantic.

His brothers, Clifford and Grafton, also struggled to maintain the basic academic standards. Clifford's social behavior was even worse. Fourteen when his father died, he seemed to instantly follow the course of many rich, undisciplined boys: utter rebellion. Spoiled by his doting mother and full of bravado, Clifford all but thumbed his nose at his grandfather, B. F. Smith, who tried repeatedly to get him to knuckle down. After Clifford was expelled from Pomfret for bad grades and worse behavior, B. F. stepped in and sent him to the Manlius School, hoping the strict military academy in upstate New York would whip the boy into shape. Instead, Clifford burned another bridge with his indifference and unhealthy influence on his younger classmates. After enrolling in and unceremoniously leaving four schools in twelve years, Clifford never graduated from any.

As was the custom for young, wealthy women of the time, after her husband's death Mabel quickly remarried a solid but rather humorless businessman from a prominent Nebraska family, Joseph Baldrige,* and moved to Omaha where her father still spent his winters. To his credit, Baldrige took charge of his lackluster stepsons and with their grandfather gave them fair warning to shape up and improve their studies or face the consequences. Dudley and Grafton struggled academically but fortunately lacked Clifford's arrogance and sense of entitlement and were therefore supported and urged on by their headmasters. Like Clifford before them, they left Pomfret and were sent to what was by then called the St. John's School in Manlius. Dudley was a valuable addition to the hockey and track teams, but he and Grafton lasted only a year before being sent on to Phillips Academy† in Andover, Massachusetts—a forgiving school, it seemed, since the

---

* Joseph's brother was Nebraska state senator Howard Hammond Baldrige, his nephew was US Congressman Howard Malcolm Baldrige, and his grand-nephew was H. Malcolm Baldrige, secretary of commerce under George H. W. Bush.

† While commonly known as Andover Academy today, at the turn of the twentieth century the school was known as Phillips Academy at Andover, which remains its formal name.

year before the incorrigible Clifford had been thrown out on his ear after a mere five months there, leaving a string of debts his stepfather had to pay.

Dudley entered Phillips Academy in September 1913 and immediately tried out for and got onto the wrestling and football teams. He also pledged to one of Phillips's oldest secret societies, the PBX or Phi Beta Chi. At the height of the club's hazing rituals in early December, he began to suffer severe abdominal pains and chronic indigestion. While a "sensitive appendix" was at first suspected, his condition stabilized and the doctors at the school said he was out of danger and recommended he stay until the Christmas break in a few weeks. Mabel saw it otherwise. Having lost her only brother to a burst appendix in 1901,* she insisted Dudley come home to Omaha immediately. On December 9 he was loaded on the Union Pacific's Wolverine Express at Boston's South Station, headed west.

A few days before Christmas the appendix was removed and in mid-January Dudley returned to Phillips and to his new brotherhood in the PBX. Phi Beta Chi employed the usual hazing ceremonies, which involved various kinds of torture for its new pledges, from being routinely punched or paddled across a bare bottom, placed in a coffin and cross-examined, or commanded to stay all night in a cemetery with only a clay pipe and a bag of Lucky Strike tobacco. The faculty at Phillips tried for decades to "crush them out" but the societies thrived and even built large private houses off campus for their meetings.

Though Dudley's stomach distress had coincidenced with his pledging, he nonetheless survived the hazing, was inducted, and was eager to return to school. Mabel and Joseph weren't so enthusiastic about his membership and wrote to the headmaster that they

---

* In 1901, B. F. had lost his only son, and Mabel her only sibling, Clifford Warren Smith, to a burst appendix. When he died, Clifford left a son, Clifford Warren Smith, Jr.

feared Dudley's involvement was "not very conducive to faithful study." Evidently it wasn't.

For the next two and a half years, Dudley fought to gain his academic footing, but, like Clifford, his grades went from poor to unacceptable. After he repeatedly failed several subjects, the school threatened to expel him. Unlike his older brother, Dudley wrote a series of earnest letters to the principal, Mr. Alfred Stearns, insisting that he was applying himself and that with proper tutoring he would be able to master the two subjects which particularly dogged him, algebra and German. Signing each, "I am, Respectfully yours," Dudley tried to impress on Stearns that he was "ready to do everything and anything" to meet the standards of Phillips Academy where he had spent, "believe me, the happiest three years of my life." Meanwhile, Dudley's stepfather wrote to Stearns commenting that while he didn't think Dudley was a "dullard, the boy is in fact very slow." (One can only hope Baldrige didn't share his opinions with his stepson.)

In the end the appeals failed; the school reluctantly refused to let Dudley return for the 1916–17 academic year. While Stearns acknowledged that the young man had made every "faithful, conscientious effort," Dudley utterly failed to meet their scholastic requirements. Writing that he didn't "know of any boy who has left us in recent years who will carry with him a fuller amount of good will and affection," Stearns expressed the heartfelt regret of an entire faculty at the school's losing Dudley.

Defeated and depressed, Dudley returned to Maine for the summer, where he worked at Old Orchard Beach in one of his grandfather's businesses. Twenty years old, overweight, and miserable, all he could think of, as he watched the tourists walk on the pier, was how to avoid a permanent move to Omaha. He realized his best option was to join the war effort in Europe. After following

Mabel and Joseph back to Omaha in the fall, Dudley was turned away from five branches of the US military, each time with his papers stamped "4-F" because of his poor eyesight and flat feet. Finally, and with few options, Dudley set his sights on the French Foreign Legion, a fighting force created for foreign nationals wishing to serve in the French armed forces. A combination of idealistic volunteers and hardened mercenaries, the men of the Legion had fought and died side by side in wars dating back to 1831. It was a perfect solution for Dudley. After he sent letters and telegrams inquiring into how an American could sign up, he discovered that the Legion had a long waiting list and he wouldn't be able to join for at least a year. Still determined, he applied to the American Red Cross's ambulance corps, which would at least get him out of Omaha and over to Europe.

With a stack of glowing recommendation letters from former teachers and headmasters, including Mr. Stearns at Phillips, Dudley easily got into the ambulance corps and talked his wastrel older brother, Clifford, into going with him.

On October 24, 1917, Joseph Baldrige, Mabel, Gwen, and Grafton all waved from New York's South Street pier as the two brothers sailed for Europe. With them on the SS *St. Louis* were six surgeons and thirty-five nurses, all bound for the front lines. The crossing was a boisterous affair of late nights in the ship's parlor singing patriotic songs at the piano, hard drinking, and close dancing with strangers, as they all enjoyed their last civilian revelry before the horrors of war became a daily routine.

Over the years Dudley Francis Wolfe had grown into an attractive, quiet, dignified young man with a shock of curly dark hair above the high forehead he had inherited from his father. He was friendly but reserved, and while he had an engaging smile, he more often looked out upon the world with a steady sober gaze from behind his round glasses. He was considered stout and would struggle throughout his life with his weight. At five feet ten inches, he weighed anywhere between 180 and 220 pounds, his heaviest being after his expulsion from Phillips at what was probably the nadir of his life. Once free of that failure, he grew up, got back into sports and steadily lost the weight, developing the solid, athletic build of a running back rather than the lithe agility of a sprinter.

When Dudley and Clifford got off the boat in Liverpool they made their way to London, where they decided to do some sightseeing before the ambulance corps training was to start. One night Dudley dined alone at the hotel, and as he bent comfortably over the oak bar waiting for his dinner, a middle-aged man who looked through thick glasses and wore a trim suit approached him and asked whether he was the American Dudley Wolfe registered at the hotel. Dudley stood and reached out his hand, affirming that yes, he was.

The man bowed slightly and introduced himself as Lucien Wolf, explaining that he had a brother Dudley who had emigrated to America many years before, and he wondered if perhaps they were related. Dudley invited Lucien to join him at the bar and, pulling his passport out of his pocket, asked him to write his name on a spare page so he could see how it was spelled. Curious at the missing "e," the two men compared genealogical notes and dates. Soon they looked at each other with widening eyes and then, somewhat awkwardly, uncle and nephew rose and embraced each other.

Dudley listened as Lucien told him the whole story. He quickly learned that his father, Dudley Wolfe, the self-proclaimed British aristocrat and businessman, had actually been born Dudley Wolf, the second son of a Bohemian Jew, Edward Wolf, who had escaped a violent wave of political uprisings and class warfare throughout Europe in 1848. Edward, a pipe manufacturer and tobacconist, and his Viennese wife, Cécili Redlich, raised their children in Hackney, a Jewish section of London. Their two eldest, Dudley and Lucien Emmanuel,* were sent to Gloucester House, a Jewish school for boys in Kew, outside of London. At some point after Dudley Wolf emigrated to America in the late 1880s and before he married Mabel Smith in 1893, he had added the "e," forever leaving his Jewish name and heritage behind.

Lucien also told Dudley, with tears coming to his eyes, that he had only learned of his brother's death the year before, and not from Mabel but from an attorney in Omaha. Lucien had told the attorney that he wanted his brother's children to be told how to communicate with him, but obviously, he knew now, that hadn't been done. They had never been told of their Jewish uncle in England. What an extraordinary coincidence that he should happen upon one of them in a London hotel! Looking at Dudley Wolfe, Lucien felt a swell of love and pride. He could see his brother in the young man's square jaw, aquiline nose, and high forehead. How Dudley would have liked to see his boy grow up! Lucien had so many questions: Why had his brother never mentioned his family in London? Why hadn't Mabel, in going through his papers, found Lucien's letters and contacted him? And mostly, why had Dudley abandoned his name and heritage after he arrived in America? But Lucien would never know. His brother's reasons had died with him.

Dudley looked at the distinguished man next to him, his uncle. This man and his mysterious father had been brothers, the sons of Bohemian Jews, refugees no less. And while Dudley Senior had apparently broken all ties with his past, before he left his home

---

* Lucien Emmanuel Wolf was a prominent Jewish diplomat, foreign affairs expert, journalist, and historian. After the outbreak of the Russian pogroms in 1881, Wolf took a leading role in the effort to aid persecuted Jews in eastern Europe and began warning the allied leaders of an ugly anti-Semitism raging throughout Europe which, if left unchecked, would only spread. However, because of his anti-Russian efforts he was perceived as pro-German. After World War I he lost his standing as a diplomat and effectively ended his career in journalism.

the Wolfs had been a loving, close family which gathered around Cécili's piano after dinner, each of them playing an instrument while "Papa" sang Dvořák *lieder* into the night. Suddenly Dudley realized where he got the "Cecil" in Dudley Francis Cecil Wolfe; he had been named for his grandmother.

Dudley almost laughed, picturing his maternal grandfather's face if he were to hear this news. B. F. and the mighty Smiths were proud of their Maine lineage straight back to 1610. He wished he dared tell him that those Smiths now had eastern European Jewish blood flowing through their heirs' veins.

Exchanging addresses with his newfound uncle, Dudley promised to visit him before returning to America after the war and suggested they might even schedule a family reunion of sorts, although his Semitic relatives might not be welcomed with open arms at the gated enclave of Warrenton Park.*

After Lucien left, Dudley sat at the bar trying out his new name and signature beneath where his uncle had written his. Repeatedly he wrote "Dudley F. C. Wolfe" and "Dudley F. C. Wolf," as if deciding which he would choose.

Once in France, Dudley drove into action behind the wheel of a small medical camion, a specially rigged Model T Ford with a wooden box frame attached to the rear to carry the wounded and the dead. For the next year, from the western front, where he witnessed the bloody battle of Soissons along the Marne, to the Italian front along the Piave River, he drove through one of history's most devastating wars. While other young men were shooting themselves in the foot or leg to get out of combat, Dudley volunteered for

---

* It's not clear whether Mabel or B. F. knew the truth of Dudley Senior's Jewish heritage, although it's hard to imagine a man as savvy and successful as B. F. wouldn't know. In a book B. F. commissioned about the Smith family in 1932, it says that Dudley Senior was "the son of a prominent wool merchant," not a Jewish pipe-maker and tobacconist, who had spent much of his youth in India.

some of the worst duty possible. He quickly learned the difference between mortar fire and shrapnel—you could possibly run from a mortar blast if you heard it coming, but with shrapnel you had to hit the dirt and pray not to get hit. He saw soldiers in hand-to-hand combat, so close he could see the color of their eyes as they pulled the pins from their grenades. After the clouds of mustard gas cleared he would walk through the fields and trenches, pulling masks full of vomit off dead soldiers, their faces purple and their lips black. He saw open trenches filled with rats as fat as otters nibbling on the dead and dying soldiers. He witnessed artillery rounds so solid he couldn't distinguish the individual explosions but merely felt and heard the constant bomb-like roar through his body. Then there were the husks of bodies, already ruined by disease and starvation, which he loaded into the ambulance. The winter of 1917–18 was brutally cold, and it was followed by an equally painful, sweltering summer. Chewing coffee beans and taking swigs of grappa to stay awake and remain numb at the same time, Dudley drove through the Austrian attack along the Piave River near Venice. Man after man, body after body, some getting hit before his eyes with their shattered legs collapsing beneath them, others blown naked of their clothes by the bomb blast, their torsos and limbs hanging from the trees above: the war became Dudley's education.

The ambulance work suited him. He found cold, narrow purpose in its physical stress and emotional exhaustion. There was no time to think about his failures at school, the disappointment of his mother, or the demands by his stepfather and grandfather that he make something of his life. Here he was, dodging bullets and bombs, pulling broken men from their trenches and driving them through a rain of munitions to the relative safety of the dressing stations. Often they would be screaming in pain and he wished for a gun to put them out of their misery, as he had the animals he had found in traps with a leg chewed nearly off in an attempt to gain freedom. But he hadn't shot the men; he had loaded their ruined bodies into the top-heavy Ford and driven them to the hospital, many of them dying on the way. Then he would turn around and go out to do it again. No one had to ask or direct him and no one ever called him slow or suggested he was a dullard. He knew the routine, he knew his mission, and he performed ably and without complaint.

In the midst of this hell, Dudley remained a gentle man. On one trip from the front, he brought a mortally wounded French soldier from the trenches to the hospital where he then watched him die. Before he returned to his camion, Dudley took out his pocketknife and cut a small lock of the man's hair, wrapped it in a square of hospital gauze, and tucked it into his coat. Perhaps he intended to deliver it to the man's mother, or his girlfriend back in Paris. But he did neither. He wrote the man's name and where he died on a slip of paper, tucked it and the small bundle of hair into an envelope, and kept it locked in his desk drawer. Whatever the gesture may have meant, the lock of hair became one of Dudley's most guarded possessions.

He wrote frequent and often funny postcards and letters to his family, making his wartime activities sound more like an extended vacation, describing his ten-day leaves to Rome and Naples and collecting the exploded shells as souvenirs for Gwen. Sitting in a café in Milan, where he was on leave from the French front, Dudley wrote to Gwen, "Heigh ho, sisterlino Gwendolino! Hope you have a fine time Christmas vacation. But don't eat too much! Give my best to all I know. Much love, Dud." In one, he described watching an observation balloon get shot down by a "Boche" sniper,* then

---

* "Boche," a term of derision meaning "rascal" or "pig-headed," was used to describe the German soldiers.

of seeing the observer come floating down in his parachute, almost at Dudley's feet. Most often he wrote in between attacks along the front and would end the letters abruptly when a call came for ambulances—"and that means me." But he always took the time to close the letters tenderly: "Give my love to all, Your loving brother, Dud." Over the years, between Clifford's rebellion and Grafton's youth, he and Gwen had become the closest siblings and wrote long and detailed letters to each other.

Finally, word came that Dudley's commission for the French Foreign Legion had come through. As he was signing his release papers from the ambulance corps he learned that he was to be awarded the Italian Croce di Guerra, the Italian Red Cross medal, and the campaign medal for the Italian–Austrian War.

On October 1, 1918, after ten months driving an ambulance, he finally donned the uniform of the French Foreign Legion but fought on the front lines for only a month. On November 11 the armistice was signed; the war was over.* Even though his active duty was short, he received more medals for his service: the French Volunteer Medal and the French Campaign Medal. After posing for a picture in his decorated uniform, one of his Grandfather Wolf's handmade pipes proudly held in his right hand, he neatly tucked the ribbons and medals into their boxes and packed them away for his mother and grandfather.

While Phillips Academy at Andover had rejected Dudley academically, after the war they proudly claimed him as one of their own, years later boasting that he had amassed more medals than any other "Andover man" during the Great War.

As he was packing for home, Dudley learned that Clifford, who had been assigned to the western front, had been captured and was

---

* The enlistment delay turned out to be providential for Dudley, as most of the legionnaires died in battle.

being held in a German prisoner-of-war camp. Dudley went into high gear, writing to the American Field Office, the Red Cross, and the diplomatic corps to get information on Clifford's condition, status, and, now that the war was over, his release. For the next two months, he badgered anyone and everyone he could find, until he finally received word on January 1, 1919, that his brother had been put on a train in Strasbourg bound for France. Clifford was free.

With Clifford's safety now assured, Dudley realized he was still not ready to return home. He lingered in Europe for almost another year, spending most of his time in Paris and then in London with his uncle Lucien, where he met an entire family of Wolf cousins he hadn't known existed. He saw pictures of his young father on Cécili's piano, which now sat in Lucien's parlor, and gave his uncle several pounds to have the photographs copied; he wanted to take a set home to Maine with him.

After months of gentle urging from Mabel and Gwen, Dudley finally returned to America in the fall of 1919 and joined his mother, sister, brother, and stepfather in Omaha, where the Smith family banking and real estate businesses still flourished. For the next four years Dudley struggled to find his way in real estate, while Clifford, who had also returned a decorated veteran, came home a changed man and immediately began learning how to manage B. F.'s vast holdings. Dudley tried to embrace the business, but as he sat in the flat, dusty cow town of Omaha bent over probate documents and land titles, he yearned for the gentle hills and ocean breezes of Rockport. Each summer he eagerly returned to Maine and his first love, sailing. He entered every race he could find, from local regattas to world-class competitions, but he also relished the times he was alone on the ocean, absorbing the quiet solitude. He realized that war and sailing had a lot in common; although one was mired in chaos and the other in calm, he felt utterly detached from the world in each, and it was the solitude he cherished. Every year his summer vacation got longer until finally, in 1924, with the excuse of at last entering college in the fall, Dudley announced he was heading back east for good. Clicking along on the railroad his grandfather had helped build, Dudley watched the parched prairie grasses give way to the rolling hills of western Pennsylvania, New York, the Berkshire Mountains, and, finally, the marble and brick office buildings of Boston. The ocean was only another hundred yards away.

When the family gathered in Maine that summer, B. F. Smith called his grandsons to his estate in Warrenton Park overlooking Glen Cove. At ninety-four, B. F. was as sharp, canny, and proud as he had ever been. He explained that the good Smith name was in danger of disappearing.

Dudley, Clifford, and Grafton looked uncomfortably at their cousin, Clifford Warren Smith, Jr., the only son of their late uncle who had died of the burst appendix over twenty years before. He was a Smith and already married; surely he would be able to sustain the Smith name? But as they glanced at Clifford Junior, they saw that he sat slumped in his chair and, although it was only two in the afternoon, he looked as if he had been drinking. The young man had been an embarrassment for years. B. F. had bought him out of many scrapes with the law; there had been an assortment of very young girlfriends; and, the family feared, a messy divorce loomed. Perhaps B. F. was right; if his legacy depended on Clifford Junior, it could be an ignoble end.

For his part, B. F. didn't want to chance his family legacy on this reckless boy having a son who could carry on the Smith name. As much as he had tried to instill the work ethic and a sense of responsibility into Clifford Junior, it was his daughter Mabel's three boys who had made him proud: Grafton was an accomplished sailor who also showed promise as a horse breeder; Clifford had finally shaped up and taken over the family business; and Dudley had come back from Europe a decorated war hero and was an even greater talent than Grafton at the helm. Turning to his three Wolfe grandsons, he offered a proposition; if they would change their name from Wolfe to Smith, he would make them direct heirs of his fortune, rather than secondary beneficiaries following the death of their mother.

Dudley exchanged looks with his brothers, but each seemed afraid to ask the obvious: What about our legacy, the Wolfe legacy? What about our family name? Dudley looked hard at his grandfather, wondering if he knew about the London Wolfs and if this had anything to do with forever burying the Wolf name and its Jewish origins. But his grandfather didn't betray a thing and Dudley didn't ask. He had too much respect for the old man to challenge him.

For his part, B. F. did not mention Dudley Wolfe Senior at all and simply went on to explain that for their trouble they would be rewarded handsomely. Variously estimated at $70 million to $100 million ($1.05 billion to $1.5 billion today), the Smith fortune was rumored to be the largest in all of New England, and certainly one of the largest in the United States at the time.

Not knowing what else to say to their formidable grandfather, Dudley and his brothers agreed. Soon afterward, they stood before a judge in Knox County, Maine, where they swore their name change into effect.

Dudley immediately felt regret at his decision. Later that summer, as he wrote his application to Harvard, he hesitated before signing the letter but finally did so as "Dudley F. Wolfe" and mailed it off to Cambridge. Days later a letter arrived from the admissions office telling him he didn't have the proper credits for enrollment.

Almost relieved, Dudley sent a letter acknowledging his lack of credentials and immediately called the Manter Hall Tutoring School in Harvard Square, where he attended preparatory classes for the next year. But when he reapplied the following summer, it was as if his heart just wasn't in it. Using many of the same answers to questions such as "What games do you especially like?" and "What is your intended profession?" as he had given in his 1924 application, Dudley wrote, "sailing, hunting and camping," and "business, most probably" but gave no indication of the man behind the pen.

Meanwhile, he struggled with his agreement to become a Smith. The name felt fraudulent to Dudley and insulting to his father and his newfound family in London. But in deference to B. F., he tried it on. In the summer of 1925 he entered his new single-masted sloop, the *Bonita IV*, in the Brooklyn Yacht Club's deep-sea Challenge Cup, as Dudley Wolfe Smith. Besting larger, more powerful boats and some of the sport's most seasoned sailors, Dudley won the race, an honor that put him among the likes of Jack Dempsey, René Lacoste, and Johnny Weissmuller in the *New York Times* listing of "Champions of 1925." It would be the one and only time he used the name Smith in a race. If he were to gain national fame again, he wanted his father's name in the records. In his next race and every subsequent race, he entered as Dudley F. Wolfe.

Soon after the race, he went to B. F.'s rambling clapboard house on the hill, Clifford Lodge, and asked to have a word. As calmly and evenly as he could, Dudley explained why he wanted to return his legal name to Wolfe—that he felt the change disrespected his late father who also deserved a legacy. Hadn't he in fact been named for his father, who had evidently shared B. F.'s desire to see his name live on? And if B. F. felt he needed his legal heirs to have the Smith name, Dudley understood; he would make his way in the world either with or without the Smith millions.

The old man sat and listened, impressed by his grandson's honesty and honor; he knew Dudley could easily have waited until his death to change his name back without any risk to his inheritance. B. F. looked at his grandson and realized he loved the boy who, unlike the two Cliffords, had never been anything but gentle and respectful, eager to excel and now proving to be a genius at the helm. And yes, Dudley Senior also deserved to have his name live on.

When Dudley was finished, B. F. slowly rose out of his chair and took his grandson's hand, assuring him that his inheritance was safe and that he had his grandfather's blessing to return his name to Wolfe.

Within the week, Dudley contacted a lawyer in Portland and had his name changed back to Dudley F. Wolfe. B. F. kept the trust as written with Dudley a full heir. Grafton and Clifford would remain Smiths the rest of their lives.

In the fall of 1925 Dudley was finally accepted to Harvard. Although he still lacked crucial credits, the college allowed him an "uncredited grade" for Latin, which he had failed.* Just as he had at Phillips, he played football, earning a coveted Harvard letter. He also immersed himself in the secret clubs society, and he was a popular member of several despite (or perhaps because of) the fact that he was ten years older than his classmates. Beginning his sophomore year with the Institute of 1770, he later joined the "Dickey," as Harvard's unofficial chapter of the fraternity Delta Kappa Epsilon was known, and finally the Owl Club.† Entry at all levels into the Harvard club elite depended primarily on wealth

---

* Harvard in the 1920s was more lenient in its academic standards for applicants, and Dudley's ability to pay cash for his education couldn't have hurt his application process. In any case, he was in.

† The Owl Club would later claim Senator Edward Kennedy as a longstanding member, until political pressure forced the senator to resign in 2006 from the still all-male society.

and family social standing, two criteria Dudley easily met. Deciding not to live on campus in Cambridge, he rented a brownstone at 177 Commonwealth Avenue in Boston. It sat just down the street from B. F.'s sprawling mansion at 21 Commonwealth Avenue in fashionable Back Bay, a neighborhood of 15,000-square-foot houses running west for ten blocks from the Boston Botanical Gardens. Dudley, a reticent but generous host, welcomed his new group of college friends to his home, offering them the finest whiskeys and cigars, and, when pressed, telling tales from the front lines of a war they had only read about and of his twenty years at the helm of his own boats.

ON MARCH 14, 1927, just shy of his ninety-seventh birthday, the family patriarch, B. F. Smith, finally died. Although he had loved him, Dudley nonetheless felt a new freedom after his commanding grandfather was gone. While he had lost a source of emotional support, he had also lost his most critical judge, the witness to his every failure.

Although Dudley realized he wouldn't meet his graduation requirements by June 1929, he knew he would earn his bachelor's degree the following year—the first diploma of his life. Perhaps as a reward, he commissioned a double-masted, sixty-foot schooner from his sailing friend John G. Alden of Boston, who modeled his boats on the Grand Banks fishing vessels: heavy, sturdy, and strong enough to withstand gales. Soon after the yacht's completion in Wiscasset, Maine, Dudley christened it the *Mohawk* at the Camden Yacht Club, just up the road from Rockport. As he walked through the venerable but rustic one-room clubhouse after the ceremony, he saw an entry notice for the King and Queen's Cup Classic, a transatlantic yacht race from New York to Spain. Knowing that races across the Atlantic had always demanded a larger class of sailing yacht of at least one hundred feet, he leaned in to read the specifications and was gratified to see that they didn't limit the class of boat. Looking out the club window at his powerfully built *Mohawk* he thought, why not?

Although no yachtsman in history had taken the risk of racing a sixty-foot boat across the ocean, Dudley was confident that the *Mohawk* could not only perform well but could maneuver easily around the larger, more cumbersome boats. While smaller yachts had certainly been sailed across the oceans, no one had ever raced one; and, as any sailor knows, pleasure-cruising from point to point, motoring into ports, even sailing off course when necessary to avoid storms, was very different from nonstop, point-to-point racing across 3,000 miles of unforgiving sea.

A week into the race, Dudley spotted a steamship off the *Mohawk*'s port side. He grabbed his field glasses and saw that it was the Italian luxury liner *Conte Biancamano* on its route from New York to Genoa. While he had never been on that specific ship, he'd been on many like it and was familiar with their luxurious appointments. Now, with seven days' worth of stubble on his chin, salt crusting his eyebrows, and sweat stains under his arms, he looked at the far-off ship; its marble baths, leather and oak bar infused with the smells of fine whiskey and Cuban cigars, and wide promenade deck seemed a world away.

With a final look at the billowing smokestacks disappearing over the flat ocean, Dudley returned his focus to the *Mohawk* and to a storm brewing in the skies behind him. He ordered the crew to lock down the hatches and prepare for the gale, trimming the sails and lashing themselves to the mainmast and cockpit. For nearly six hours the *Mohawk* heaved from side to side, the storm soaking her decks and battering the men. Several times a crewman lost his footing and was nearly washed overboard, but his lash kept him on the boat, albeit bruised and exhausted. Finally, the gale moved off and calm returned to the sea and the *Mohawk*. Those would be the only rough seas of their nearly month-long race. Most of their remaining days to Spain were spent like any other enjoyable sail in fair weather off the New England coast, with Dudley watching the woolly telltales tied to the bottom of the sail for any whisper of air to be captured in the thousands of square feet of canvas above. Their nights were spent quietly, even serenely, as each man took his turn at the helm while his mates caught a nap or ate. One night Dudley watched a pod of porpoises play alongside the *Mohawk*, jumping through its wake as if through an invisible circus hoop. Then, as if touched by a giant torch, the seas lit up with phosphorescence through which the *Mohawk* sailed, leaving an aisle of shimmering green light in its wake.

Twenty-five days after leaving New York, the *Mohawk* raced to a second-place finish in Santander, Spain. Her crew looked more like a band of pirates than Ivy League men, each sporting a beard and their tattered college sweaters. Welcomed like heroes home from a successful battle, the men of the *Mohawk* accepted an enormous silver chalice from King Alfonso XIII and Queen Eugenia Victoria. That night, the streets of Santander were alive with celebration, and everywhere the crews of the various yachts went they were feted by handsome, dark-eyed women offering the men bottomless carafes of sangria.

In every race he entered, Dudley listed himself as "owner and captain." While he enjoyed the trappings and gentility of the sport, it was more about the boat and the ocean and the race and he wanted to be crucially involved at its heart—the helm. It was a love he shared with his younger brother, Grafton.

Grafton Wolfe Smith was a charming man with a beauty that

was almost ethereal. From his earliest days he attracted friends and lovers and gained easy entry into high society's finest clubs and private organizations from Maine to Palm Beach. Like Dudley, he owned and sailed his own yachts, and for years, on any given weekend, at least one of the Wolfe/Smith brothers could be found racing in regattas off the eastern seaboard. Grafton also developed a love for horse breeding and racing, and, in September 1931, while driving his new car home to Hamilton, Massachusetts, from the racetrack in Saratoga, New York, he lost control and hit a telephone pole. The car had been going so fast and the impact was so violent that three wheels were sheared off. Grafton was thrown clear of the wreckage, unconscious but still alive. Passing motorists stopped at the scene, piled him into their car, and drove him to a nearby hospital. His wife, Janice, was called, and she raced through the night to the hospital. But when she arrived, he had died of head injuries. Perhaps suspecting that alcohol may have been involved, the family ordered a toxicology report which came back clean; no alcohol or drugs were found in his system. The young man had simply been driving too fast.

After Grafton's death and perhaps growing weary of New York, Boston, and Maine society, Dudley decided to return to Europe where the parties had more dignity and the sports more adventure.

Having driven through the Alps during the war, Dudley was familiar with the premier climbing and skiing areas of Europe: Zermatt, Chamonix, the Arlberg, and Davos. There, he hired renowned mountain guides to help him become proficient in his new sports. Solidly built and strongly muscled, he always showed resolute determination and good humor as he struggled to master the ropes, crampons, and ice axe maneuvers of climbing. But on skis, as he had on deck, he found that he had a natural sense of balance and coordination which allowed him to excel. As with sailing, he found he loved the thrill and speed of racing and entered many regional competitions. At the sharp pop of the gun, he would throw his weight down the slope, his strong legs hugging the heavy wooden skis close together, almost casually transferring his weight back and forth along the carved edges, the tips clattering along the icy course as he sped to the bottom of the steep runs. Because he competed against much younger men who had been reared on the racecourses, he never won an event, but he always crossed the finish line. He also loved the physical challenge and exhaustion of ski touring, and while exploring and conquering largely untouched peaks on his skis and skins, he achieved over thirty difficult summits and traverses, chief among them a ski traverse of the Mont Blanc massif.

Over twenty years before the famed Telepherique de l'Aiguille du Midi was built, enabling tourists, climbers, and skiers to ride up the side of the massive mountain, Dudley and his party climbed over 9,000 feet from Chamonix village to the Vallot hut on their skis. From there he performed an early and still rare ski traverse of Mont Blanc to the Mer de Glace. He also climbed rock faces on the Brevant and reached scores of summits in the western Pyrenees, the Alps—including Mont Blanc and the Matterhorn—and in the Bregaglia group of the Engadine along the Swiss–Italian border.

While skiing in the Tyrol above St. Anton in the Arlberg district of Austria in the spring of 1934, Wolfe watched as an attractive woman with a heroically female body—curvaceous, strong, and statuesque—slalomed down the slopes, effortlessly mastering the icy course. At the bottom, he watched as she tore off her ski hat, releasing a thick crop of short, dark curls, and smiled broadly at her companion. Inquiring, he was told her name was Alice Damrosch.

Alice Blaine Damrosch was born on May 18, 1892, the eldest daughter of the famed conductor of the New York Symphony,

Walter Johannes Damrosch, and the granddaughter of James Gillespie Blaine, secretary of state under presidents Garfield and Harrison. The Damrosch dynasty, as one writer called it, included several generations of European musical heritage, and after Walter Damrosch and his brother Frank immigrated to America in 1871, they began building a musical tradition in their new country. Walter had four daughters, who grew up in a house where there was always a guest musician visiting, his cello leaning against the door frame or his sheet music on the piano.

Alice's first marriage in 1914 to Hall Pleasants Pennington, whom the *New York Times* described as a man who "gardens," ended almost before it began. The ceremony was on Lake Champlain in upstate New York, after which the newlyweds canoed off in a flurry of rose petals as musicians played on the shore. But that was evidently the end of the romance; early the next morning, Alice canoed alone back to where her family was staying on the lake and spent the rest of her honeymoon with them.

Alice went through romances quickly. No man, it seemed, quite lived up to her family's artistic or intellectual standards. A man had to be someone and do something, and while her beaus entertained her in the short run, none seemed to measure up for the long haul. Pleasants was no different. While they stayed married for years, they remained childless and she lived more or less a single woman's life, splitting her time between New York society and long vacations in Europe. When they finally divorced in the late 1920s, she escaped to the mountains of Austria, where she found a new life of hunting and skiing with a host of creative and accomplished friends. After killing her first ibex, she wrote to her family in New York, "The blood was so hot you could have boiled an egg in it!"

While children bored her and she never sought to have her

own, Alice was a powerful presence whose nieces and nephews adored and feared her in often equal measure. She could be ruthless in her comments, cruelly pointing out if one had gained weight or had an unsightly blemish. After the mortified niece fled to her room sobbing, Alice would wave off her biting criticism with "Well, that's the way I see it." When she took her niece Lisa shopping for her first evening gown, what should have been a pleasant outing became an ordeal when Alice demanded, "Why can't you stand up straight?" and made cutting remarks about the adolescent girl's lingering baby fat. But Alice was also tough on herself and fanatical about her own appearance. Rising before dawn every morning of her summer visits to the family house in Bar Harbor, Maine, she would climb to the summits of nearby mountains in Acadia National Park before breakfast in order to stay in shape. In the 1930s, when she was well into her forties, she became one of the first women to ski the unrelenting ice wall of Tuckerman's Ravine, a glacial cirque on Mount Washington's southeast face in New Hampshire.

She was also a gracious hostess, inviting those same nieces to Austria for extended vacations, sitting for hours showing them the art of needlepoint, and teaching each of them how to ski, although the lessons were far from gentle. "That is a stupid way to ski! Bend your knees, for heaven's sake!" she would yell down the slope. Still, her nieces looked forward to their visits. Her apartments in St. Anton and New York always had the best of everything. The bed linens were Egyptian cotton and professionally laundered so that the creases were crisp. The lavender soap was imported from England, the towels monogrammed, and always there were cut flowers in every room.

Part Jewish, Alice had an abiding hatred of the Nazis and their rapid encroachment on her beloved second home of Austria.

Although deeply political and entirely outspoken, she would don her white gloves and society hat and play the role of pampered, ignorant American matron presenting herself at Third Reich military offices in order to gain the release of her detained Jewish friends, among them Hans Kraus, a famed orthopedic surgeon.*

In 1931, at the age of thirty-nine, she won a gold medal at the Parsenne Ski Derby at Davos, Switzerland. Three years later, while skiing above St. Anton in the spring of 1934, she met a gentle, soft-spoken, and earnest yachtsman and budding ski racer. Soon, the feisty divorcee and the understated bachelor realized they shared a deep passion for all things outdoors, not only skiing and touring but hunting as well. While Dudley lacked a profession, he nonetheless was a charming, generous man who didn't throw his money around garishly, as so many wealthy Americans did, and she knew he loved her. She feared her family would take issue with his apparent idleness, but they took issue with everybody, and besides, she and Dudley would spend most of their year in Austria, thousands of miles away from her family's critical eyes.

In late October 1934 Dudley and Alice cabled home to America: they had gotten married in Geneva and would be sailing to New York on the SS *Bremen* in early November for the obligatory celebrations. Alice was also organizing a fundraiser in New York in December for what would become America's first women's Olympic ski team, after which she and Dudley would return to Austria for her favorite season, Christmas. She loved him dearly, but her family, true to form, thought him a somewhat bland playboy. Hoping to soften at least one of her sisters' edges, Dudley bought Anita Damrosch a Cartier gold watch. Whether or not it changed her

* Kraus, an early proponent of using physical therapy and exercise rather than surgery to treat weak and wounded spines, went on to become President John F. Kennedy's primary back specialist.

opinion of her brother-in-law, she cherished the watch the rest of her life.

For the next three years, the couple criss-crossed the Atlantic, traveling between their homes in New York, Maine, and Austria. In Europe, Dudley bought a Buick Phaeton roadster, and the two toured the mountain towns and villages, stopping for the night only when they found inns which looked suitably quaint and clean. But it was in Alice's small and cozy apartment at the Haus Angelika in St. Anton, and at her tranquil hunting preserve in the mountains above, where Dudley felt truly at home, perhaps for the first time in his life.

Dudley was comfortable and loved the mountains of Europe, but by early 1938 he was spending more time on his own than with Alice. With the excuse of pursuing his new passion, climbing, he spent huge chunks of time in Zermatt, Chamonix, and Trento. After only four years of marriage, he realized that he preferred his solitude, his freedom. He loved Alice, but it wasn't enough to maintain a marriage and he told her he wanted a divorce.

In one of the rare times in her life that she showed weakness, Alice sat in her small living room in the Haus Angelika, put her head in her hands and cried. Her niece, who was visiting from America, watched from an alcove, stunned into silence at her aunt's display of raw emotion. She had never seen it before and she would never see it again. Over the course of the next several months, while Dudley returned to Maine for the summer and Alice remained in Austria, they wrote many letters to each other about the failing marriage. She begged him to reconsider and return, hoping that he missed her as much as she missed him. But it was to no avail. The marriage was over.

While Dudley and Alice weren't very good at marriage, they were wonderful friends and would remain close. In October they met in New York, and, after discussing some of the more mundane details of the divorce—her alimony, dividing the wedding gifts, and how long he would pay the rent on the apartment—they decided to have a party, show Dudley's slides, and celebrate the fact that, divorce or no divorce, they were still the best of friends.

As Alice sat down to write out the invitations, she playfully wrote out the phonetic spelling of a guest's name.

"Dear Mr. Vissner," she wrote, inviting Fritz Wiessner to the slide show and dinner party, adding a PS: "Black tie!"

Chapter 3

Climbing's Controversial Genius

Whatever you can do, or dream you can, begin it.
Boldness has genius, power, and magic in it.

— GOETHE

Fritz Wiessner, 1939. *(Courtesy of the George C. Sheldon Family)*

A t the start of the twentieth century, the earth's highest places, fourteen peaks that stand above 8,000 meters (26,240 feet), were little known and entirely unconquered. While Dudley Wolfe was learning the ropes and anchors of sailing, adventurers across America and Europe were learning the ropes and anchors of a new exploit, extreme high-altitude climbing. Although the summit of 15,781-foot Mont Blanc had been reached in the late 1700s and the 14,692-foot Matterhorn had been first scaled in 1865, little was known of the mountains of the vast Himalayan range, or of man's ability to survive at nearly twice the altitude of the roof of the Alps. But scientists, explorers, and mountaineers alike were determined to find out.

With the wildest edges of the earth thoroughly discovered, adventurers at the turn of the twentieth century set their sights on the far-off peaks of Nepal, Tibet, and India, and mountaineering clubs in London, Milan, Berlin, and New York organized expeditions to the still untouched giants.* After early British and Italian explorers had tried and failed to climb K2, the world's second highest peak, in remote northern India, they declared the mountain's sheer cliffs, unrelenting avalanches, and brutal weather unconquerable. Then, because Britain's "Great Game" with Russia after World War I determined which power would control central Asia, the British turned away from K2 and focused their attention on the world's tallest (and therefore in the eyes of many, best) mountain, Everest. Not to be excluded from the great conquests, German climbers set their sights on Nanga Parbat, a 26,660-foot peak near

---

* As early as 1577, astronomers were measuring not only the distance of stars but the elevation of mountains, and by the time the British Trigonometric Society sent out its cartographers to the ends of the earth in the nineteenth century, the world's highest peaks had been measured to within inches of their actual height.

K2 at the western edge of the Himalayas in northern India, and the Americans were left with the seemingly impossible K2.

Ironically, it would be a German immigrant built like a fireplug who was the driving force behind the American Alpine Club's dedication to K2.

BORN IN DRESDEN in 1900 into a prosperous but not wealthy family, Fritz Hermann Ernst Wiessner developed a passion for art, architecture, and opera, learning to love beauty and perfection, particularly in nature. He was also a patriot, and even though Germany was apparently losing the punishing Great War once the Americans entered it, as soon as he legally could he joined a special military unit called the Schützen and was shipped to the front lines near Belfort, close to the Crown Prince's army. Luckily, the armistice was signed before Fritz saw any active duty, as most of the Schützen youth were killed within weeks on the front.

When the war ended, Fritz returned to his first love, the outdoors. Spending untold hours devouring his father's mountaineering books, he read of the great exploits of the nineteenth-century climbers, from Charles Barrington on the Eiger in 1858 to the Matterhorn's first and deadly ascent in 1865, when the Englishman George Hadow slipped on descent, pulling two other climbers in his party away from the face. A fourth teammate was able to wrap the rope around a rock but it snapped, and all of Zermatt watched through field glasses as the four men fell thousands of feet to their deaths down the north wall. The disaster would forever mythologize the mountain, and with every new generation of climbers there would be a fresh crop of men eager to challenge its deadly legacy. Still a teenager, Fritz Wiessner became one of them.

Throughout his life, Wiessner had a pronounced, almost

balding forehead, yet retained a boyish face and impish smile. At only five feet five inches and with a body that was all sinew and muscle, he had the perfect physique for scaling rock walls using primarily his fingertips and toes. Fritz learned how to climb with his cousin Otto Wiessner, and together the two would travel to the sandstone towers of the Elbsteingebirge district south of Dresden. One weekend, Fritz took the train with some other climbers from a local club to a rock tower near the Czech border. Otto was delayed but planned to catch up with Fritz and the others at the wall; when Otto couldn't find them, he ventured off on his own, soloing the so-called Winklerturm. As he descended he saw that another group on the wall had gotten into some trouble and went to assist them. Suddenly a sandstone block under his fingers came loose and he fell. Later that evening, Fritz walked through the small town near the wall and noticed that several locals who knew him were looking at him very oddly.

"What's the matter?" Fritz finally asked a shopkeeper he recognized.

Without a word the man took him to a small house near the town's inn. Entering the dark parlor, he could see that there was a body laid out on a table. Moving closer, he suddenly stopped, stunned and horrified. The bloody, crushed face was Otto's.

At just twenty-one, Fritz suffered his first climbing death. It remained his most horrifying.

Otto's death, though, did little to curb Wiessner's love of the rock, and soon he was pioneering some of the hardest rock climbs in Europe, defining a new standard for technical difficulty while spurning the use of protective pitons to ascend the cliff walls. Throughout the Alps, his feats would go largely unchallenged for decades. His love of the mountains in large part dictated his life goals, including deciding he would climb every mountain in the

Alps above 4,000 meters, or 13,000 feet. (Like the Himalayas, the Alps are measured in meters and those who climb them set goals to achieve the highest in each range.) No one could deny that he was fabulously talented on rock, but he was less gifted on snow, ice, and at high altitudes, once collapsing from mountain sickness at 12,800 feet on Mont Blanc and again at the same height on Mount Rainier outside of Seattle, Washington.

Famous as Fritz was for his brilliant and fearless climbing, he was infamous for his silent brooding and violent temper. When asked to describe him, everyone from his children to his worst detractors used words like "sullen," "stubborn," "temperamental," and "explosive." Some offered "romantic," "depressive," and "Germanic." With fierce mood swings that would take him from cheerful and engaged to raging and resentful within seconds, Wiessner was a complex and driven personality. The term "he does not suffer fools gladly" could have been coined to describe him. He could utterly dismiss a person who lacked the proper social standing, and he refused to even look at a climbing partner while the man's elbows were on the table or if he held his fork like a shovel rather than a pen. But Fritz could also show enormous patience when talking to a novice climber, explaining the differences between climbing on limestone and on granite, or how to properly use one's toes to power up the rock while the fingers merely acted as guides up the wall. As much as he could be a snob about poetry and etiquette, he would take anyone who asked into the mountains, proud to introduce the man or woman to their pristine beauty and complicated rock walls. While he was something of a feminist, including women on rock and mountain climbing expeditions at a time when women had barely been allowed to vote, never mind belay a man on a rope, he also shared a tent with many of them, which begs the question of his motivation. Nonetheless, his inclusion of women on some of his tough expeditions indicated a liberalism not often in evidence in the early days of American, British, Italian, and German climbing.

In short, Fritz Wiessner was admired and hated, respected and reviled. For Fritz, it was simply all about climbing. The main things he wanted to know about others were: Did the man use fixed protection? Did he climb unsupported or did he need a phalanx of gear and men below him? Did he leave the rock untouched by his having been there? Did he puff up his own resumé, claiming a height never reached or a new route not actually achieved? And mostly, did he make the summit?

While he could be quite charming, he was also unabashedly German. On a climbing trip to Communist-controlled Dresden in the 1970s, he took his daughter to a restaurant unfortunately situated near a pig farm; he marched into the dining room with his pigeon-like strut and loudly exclaimed to the largely military diners, "Phew! One can smell the influence of the Russians!"

He was also notorious for his abhorrence of all things mechanical: radios, cameras, even bicycles. If it had a moving part which he might at some point have to adjust, Fritz avoided it whenever possible. Automobiles were his Achilles heel, which may have accounted for his appalling driving habits. Hunched forward with his chin nearly on the steering wheel, he commandeered the road as if every car in front of him were there to be overtaken, all the while jerking and lurching through traffic because he was never able to master the clutch. Once, while driving through East Germany with American climber Henry Barber in 1972, he became increasingly frustrated and confused by the traffic patterns and pedestrian paths and turned sharply between the lanes of traffic onto a footpath. Police in stiff blue uniforms and large black hats came from every direction trying to get him back on course, but Fritz waved them off, as if they were pesky flies rather than members of the Communist military police. He kept going on the footpath until he reached a break in the cement barrier and finally drove back onto the road. He never understood even the basic mechanics of a car, starting with filling the tank. On that same trip to Germany with Barber when Fritz was in his early seventies, he walked around the car at a gas station with the nozzle in his hand, scratching his head trying to figure out how the fuel got into the car. Reaching the end of his tolerance, he merely stuck the nozzle into the wheel well and started pumping. The irate attendant came running and, after a lot of shouting and gesticulating by both men, told Fritz to get back in the car while the man pumped the gas himself. Fritz blamed the incident on the car's poor design, rather than his own inability to understand its mechanics. Fritz was a man who couldn't be wrong.

By the late 1920s, with the post–World War I depression lingering throughout Europe and business increasingly difficult in war-torn Germany, Fritz decided it was time to leave his beloved Saxony and live in America, even though he knew there was a risk that he might one day have to bear arms against his own homeland.

After making his way to America on the SS *St. Louis* in March 1929, Wiessner found work as a chemist and engineer in New York City, but money was always tight and he supplemented his income with a variety of odd jobs. Oddest among them was washing the windows on the world's highest building at the time, the Empire State Building. Unlike today's unionized window washers, who work on protected scaffolding and in limited shifts, Fritz washed the windows while hanging off the building on a single hemp rope tied around his waist, from sunup to sundown, as long as the daylight allowed. Floor by floor, with just his squeegee, a bucket, and the rope, he worked his way up and across the building several stories at a time. He loved the work and would hang high above

New York feeling not like an hourly laborer but like a Titan in command of the city beneath him.

While his work as a chemist was interesting, it did not pay well and Fritz struggled to make ends meet. Still, with every spare dollar he scraped together, Fritz would venture on the weekends to the rock climbing areas scattered throughout the Hudson Valley, Connecticut Valley, and New Hampshire, where he soon became acquainted with America's still nascent climbing community.

The American Alpine Club, hoping to replicate London's venerable Alpine Club, had been established in 1902 by a handful of well-heeled industrialists and intellectuals who had the time and money to climb mountains. In this era, before corporate sponsorships and lucrative media deals, climbers paid the entire cost of their expeditions themselves, which meant that the mountaineering community was limited to affluent adventurers and those whom they invited to join them. By the early 1930s, the club rented space in lower Manhattan for its meetings, charged ten dollars in annual dues, and hadn't grown much beyond the tweed and leather set that founded it. But it was nonetheless the sole representative of a climbing class in America and, when one of its most respected members, Robert Underhill, agreed to sponsor him in 1932, Fritz readily joined. He had a rich man's tastes if not a rich man's resources, and his enormous talent for climbing and his extensive history of record-setting climbs made him an immediate force in that company.

With his transatlantic connections getting stronger every day, Wiessner was asked to help organize a German–American expedition to climb Nanga Parbat. It would be his first venture to extreme high altitude and a bid to make history. With money a persistent problem, Fritz brought in one of his well-heeled climbing partners from New York, Rand Herron, an aesthete and poet who by the age of thirty had also achieved a long list of first ascents, from the High Atlas in Morocco, to the Russian Caucasus, to Lapland, where he traveled eight hundred miles on skis. Rand then invited his girlfriend to join the climb. She was a journalist named Elizabeth Knowlton, whose articles for the *New York Times* would help raise money for the expedition.

With degrees from both Vassar and Radcliffe colleges, Knowlton was the second woman to set foot on one of the Himalayan 8,000-meter peaks (the first was fellow American Fanny Bullock Workman, who explored the Karakoram with her husband in the late 1890s and early 1900s). Although Knowlton was a strong climber, when Wiessner's team reached 21,000 feet on Nanga Parbat it was decided that she would not continue any higher. In her excellent book about the expedition, *The Naked Mountain*, published in 1933, she expressed no anger or resentment at not remaining a member of the climbing team. Instead, she acknowledged that she was there primarily as a writer, not a high-altitude climber.

As the men continued without her, they faced a series of setbacks. They had been forced to hire inexperienced Kashmiri porters from Hunza in northern India because the more skilled Darjeeling Sherpas (Tibetan for "east people") had already been taken by another expedition. Wiessner described the Hunza as "strong, tall men of the Aryan race," but they nonetheless suffered from the high altitude and increasing fear of mountain spirits.* Fritz reported that when they finally reached 21,000 feet, the

---

* From the early Egyptians to present-day Tibetans and Nepalese come tales of spirits and monsters which live in and, some believe, protect the mountains as the seat, house, or throne of gods. To trespass on that sacred land, particularly the summit, is a fool's endeavor. Nepal's Kangchenjunga, the world's third highest mountain, is considered by the Nepalese to be the most sacred of all the 8,000-meter peaks and for many years after climbers first reached the top, they respected that belief by not setting foot on the actual summit. However, many recent climbers have violated that respect and left their footprint, and their vainglorious keepsakes, on the true summit. Some believe that, as a result, Kangchenjunga remains one of the most difficult to ascend, and survive, of all the fourteen 8,000-meter giants.

porters were "of no use whatsoever." Fritz left them there to rest for a few days with instructions to resume carrying loads up the mountain for the team as soon as they were able. Meanwhile, he and the other climbers toiled on and managed to reach a height of 23,000 feet on July 29. A series of storms dumped monstrous amounts of snow on the mountain; in some places it was up to their necks and they had to "swim" through it using both arms and legs to propel themselves forward. Having no communication with the support team below, they had no idea that the porters weren't merely resting but had called it quits, refusing to climb any further. Fritz, Willy Merkl, and the summit team sat for nearly a month, their strength slowly withering, their stamina and drive dissipating day after day as they waited for food and fuel that never came. On August 20 they were "finally obliged" to retreat down the mountain. After five weeks at 23,000 feet, Fritz found the thicker air and fresh food a "great relief and immediate benefit." While little was known in 1932 of the physiological devastation of long exposure to high altitude, Wiessner knew first-hand that he and his men had suffered from their thirty-five days on the mountain. After two years of planning, fundraising, training, and arduous travel to reach the foot of the mountain, the team was finished. In *The Naked Mountain*, Knowlton described the expedition as an exercise in "frustration and futility."

The team failed to reach the summit, but great heights had been reached on an 8,000-meter peak and, more important, no man (or woman) had been lost. All in all, it was not a bad showing for a Himalayan expedition in the 1930s.

However, when Fritz returned to New York, he was not greeted by plaudits. America was reading every day of Adolf Hitler, a short, strutting, autocratic, volatile dictator who bore an unfortunate resemblance to Fritz himself. Then, in 1934, another German expedition to Nanga Parbat lost ten members, including its leader, Willy Merkl, who had also led the 1932 trip. Climbers in the American Alpine Club were beginning to wonder if the Germanic temperament coupled with the demands of the Third Reich to summit against all odds was not a lethal combination. Several club members began to challenge Fritz Wiessner's membership, and unsubstantiated but persistent rumors spread that he sympathized with and perhaps was even spying for the Third Reich. After the Nanga Parbat disaster, several members called for his resignation from the club. But Fritz also had his defenders, chief among them his good friends Robert Underhill, one of America's esteemed fathers of rock climbing, and his wife, Miriam Underhill, a talented and pioneering climber in her own right. In a letter of apology to Wiessner for the club's "grave mistake" in publicly challenging his membership, Underhill told Fritz how personally frustrated he was that Americans were somehow unable to "understand Hitler and what he has done for Germany." He went on to lament that Americans "cannot realize the moral and spiritual revival which . . . Hitler seems to have been able to bring about. You have no doubt long since made up your mind simply to endure this almost universal misinterpretation of Hitler and Germany, but I am terribly sorry to see it break out in our club, in such a way."

Anti-German sentiment had been rampant in the United States ever since the start of the Great War two decades earlier, and Fritz felt the sting of prejudice in other places as well. Eventually, the threats of expulsion from the AAC subsided, but the rumors never did, and while not a shred of evidence ever surfaced to suggest that Wiessner was working with Germany after he emigrated, many in the club deemed him a Nazi spy to their dying day.

In the spring of 1935, Wiessner and a group of his European friends, who had all cut their climbing teeth in the Alps, were cresting a cliff in the Shawangunk (pronounced Shon-gum) Mountains one hundred miles north of New York City when they looked to the north and saw a long, high line of white quartz cliffs in the distance. Returning the next weekend, Fritz found a 230-foot-high, eight-mile-long band of seemingly endless climbing routes. His subsequent establishment of the northeast's most famed climbing area near New Paltz, New York, called the Gunks in climbing circles, is legendary. He and Austrian climber Hans Kraus (Alice Wolfe's friend whom she helped free from Nazi detainment) used only three pitons in the upper section of their otherwise free ascent of High Exposure, one of the "jewels of the Gunks," an overhanging cliff of serrated bands hundreds of feet above the alluvial plains of the Hudson River Valley. Wiessner's climbing broke such new ground that at a meeting of the American Alpine Club in 1964, when a climber was crowing about having made a first ascent on a crag in Connecticut, Fritz tactfully interrupted and told the man that he in fact had pioneered the route over twenty years before.

From upstate New York, Fritz traveled west in the summer of 1936 to the Canadian Rockies, where the Coast Range's highest and still unclimbed mountain stood waiting: Mount Waddington. After sixteen attempts had failed and two climbers had died trying, many believed the 13,260-foot Waddington, more of a stark rock icicle than a real mountain, was simply not climbable. Fritz, however, considered it a puzzle to be solved. For his expedition he chose a small and eclectic group of close friends and stellar athletes, among them William House, a twenty-three-year-old forester from New Hampshire who had relatively little expedition experience but had already gained a name for himself on the rock walls of the White Mountains. And, echoing his inclusion of Elizabeth Knowlton on Nanga Parbat, Fritz included Betty Woolsey, who had raced on Alice Wolfe's women's US Olympic ski team in Garmisch the previous February. Not only were Woolsey and Knowlton strong athletes, their very presence helped Fritz to raise awareness and much-needed funds for a string of climbs in the 1930s and 1940s. But, like Knowlton, lacking climbing experience, when summit day came Woolsey was relegated to the support team, and was not one of its stars going for the top.

After weeks of preparation lower on the mountain, on July 26 Fritz and Bill House rose at 2:45 a.m. and began their thirteen-hour assault. Climbers who had already tried to reach the summit and failed watched the two men's progress through field glasses, spying them at 10:30 a.m. carefully traversing a narrow snow patch that clung to an almost vertical face. At 3 p.m., the glint of an ice axe near the summit was spied from ten miles away. And finally, at 3:40 p.m., Fritz was seen inching his way along a knife-edged snow ridge the final feet to the summit, with House close on his heels. Two Americans had conquered Canada's most sought-after peak and Wiessner's reputation as a fearless climber only increased.

Wiessner quickly followed that exploit by aiming for Wyoming's Grand Teton and its unclimbed north face. After examining topo-graphical maps of the mountain and repeatedly climbing to the base of the route to stare at its jagged cliffs, he finally decided on his course up the sheer rock wall. On August 10, 1936, he posi-tioned himself at the base of the route and, again with the formi-dable Woolsey there for the press rather than as a summit partner, organized his gear for the morning's climb.

Earlier that evening, Wiessner had run into a Teton guide whom he pumped for information about the route and the conditions on the mountain. The guide, Paul Petzoldt, answered all of his ques-tions, bid him goodnight, then raced down into the valley to roust his brother, Eldon, and his summer hired hand, Jack Durrance, out of bed. Explaining that Fritz Wiessner was at the base of the Grand and poised to make its first ascent, Petzoldt insisted that they, not Wiessner, should have the honors of the great North Face prize. Less than an hour later, packed and ready for the assault, the trio tiptoed past Wiessner's quiet tent, where he and Woolsey slept. Working through the night and into the morning, with Durrance leading the route most of the way, the three men made the much-coveted summit by midday. When Wiessner rose he learned that Durrance and the Petzoldts had in effect stolen his first ascent. He went ahead anyway, making what was then the second ascent. The insult so infuriated Fritz that two years later, when Paul Petzoldt applied for membership in the American Alpine Club, Fritz lobbied hard against his inclusion, telling a club official that Petzoldt was "not the kind of man we want as a member."*

After his bittersweet success on the Grand, Fritz set his sights on an odd geological rock formation in eastern Wyoming which had beguiled countless generations of Native American Indians and pioneers: Devil's Tower. Looking somewhat like a ruined Bundt cake on an empty banquet table, the 2,367-foot plug of igneous rock juts out of the ground in the middle of the plains thirty miles from the South Dakota border. According to Sioux legend, the tower was created by the Great Spirit, who lifted the rock high above the Belle Fourche River Valley to save three maidens being pursued by bears. As the bears tried to reach the maidens on the elevated rock, each slipped and fell, leaving claw marks that give the rock its distinctive, fluted surface. After the bears fell to their deaths, the maidens slid down from their lofty perch on a rope of wildflowers.

The first recorded climb of Devil's Tower was in 1893 when two

---

* Correspondence between Henry Hall and Wiessner, December 1938.

ranchers, dressed in overalls and cowboy boots, assembled a ladder of individual wooden pegs which they pounded into the deep cracks, remnants of which can still be seen. On the top, they left a large American flag.

Theatrics aside, the man most famous for his ascent is Fritz Wiessner, who in 1937 not only climbed it without a ladder (or flag), but without any protective gear save a single piton near the top which he later regretted, saying it was unnecessary. Breathing in great huffs and puffs from the effort, Wiessner inched his body up the cracks and crags, leading partners Bill House and Lawrence Coveney the entire route. Nearing the top, he shouted down to his partners. While the words were unintelligible, their meaning was clear to House, who had heard them before on Waddington. The words meant "We are going to the top."

With an odd sort of fate cementing their relationship, the next man to climb Devil's Tower in a style which would become legendary was Jack Durrance, in September 1938. Like Wiessner, he and his partners climbed it "free"—without protective gear anchoring them to the rock in case of a fall. The line he chose to ascend was named the Durrance Route and has become the Tower's most common ascent for today's climbers.

Even while he was making headlines on American mountains and rock walls, Fritz remained fascinated by the mountains in remote southern Asia. Those stunning peaks were majestic, never scaled, and twice as high as anything in Europe or the American lower forty-eight, and Wiessner knew that if he succeeded in reaching even one of the summits, he would secure his future as well as a place in climbing history. He had seen the way Knowlton's articles and book on Nanga Parbat had gained her fame and a certain measure of fortune; if he were to actually come home with a summit, he thought his story would be invaluable.

Having proven himself an able high-altitude climber on Nanga Parbat (although Willy Merkl told the president of the Alpine Club in London that he didn't trust Wiessner on snow enough to invite him to join Germany's 1934 attempt*), Wiessner lobbied the American Alpine Club to give him control of America's first major assault on K2 in 1938. However, when India finally issued a permit in October 1937, Wiessner didn't have the money to leave. He had recently started his own business making and selling ski wax and it was struggling; to leave it for several months was financially impossible. He handed the reins over to one of his climbing partners, a young man who was in his third year of medical school at Columbia, Charles S. Houston (pronounced How-stun, like the street in lower Manhattan).

Fritz and Charlie were good friends, having spent years skiing in New Hampshire and climbing the rock walls near New Haven, Connecticut, together. Although Fritz was thirteen years older than Charlie, both were new members of the American Alpine Club, and they enjoyed each other's company. But when Wiessner turned down the leadership of the 1938 expedition for which he had lobbied so hard, many, including Houston, suspected ulterior motives, namely that he was waiting for another team to do the Herculean work of finding the best route up the mountain, a route which Wiessner could then merely climb, saving weeks of valuable expedition time and energy. Before stepping aside, Wiessner made it clear that he wanted the 1939 permit for K2, if granted. Meanwhile, Houston assumed leadership of the 1938 attempt. Before Charlie left for the mountain, Fritz told his friend that it

---

* Germany's 1934 attempt on Nanga Parbat is generally considered unparalleled for sheer agony; ten expedition members, including Willy Merkl, died of exposure and sickness. Only one other team has lost more lives in the long and deadly history of Himalayan climbing: Germany's 1937 attempt on Nanga Parbat, in which no fewer than fifteen members and Sherpas died in a single avalanche. Small wonder Nanga Parbat is known as the Man-Eater in many climbing circles.

was much more important to come through "without the loss of life rather than a brilliant success brought through being reckless."

Over seventy years later, Charlie Houston's 1938 American expedition to K2 is still singled out as one of the finest in Himalayan climbing history on all fronts: the talent of its climbers, the preparation and execution of their goal, which was to ascertain the most climbable route, the hard work and careful risk management, and the cooperation, respect, and even love among the members of the team.* Except for some ugly business after the expedition involving Paul Petzoldt and an American missionary's wife,† the team was hugely successful. Houston and Petzoldt climbed thousands of feet higher on the mountain than any man ever had, and there was speculation that they might even have made the summit if not for a limited supply of matches—needed to melt snow for cooking and, more important, drinking water. However, Houston said later that even if he had had more matches, he could not have gone farther. He had reached his climbing ceiling. Those moments at 26,000 feet, his personal altitude record, were crystallized in his brain as the most emotionally charged minutes of his life, as he struggled to control his racing pulse and mixed feelings of regret and relief at deciding to turn back.

Charlie and his "brotherhood of the rope" returned to the States and were celebrated coast to coast as conquering heroes, feted with extravagant dinners and given a lucrative book contract. Their reconnaissance of the mountain had been successful, and

---

* The only expedition in American climbing history which carries more respect and admiration than the 1938 trip is Houston's 1953 return to K2, where, trying to rescue a fallen comrade from high on the mountain, he and the rest of his team survived a freak fall and in the process defined for many what the true "fellowship of the rope" is.

† Petzoldt stayed on in India after the expedition, having become enamored with Eastern religion, as well as a fetching American missionary's wife. In a still mysterious accident, Petzoldt and the missionary were arguing when the missionary fell, hit his head, and died. Petzoldt made a frantic appeal to Houston back in New York for money to buy his way out of jail, which Houston sent.

Charlie and the team reported that the Abruzzi Ridge up the east spine of the mountain provided the best chance at the summit. While steep, unforgiving, and providing little by way of proper campsites, the route was, except for a section between Camps VI and VIII between 23,000 and 25,000 feet, relatively free of avalanche danger.

With Houston's team home and priceless new information about the route in hand, it was now Fritz's turn. Charlie shared every detail of his own expedition with Fritz, from the grueling 330-mile trek to the mountain to 26,500 feet on the Abruzzi Ridge, the point he and Petzoldt had reached before turning back. Houston even wrote Wiessner a two-page, single-spaced note in which he delineated the climbing route from base camp, up the glacier to the base of the route, through each of the high camps, to his and Petzoldt's high point, explaining every major rock formation, obstacle, tent platform, and avalanche-prone slope on the 12,000-foot ascent. He also sent photos and amended the Duke of Abruzzi's maps of the mountain, explaining in careful detail where and why they chose the route and camps they did. Fritz now had a virtual blueprint for his climb.

Fritz turned his attention to building a strong team. He was at a crossroads in his life and he wanted K2. He needed K2. He was thirty-eight years old, single, and not yet an American citizen. He was living in a small apartment in the Columbia Heights section of Brooklyn and his ski wax business was barely covering his bills. With business only getting worse as the Depression rolled on, he was forced to send solicitation letters to friends and colleagues, many of them in the Alpine Club, asking them to invest in his company. When they did, it was rarely more than twenty-five dollars. To make ends meet and to stay in shape, he worked several jobs, including washing windows on the Empire State Building.

Every day he dealt with the growing anti-German sentiment, not only in the club but in the country as a whole, as another world war looked more probable every day. He had always hoped to find a rich American widow and live the good life, but so far that hadn't happened. K2 was his chance to move beyond his modest life and to make something of himself. After Knowlton's success, he saw that America had a fascination with the Himalayas and that a living could be made climbing them. If he were to climb this so-called unclimbable mountain in India, he would be set for life, possibly even as a guide for his well-heeled friends in the AAC who were itching to explore the giant peaks. He had been dreaming of K2 for years, mapping out every aspect of the expedition in minute detail. But with only a couple of months before he was to leave for the mountain, he still hadn't nailed down his team or its funding. His whole dream could vanish if he didn't recruit enough team-mates to cover the $15,000 cost of the undertaking.

Then Fritz received a note from Alice Wolfe inviting him to attend a black-tie dinner party at the Wolfes' Fifth Avenue pent-house where her husband, Dudley, would show some of his climb-ing slides from Europe.

Suddenly, the expedition's future looked much brighter.

Chapter 4

The 1939 American K2 Expedition Team

When men climb on a great mountain together, the rope
between them is more than a mere physical aid to the ascent; it
is a symbol of the spirit of the enterprise. It is a symbol of men
banded together in a common effort of will and strength against
their only true enemies: inertia, cowardice, greed, ignorance,
and all weaknesses of the spirit.

—CHARLES S. HOUSTON

The 1939 American K2 team: Back row, left to right: George
Sheldon, Chappell Cranmer, Jack Durrance, George Trench; front
row, left to right: Eaton Cromwell, Fritz Wiessner, Dudley Wolfe.
(Courtesy of the George C. Sheldon Family)

Within weeks of seeing Fritz at the slide show, Dudley had committed to going to K2. He booked his passage to Europe, sublet the penthouse, updated his will, and ordered the necessary equipment and clothes: a new ice axe, two pairs of leather mountaineering boots, the best steel crampons he could find, and layers of wool and silk underwear. What he hadn't done was tell his family, in particular his older brother, Clifford.

From the day the brothers had returned from World War I, Clifford had taken charge of running the family and its businesses. Their grandfather had been close to ninety at the time and Clifford was the eldest of his male heirs, so it had fallen to him. While Clifford and Dudley were close, loving brothers, they were very different men. Each was reserved and conservative, both politically and socially, but Dudley made adventure his life while Clifford donned a three-piece suit and polished brown leather shoes and made his life the family business. While he had no control over his younger brother, Clifford nonetheless judged Dudley's lifestyle that of a playboy and not a serious man. When Dudley wrote of hunting in the hills above St. Anton and skiing down the couloirs of Chamonix, Clifford responded rather stiffly how "grand it must be to have the time for such exploits." In the year before the expedition, Clifford had had enough of bearing the entire burden while Dudley played and had suggested that perhaps Dudley should spend some time with him on Wall Street and learn the family business.

For his part, Dudley knew Clifford was right. His brother had taken on managing the estate and overseeing the books of the vast Smith fortune, and done a damn fine job of it, while he merely had his name on the door at their New York offices. And yet Clifford seemed to thrive on the spreadsheets and business pages of the *New York Times* as Dudley never had. Instead, he had tried to define himself through ever more daring challenges. Rather than let his poor eyesight allow him to sit out the war, he had gone to Europe and volunteered with the French Foreign Legion. In deciding to race across the Atlantic, he had shown the world it could be done in a sixty-foot schooner. In climbing in the Alps he had fought hurricane winds and traversed crevasses where only days before men had been lost.

But Clifford did not consider his brother's exploits a legitimate use of time, and as Dudley packed his bags for yet another adventure, this one nearly a year long by the time he would finally set foot back in America, he put off telling his brother of the expedition. Instead, he left Boston before the Christmas holidays giving the impression that he would return to Maine in time to put his new sleek, single-masted racing sloop, the *Highland Light*, in the water for the season, most likely by mid-May. With his ticket to Bombay already in hand, he had no intention of doing so.

Before leaving for K2, and with a list of things to accomplish before he did, Dudley went to New York and hurriedly met with his attorney to draw up a new will. While in the city, he went to see his cousin, Clifford Warren Smith, Jr. Just as B. F. had feared, the man, now thirty-seven, was steadily killing himself with a fast life, well lubricated by alcohol, illegal drugs, and a revolving door of women, the latest being a Ziegfeld Follies cigarette girl. While even Clifford Junior's mother had written him off as irredeemable, Dudley remained in touch with his cousin and even considered delaying his trip overseas when he seemed close to death. But, having been assured by the doctors that Clifford Junior wasn't in imminent danger, Dudley continued getting his own estate in order for his protracted absence.

From New York, Dudley traveled to Boston where he made sure to buy some items which would be with him every step of the way: two pairs of double-layer khaki pants from Blauer's in Harvard Square and a pair of Asa Osborne's world-famous leather and canvas gauntlets with fitted wool liners. He had walked to Osborne's store on Beacon Street himself, just to make sure of the fit. They were the best cold-weather gloves made, and Dudley felt a certain satisfaction flexing his hands in the soft leather mitt. As he had in the ambulance corps and before each sailing race, Dudley pulled out a fine-tipped fountain pen, carefully spelling out "w o l f e" on each of his items, from his fleece-lined anorak to the cuff of his Osborne gloves. One afternoon he stood like a model in his new gear, turning this way and that in front of a tall standing mirror in his bedroom, making sure everything fit and had no loose seams. His nephew walked by the open door and couldn't resist telling his uncle he looked like a page out of the L. L. Bean catalogue. Dudley smiled and nodded.

On December 10, 1938, Dudley made a final check of his gear and papers before leaving for the harbor where the SS *Georgic* waited to take him to Europe. As he left B. F.'s house at 21 Commonwealth Avenue, where Mabel had spent more and more time during the old man's last years, Dudley was suddenly glad his mother had died several years before.

One of the last times he had seen his mother, he had joined her in her favorite holiday event, something she called "contributing to the Police Fund." Every Christmas she would dress in her Sunday best, down to the velvet blouse with her grandmother's cameo at her neck and a sable shawl wrapped loosely around her shoulders, call for the car to be brought around to the front of the house, and then be driven the length of Commonwealth Avenue. Whenever she saw a policeman, she would have the driver pull over so that she could extend her gloved hand through the window to give the officer money. The cop would tip his hat and bow with a "Thank you, Miss Smith," as he tucked the bills into his heavy overcoat. It was a tradition she had learned as a girl first in Omaha and then here in Boston, driving the rounds with B. F. In those days, of course, she and her father had ridden in a horse-drawn carriage and B. F. had brought a bottle of whiskey and cups and would stop and drink with each man as if he were a cousin. Like her father, she believed the tradition helped keep their lavish home and property safe from criminals.

Mabel had always worried more about him, Dudley thought, than she had about either of his brothers, even though Grafton, as it turned out, was the son who had needed the extra concern. He, Dudley, had always managed to balance his adventure with prudence and planning. From his trench warfare to his transatlantic racing, he had respected danger, not challenged it, and had known when to pull back, on the gas and on the tiller, in order to remain within a safe margin while staying in the game.

Dudley closed the three-inch-thick mahogany door and walked across the brick sidewalk and cobblestone street to his waiting car. Although he had already experienced many adventures, Dudley knew he was taking the first steps on the journey of his lifetime.

Before he climbed into his car, he counted all of his new Abercrombie and Fitch duffels and assorted hard leather cases with his cameras and filming equipment. Assured they were all there, he took a final look at the grand house and its expansive gardens, now covered in a pre-Christmas snowfall. He would miss an entire year of seasons. Between the travel and the time on the mountain, he wouldn't return to Boston until next October or November, just as the first snows of winter were falling.

He reminded his driver which pier the boat was leaving from

and sat back as the car slowly pulled away from the curb, its tires crunching on the icy snow.

As excited as he was about the expedition, he was also glad to be spending another Christmas with Alice in St. Anton. Their divorce, while heavy with her grief and his guilt, had nonetheless been as gentle as their marriage, and when she had asked him to come for her annual Christmas celebration he happily accepted. She made much of the season, particularly a tradition she had begun with the local children who would clamor beneath her windows yelling "*Danke*, Auntie Alice" as she threw sweets and candies to them from above. These holiday traditions gave her what she called her "annual dose" of children and she enjoyed playing the extravagant and eccentric American aunt, if only for a week at a time.

After Christmas with Alice, Dudley traveled to Switzerland for the New Year celebrations and to spend two months skiing and glacier walking. When he got to Davos and settled into his room at the Derby Hotel, he sat down to organize his thoughts. It was finally time to tell Clifford of his plans. As he began the long letter, he first detailed his climbing resumé over the past five years, assuring Clifford of the difficulty, danger, and rarity of some of his achievements:

> Please do not think I am blowing my own horn; you will understand when you see what I am leading up to.
>
> A short time ago[*] I received an invitation from Fritz Wiessner, leader of the American Alpine Club expedition to the Hymalia [sic] to join the expedition in an attempt to climb Karakoram (K2) 28,600 [sic] ft, the world's second highest mountain. This invitation, after carefully looking into the expedition, I have accepted.

---

[*] Here Dudley fudged a bit, as the invitation was proffered back in New York the previous fall.

After detailing the seven team members, Dudley explained that the entire cost of the expedition would be $17,500 ($262,500 today), with each of the seven contributing $2,500,* a sum Dudley thought a bargain:

> In other words, $2,500.00 covers all my expenses from March 15 until about October 1 when I am back in New York. I would say it was very cheap.

Considering what the same amount of time at the Derby in Davos or the Ritz in Paris would have cost, he was right.

Dudley continued:

> On this expedition there will be no professional guides, but Wiessner is as good as the best guides and will have the complete planning of the climb. As he reached one of the highest points on Nanga Parbat and has had much other experience, I feel that he will be most conservative. He impresses me as being a most careful climber. Finally, realize that the men taking part in this trip are mature, responsible, professional men and married men, some with families, who will not take foolish risks.†

Dudley described the climbing route they would tackle up the mountain and wrote that, because it was primarily along a rock ridge, there was less danger of avalanche than on an otherwise easier slope. Finally, and with an eerie prescience, he spoke of the danger above the high camps, assuring Clifford that "if risks are

---

* $37,500 today. Expeditions in the early twenty-first century to K2 cost each climber less than half of that, or approximately $15,000. But in 1939 it took months versus weeks to get there.

† Fritz had given Dudley a list of team members whose experience and maturity boded well for the expedition. Unfortunately, none of those men ended up going on the trip.

taken it will be between the last camp and the top." In closing, he told Clifford that "my house is completely in order" and that he had drawn up a new will just before leaving the States, things he pointed out not to alarm his brother but to assure him of his "good sense."

With that he wished Clifford a fine winter and said that he would see him on his return sometime in October. In a postscript he asked Clifford to send American, state of Maine, and Harvard flags so that he could raise all three at base camp.

Clifford responded immediately to what he called Dudley's "most interesting letter," and agreed that this adventure could be a defining moment, as if his brother's life to this point had been rather unremarkable:

> I think you are doing it with a minimum of risk and after all, if you do climb this mountain you have certainly done something and made a wonderful record.

In February Dudley went to Chamonix to climb Mont Blanc. Climbing a ridge above the Vallot hut, he and his French guide struggled through subzero temperatures and 50–60 mile-per-hour winds, climbing only one hundred feet in an hour before they finally turned back. The guide, freezing cold with an already white nose from frostbite, was desperate to get back to the hut and had them traverse the crevasse-littered glacier unroped, something Dudley thought very careless. A few weeks later he attempted the Piz Palu (12,800 feet) on the Italian–Swiss border with his favorite guide, Elias Julien, and an English client. Again with temperatures close to minus 20 degrees Fahrenheit and winds threatening to blow them off the ridge, the men roped up and continued on toward the summit. Dudley was going well but the Englishman began to suffer from the cold. Knowing it would be harder to get the man down once hypothermia and frostbite took hold, Elias turned them back only twenty minutes from the top—a tantalizingly close distance for anyone who has overcome the odds and paid good money to reach a summit. However, rather than insist on continuing, Dudley agreed completely with Elias's decision to retreat and thought the guide a fine man as well as a splendid climber.

In early March he received a letter from Alice full of teasing urgency: "The reason I particularly wanted to see you [in Paris] was to beg you, for God's sake, to be careful on this K2 trip. Remember, Dudley Francis, it's a big grim proposition and you won't have Elias. *Please* don't take any risks and for God's sake be careful—sweet Gingus!" Her pet name for him always made him smile, even if she did continue to misspell "Genghis." He tucked the letter into his etui; it would travel with him to the mountain.

Finally March 16 arrived and Dudley traveled to London to meet Fritz Wiessner as he disembarked in Southampton. From there they went on a ten-day buying trip for the team's provisions: wool hats and gloves in London and hobnailed leather boots in Germany, steel pitons in France, snow goggles at Hamblins and heavy canvas tents and duffels at Abercrombie's, Primus stoves, English oatmeal, and Danish canned pemmican, a foul-tasting but lifesaving mixture of fat and protein invented by Native American Indians and Eskimos which helped them survive the brutally cold North American and Alaskan winters. The list seemed endless. Dudley was excited to be involved in the expedition's early planning, but his early excitement soon became concern as time after time Wiessner came up short at the cash register and Dudley was forced to step in to pay the bill. It was also becoming very annoying to have it assumed that he would pay for their expensive dinners and cab fares. There seemed to be an unspoken "Oh, it's nothing to you" attitude, and he was increasingly chafing at it. He had encountered such attitudes his entire life, from sailing across the ocean with young dock workers to skiing above St. Anton with Alice's wonderful but financially struggling friends. He had always been the one to settle the bill, and while they were right in that he barely felt it financially, perpetually picking up the tab did make him feel as if he were merely the purse behind the activity and not an active participant in its gaiety.

Here he was again, feeling like the chauffeur who pays his boss's bar bill, following Wiessner around with his wallet, settling his accounts. What Dudley didn't know was that the expedition had all but bankrupted Fritz, who had been forced to give up his apartment before leaving for the expedition and now lived out of his small office. While Fritz always assured Dudley that he would be repaid, Dudley couldn't help but wonder how. After one too many of these shopping incidents Dudley cabled his secretary, Henry Meyer in New York, and asked him to determine if every member of the expedition was paying what he had and to ascertain the ability of the expedition's coffers to repay Fritz's ever-growing debt to him. Meyer called Joel Fisher, the American Alpine Club's treasurer, and over the phone was quoted how much each member had paid. Fisher also made it a point to tell Meyer that the team was not financially tied to the club in any way. Meyer cabled Dudley back within the day, assuring him that the other three members already on their way to Europe had all paid the same amount. But he also told Dudley something that Fritz had not: a couple of the team's strongest members had dropped out of the expedition and, with Fritz in Europe, the American Alpine Club was now scrambling to find replacements. The club was hoping to confirm one of Fritz's alternate choices, and if this man joined, he would do so at a discounted rate of only $1,500, most of which the club itself would pay because the man didn't have it personally and no one in the club had been found to subsidize the expedition.

Having already paid his full $2,500 fee as well as countless chits for equipment and dinners, Dudley decided to step back and let Fritz figure out how to pay for his expedition on his own. Enough was enough and they weren't even on the expedition yet.

Before heading to Italy to meet the rest of the team, Fritz went to Munich where he had several meetings. He didn't tell Dudley what the nature of the meetings was, nor did Dudley ask. When they parted, Dudley got into his Phaeton roadster for one last drive through his beloved Alps, across the Italian border and south to meet the team in Genoa, the port from which they would sail as a team to Bombay.

For over two years, since October 1937 when India had granted the first permit to climb K2, Wiessner had been sending out letters of invitation, trying to assemble the team to end all teams. Unfortunately, many of the already small crop of America's top-notch climbers experienced enough to tackle a mountain of K2's demands had gone to the mountain the year before with Charlie Houston, and none was willing or able to take another six- to seven-month leave of absence from his life so soon after.

By early February 1939, Fritz's invitation to join the team had been turned down by an august list of America's finest climbers, including Adams Carter, Alfred Lindley, Sterling Hendricks, Lincoln O'Brien, Lawrence Coveney, and brothers Hassler and Roger Whitney, who, when he wrote Fritz his regrets, indicated a certain alarm at the team's lack of strength and experience: "Your crowd is very different from the men I had supposed you were going to have, but it sounds like a good one and I congratulate you on your progress so far." Fritz also approached the men who had been on the 1938 expedition whom he'd hoped to re-enlist, including Bob Bates, Dick Burdsall, and finally his partner on both Devil's Tower and Mount Waddington, Bill House. Fritz never invited Charlie Houston to join the expedition, a decision Houston saw more as a necessity than a snub, years later admitting, "A team could only have one leader and for him and me to have been on the same expedition would have put us into a power struggle from the start." Reading through many of the other climbers' cordial letters of regret, it is hard to discern whether family, school, work, and money commitments were the real reasons or whether they said no because of Wiessner. Not only was anti-German sentiment wide-spread throughout America, but his reputation as a difficult and demanding leader had become well known in the small climbing community. Years later Bill House would admit that his decision to climb with Houston's team in 1938 and not Wiessner's in 1939 was because he "did not want to be on another major expedition with [Wiessner]. Too many personality clashes between us."*

One man, Bestor Robinson, a climber and full-time attorney, wrote to Fritz that the expedition would be "the finest summer possible to climb on one of the big peaks under your leadership" even though his work schedule might make the trip an "irrational" shirking of his responsibilities. Still, Bestor thought that if he were able to travel straight to the mountain, he might be able to enjoy what Fritz had described as "an opportunity of a lifetime." But, his work and family obligations were a concern, so he held back on giving Fritz a definite yes until he figured out the details of what a prolonged absence would take.

Even if Robinson was able to join, Wiessner was still at least two climbers short of a competent team for a mountain of K2's size. However, he refused at least one man who had approached him to

---

* House filled out a questionnaire for a biography on Wiessner in the 1980s. That biography was never written.

be on the team: Paul Petzoldt. The American Alpine Club was still smarting from the black eye he had given the club the year before with the missionary's mysterious death, and some club directors doubted whether he could even get back into India. Further, Fritz had not forgotten the Grand Teton hijacking. Even though many credited Petzoldt as the strongest climber on the 1938 team, something Fritz desperately needed to bolster his weak roster of members, he refused to include him on the expedition.*

Nevertheless, Fritz went out of his way to encourage another climber from the Teton offense to join the team: Jack Durrance. While many imagined that Fritz harbored a resentment toward Durrance for the Grand Teton incident, he had actually been impressed by his climbing, both on the North Face and on Devil's Tower, and considered that more important than the prank. When he had finally met Jack face to face in 1938, he thought him very respectful, and he particularly liked the fact that Jack was fluent in German.

John Randall "Jack" Durrance was born in 1912 in the heavy Floridian heat of late July. His father, John Rufus Durrance, was a school principal and his mother, America Fair Durrance, was a free and restless spirit who, after being told that the German school system was far superior to anything available in the United States, to say nothing of Florida, packed up her five young children (the youngest girl, Ada Mae, was only an infant) and traveled off to Garmisch in Bavaria. It's not known whether she said goodbye to her husband, but it's clear she never returned to him and instead lived the rest of her life a single mother and eccentric soul.

Once in Germany, America Durrance set her children loose on the mountains above their village, and, learning at the heels of

---

* Letter from Fritz Wiessner to Henry Hall at the American Alpine Club, December 28, 1938.

European masters, Jack and his younger brother Dick developed a lifelong passion for skiing and climbing. Ruggedly handsome with a shock of thick dark hair, light blue eyes, and a sardonic smile which flirted at the edge of his mouth, Jack was the epitome of a ladykiller. Wherever he went, women were never far away.

When America and her four younger children returned to Florida in 1933, as Hitler's Third Reich began to consume an ever larger swath of Europe, Jack stayed on in Germany to work. He began to notice that his company was quietly retooling so that it could manufacture armaments. Told to keep his mouth shut, which he did, Durrance finally decided that dangerous and irrevocable change was imminent and left Germany in 1935.

Back in the States, he entered Dartmouth College on an athletic scholarship in skiing, awarded in part because his younger brother Dick was already a sensation at the college, winning nearly every ski race he entered, and dubbed by the *New York Times* "this nation's best all-around skier." Immediately, Jack fell into Dick's shadow at Dartmouth. He simply didn't have his brother's natural talent and was often an afterthought in the glowing newspaper accounts of Dick's shining career. He struggled academically and feared losing his scholarship once the school discovered he wasn't the skier his brother was. Miserably, he wrote his father of a terrible insecurity, not only athletic and academic but financial as well, and that he felt shabbily dressed among his better-heeled classmates. It would be a rare confession of his deeply felt insecurities.

Then, in October 1937, Jack received a letter from Mr. Fritz H. Wiessner. Opening it with some trepidation, expecting a rebuke for his rather ignoble theft of the North Face ascent the year before, Jack was thrilled to find it contained an introduction and congratulations on his North Face climb. Wiessner told Jack he had recommended him for a guiding job, which Jack had to politely decline because of his studies—he had already needed to work outside school so much that his grades were suffering. Still, he returned the favor by inviting Fritz to speak at Dartmouth and assured him that "the door to my room [is] open at all times and I only await your letter when you will arrive in Hanover." In following up, Fritz scheduled a slide show for the Dartmouth Mountain Club using Elizabeth Knowlton's photos from Nanga Parbat, and asked Jack for help in organizing it. He also said he was confused about the slides and the projector and asked Jack if he knew how to insert them properly in the slots—yet another machine that baffled Fritz. Asking if he could call Fritz by his first name, Jack obliged, delighted at having been noticed by the man many Americans were calling a legendary rock climber.

In the fall of 1938, as Fritz focused on organizing his K2 team, he realized that Jack Durrance would be a huge asset. Not only was he a gifted rock climber, he was also a seasoned mountain guide and would be able to assist Fritz with the less experienced men on the team. As a sort of test, Fritz organized a climb in the Gunks early the next month in which he, Jack and Dick Durrance, and two other hopefuls for the K2 team, Chappell "Chap" Cranmer and George Sheldon, spent a Sunday afternoon exploring the routes, many of which Fritz had pioneered. Thoroughly impressed by Jack's climbing, Fritz invited him to join the K2 expedition. Jack was thrilled and honored by the invitation and at first accepted, but when he learned of the $2,500 fee each member had to contribute, the penurious student again had to decline; he simply didn't have the money. Fritz told him that he would be a reserve member on the team while Fritz lobbied for funds on his behalf. Durrance was one of the few talented climbers available to join the expedition. Fritz turned to some of the deeper pockets at the American Alpine Club to help with finding funds for Jack's fee, most notably A. Lincoln Washburn of New Haven, Connecticut, and Henry Hall, the club's secretary and future president. Washburn apologized to Fritz that his "every available penny" was tied up in an Arctic geological trip but sent along twenty-five dollars, hoping it would help. Hall, however, took a personal interest in advancing Jack's presence on the expedition, insisting to Joel Fisher, the club's treasurer, that "we shouldn't let a man as good as Durrance stay at home if it is simply a matter of funds" and suggested that this might be a case for their "white rabbit" funds. He immediately wrote a letter to several of the wealthier members suggesting a $100 contribution each.

Fritz had also decided to invite the two other young Dartmouth men to join the team: twenty-one-year-old George Sheldon, whose inclusion Fritz called a gamble given that he was untested for the "terrific and long strain" of a Himalayan expedition, and Chap Cranmer, a scion of the Denver Cranmers for whom Cranmer Park is named. At just twenty, he was the team's youngest member and considered by many to be "Fritz's boy" after he had climbed well with Wiessner in Canada the previous summer. Although Cranmer had been on various climbs in the Alps with his family, K2 would be his first experience on a mountain above 15,000 feet. His performance in Canada notwithstanding, his inclusion had more to do with his loyalty to Fritz and his ability to pay the fee than with his mountaineering skills. Not only were his credentials lacking, but he had suffered from poor health since childhood, spending many family vacations in the care of a nurse while the rest of the Cranmer brood explored the sights of the world, from the pyramids of Egypt to the Coliseum in Rome. Hoping to alleviate his concern, Fritz asked Chap to have the doctor who gave him his physical check for heart and lung problems in particular. Although the doctor gave Chap a clean bill of health, both Mrs. Cranmer and Fritz worried about him heading into the wilds of

India; the last thing Fritz needed was a medical emergency two weeks away from the nearest telegraph station. In fact, having been to Nanga Parbat and seen first-hand how primitive that area of India was, Fritz knew that if something catastrophic were to happen to Chap's health, there simply wouldn't be time to get him to a hospital. But by Christmas of 1938 Fritz was out of options; he had to take both Cranmer and Sheldon and hope that their youth, hunger, and relative strength would serve the team adequately.

The final member of Fritz's lopsided team was Oliver Eaton "Tony" Cromwell, a Yankee blueblood born into great wealth. Others said of him that he was of the "idle rich," and he used a lot of that money traveling to Europe and around the United States, where he had climbed a long list of rock walls and mountains— invariably at the end of a guide's rope. Fritz and Tony had been friends and occasional climbing partners for several years, but Fritz tended to invite the well-heeled Cromwell on trips with a larger budget. Divorced, with a grown son, and nearly forty-seven years old, Cromwell told Wiessner when he signed onto the K2 expedition not to count on him for climbing or carrying loads above Camp IV. Instead, he would help Fritz with organization, both before and during the expedition. (One of his early contributions was to urge that Fritz refuse Paul Petzoldt as a member of the team because of Petzoldt's increasingly outlandish behavior.*)

The team was now a dangerous mix of unearned arrogance and grievous inexperience, and it suddenly got much worse. Just a few weeks before Fritz's departure, disaster struck. Bestor Robinson fell while skiing and broke his leg. After all his indecision and concerns over his schedule, Robinson was now most definitely not going on

---

* Letter from Fritz Wiessner to Henry Hall, December 28,1938.

the expedition. Although many feared the team was too weak for a Himalayan climb and questioned whether it should be scrapped, Fritz wouldn't consider it.

One of the last things Fritz took care of before he left New York was to finally become a naturalized citizen of the United States. Now the team was officially an American one.

When Fritz embarked for Europe a few weeks later, Hall and Fisher worked furiously to raise money so that Jack Durrance could go. Hall also urged Fritz to reconsider the addition of Paul Petzoldt, advising that so long as the teammates did not let Petzoldt near the finances, they should be able to avoid trouble. Fritz again refused, even though he knew, after Nanga Parbat, that in order to climb a peak of K2's size, a veritable army of support was needed. Instead of that desired regiment, Fritz had Dudley Wolfe and Tony Cromwell, both of whose mountain experience was limited to guided climbs in the Alps, and Chap Cranmer and George Sheldon, two men who were barely old enough to vote—and in fact Chap wouldn't turn twenty-one until after the expedition in October 1939.

With time running out and the American Alpine Club nervous about the team's lack of experience, Joel Fisher and Henry Hall decided that Fritz needed Jack Durrance on the team. Fisher cabled Jack at Dartmouth and told him he was in. Fisher and Hall had been able to raise only $900 of the necessary $1,500 of his expedition fee* and Fisher asked whether Jack could raise the last $600 from friends and family. Within a few phone calls, Jack had received four pledges totaling the $600. After selling three pairs of skis for "pocket money," buying a life insurance policy, and breaking the news to his girlfriend, Maria, and his mother, America, in Florida, he was on his way to K2.

---

* $1,500 was evidently considered the rock-bottom amount required to get Durrance onto the expedition.

On the night of his departure, Fisher held a dinner party in Jack's honor at his Fifth Avenue apartment overlooking Central Park in New York. Sitting at Fisher's dining-room table that night, Jack listened as another guest, Charlie Houston, voiced his concerns that Fritz's team was "seriously weak in its composition and experience." Although he was a year younger than Jack, Houston commanded the conversation around the long table, his bright blue eyes sparkling.

A year before, Houston and Bob Bates had painstakingly chosen from scores of would-be teammates the six men who would perform well as a team, on and off the mountain. Houston knew that above all else, the friendship and respect between members went a lot farther than mere climbing resumés to get a team safely up and off an 8,000-meter peak. He didn't see either on Fritz's ragtag team. Privately, Charlie also worried that his old friend had dangerous ambitions. Before leaving, Fritz had told him, "If I can climb this mountain, I'll be set for life. Then I can come home, marry a rich girl, and retire." Charlie couldn't help but think it was an odd way to approach a mountain, any mountain, and K2 was not just any mountain; to set such ironclad goals for so unforgiving a peak was pure folly. But Fritz was struggling, privately and professionally. It was a bad time for Germans in America, and Fritz seemed to need K2, rather than just desiring it. That, Charlie thought, made this a doomed undertaking.

As Charlie looked across the table at Jack Durrance, he sized up the man. He liked him, liked his confidence and his movie-star good looks. But he also worried that the handsome medical student and brash skier had a swagger about him that might clash with Fritz. Charlie knew that there can only be one leader on an expedition and on this expedition that leader was Fritz. It had been one of the reasons he had not wanted to go to K2 with Fritz;

as much as he liked the man, he knew that he and Fritz would lock horns over who was in charge.

Finally, Charlie offered Jack some valuable high-altitude medical tips, as he would be the assumed expedition doctor heading into the wilds of the Himalayas. Frostbite, Charlie told him, would be the team's biggest concern. The treatment was basic: descend to base camp at once and keep the damaged skin dry, clean, and in the sun, without doing further damage through sunburn.

With that, Charlie rose from the table without ceremony or excuse, thanked Joel and Mrs. Fisher for dinner, wished Jack well, and quickly left the apartment. His failure to reach the summit of K2 the year before still irked him. He had been so damn close and it still ate at him that it had come down to a handful of matches, matches that he himself had miscalculated. Years later Houston would admit that he had climbed as high as he was able, but in 1939, only months after he returned from the mountain, he still believed it had been in his grasp. That evening, seeing Jack heading to what had become his K2 suddenly felt more painful than he cared to admit. He walked the deserted streets of Manhattan's Upper East Side for hours, alone and lost in his thoughts.

After a glass or two of celebratory cognac, Fisher escorted Jack to the harbor where the SS *Europa* was loading its passengers for a midnight departure. Fisher showed him around the boat and then stood waving on the shore while the steamship slipped from the pier toward Europe. At about only half the cost of what the other team members paid, and almost none of it from his own pocket, the young pre-med student was on his way to the other side of the world. It was March 21. The cable from Fisher had come only three days before. He hadn't even had time to get a proper pair of boots; they would have to be bought in Switzerland on his way to embarkation in Italy.

Jack traveled third class on the German ship, which had an unfortunate reputation as a rust bucket and a vibration from the engine that rattled Jack's molars. It had few or no comforts outside of first class, including a ban on butter many thought to be at Hitler's dictate. Even though it was an uncomfortable journey, Jack was pleased that he did not suffer the seasickness that he had on his other passages to and from Germany, writing in his journal that he "failed to nourish the aquarium."

Once on dry land, he headed to Paris and enjoyed champagne lunches and wine-soaked dinner parties with an odd assortment of expatriate Americans. After dinner he and some Dartmouth classmates frequented Parisian speakeasies where "girls dressed only in panties swarmed" the handsome young Americans as they sat at the bar. The air was full of talk of *la guerre* and his friends told Jack that every Thursday night there was a city-wide blackout and air raid drill. Jack found the French girls "pretty," the lifestyle rather "aimless," and the French men effeminate to the point of being "fairy."

From Paris he took the train to Bern, Switzerland, for forty-eight hours of all-day skiing and all-night drinking. Unsuccessful in finding a proper pair of boots, he ordered a pair which would have to catch up with him at base camp. He then downed countless pints of the local beer with his guide, Fritz Oggi, before stumbling semiconscious onto a train for Milan, where he connected to Genoa to meet the team.

Last to leave America, Jack was first to arrive at the pier in Genoa where the Italian steamship *Conte Biancamano* waited. It was the same ship that Dudley had spied eleven years before as he and the *Mohawk* raced to Spain in the King's and Queen's Cup. When Jack was shown to his room, he was thrilled to realize that, rather than descending into the boat's steerage, he was being to led to the first-class deck. Dudley, although concerned that he was contributing more than his fair share toward the expedition, had upgraded everyone's accommodations to first class, not just his own.

Throwing himself onto the luxurious bed after his alcohol-soaked and exhausting journey from Hanover, Jack had barely closed his eyes when a "uniformed dark eye" ship steward rapped on his door and told him that an elderly gentleman was asking for expedition members and was waiting in the Smoking Room. Assuming it was Fritz, Jack quickly changed his clothes, combed his unruly hair, splashed water on his face, and sprinted up to where a diminutive and distinguished man awaited him. It was not Fritz Wiessner.

Instantly recognizing the elf of a man, who resembled Sigmund Freud with his white hair and goatee, Jack stretched out his hand and bent ever so slightly in a sign of respect.

"Signore Sella, I am honored to make your acquaintance," Jack said as he took the man's frail hand into his own.

Vittorio Sella had made a name for himself by beautifully capturing in photographs the magic and majesty of K2 during the explorations of the Karakoram by Luigi Amadeo di Savoia, the Duke of Abruzzi, in 1909, thirty years before. As Sella pumped Jack's hand and excitedly asked about the expedition, he became emotional in trying to convey his feelings for the far-off peak, wiping away tears as he spoke. Jack tried his best to understand Sella through his thick accent and hurried speech. As Jack leaned toward the old man, listening so intently it hurt his already aching head, he was suddenly aware of another presence and looked up to see Fritz approaching with a man Jack took to be Dudley Wolfe.

Fritz quickly stepped into the conversation, extending his hand to Sella and assuming his role as trip leader. After he had introduced Wolfe to Sella, he introduced him to Jack. While Fritz was disappointed that Bestor Robinson, his old partner and proven talent, was not going to be with them, he nonetheless had Jack Durrance, a professional mountain guide, on board. Although the younger man was not as experienced on ice, Fritz had lobbied hard for his inclusion knowing that he was a workhorse in the mountains who had more than proven himself on steep and unforgiving terrain, something they had a lot of in their future.

Last to meet up with the team were Chap Cranmer, George Sheldon, and Tony Cromwell, all of whom embarked in Naples and marveled at the opulence of the boat, with George and Chap whooping and clapping each other on the back as they found their way to their sumptuous cabins. Once settled, the men gathered at the oak and leather bar for several rounds of celebratory drinks, most of which ended up on Dudley's bill.

As the great ship's horn blasted notice of their departure, the 1939 American K2 expedition raised the first of many glasses of the *Biancamano*'s house Chianti. The steamship pulled away from the pier and the men were en route to the definitive summer of their lives.

Chapter 5

The Getting There

Is it not better to take risks . . . than die within from rot? Is it not better to change one's life completely than to wait for the brain to set firmly and irreversibly in one way of life and one environment? I think it is . . . taking risks, not for the sake of danger alone, but for the sake of growth, is more important than any security one can buy or inherit.

— CHARLES S. HOUSTON, K2 diary, 1938

Never was a country more ruggedly beautiful and at the same time more wretchedly ugly.

— GEORGE C. SHELDON, K2 diary, 1939

Crossing the Braldu River on approach to K2. *(Courtesy of the George C. Sheldon Family)*

Although 200 feet shorter and half the weight of the *Titanic*, the *Conte Biancamano* resembled the famed ship in its five-star service. From the potted palms lining the promenade deck to the painted ceiling of the music salon to the leather wingbacks and oriental carpets of the library and bar, the boat celebrated luxury with every carved pillar, recessed ceiling, and arched entranceway. As with most steamships before and since, its many meals were the focal points of each day. At dinner the men would dress in dinner jackets and gather in the dining room for the finest wines and culinary fare, its two-story ceiling with a *trompe l'oeil* vault and its carved balconies resembling an opera house.

In April 1939, the ship was crowded with tourists as well as one thousand German Jews fleeing the Third Reich and heading for Shanghai. While many could only afford third class, those who were in *primo classe* entertained the other first-class passengers by singing songs and playing the piano and the accordion into the small hours of the night. While Jack dubbed the ship "Little Jerusalem," Dudley, remembering the exuberance of his Jewish cousins in London, thought these refugees were "the only people on the boat with any personality at all."

The team enjoyed the week-long passage, particularly George Sheldon, who had never traveled outside the United States. Film footage shot by Dudley reveals a group of boisterous companions, frolicking like the college men some of them still were, playing deck tennis and golf, more than once scorching their skin in the Mediterranean sun, doing back flips into the swimming pool and mugging for the camera on the aft deck. The younger men drank hard and danced late, sweat soaking through their white linen jackets. At every port they all left the ship and toured the exotic harbors and villages along their route, becoming accustomed to the "baksheesh beggars" who pleaded with the rich Americans for money. As the boat left the Mediterranean Sea and began its passage past Port Said and Ismailia and into the Red Sea, Jack marveled that the sea was as "placid as castor oil" under the full moon. They absorbed one exotic vista after the next and the Dartmouth men relished the fact that their classmates in Hanover were in the late doldrums of a New England winter halfway around the world. Finally, they passed Massawa, Ethiopia, sailed through the Gulf of Aden, and headed out across the open Arabian Sea to Bombay. For the most part, the men were pleased with their fellow teammates, although Chap thought Tony rather dull, adding not even a touch of "sparkle" to the group.

For his part, Dudley wasn't feeling his best. He was suffering from his second typhoid inoculation and the hot days and crowded ship only made him feel more miserable. He spent most of his days resting in the privacy of his stateroom, writing to Alice and Clifford and rereading a small stack of old letters Alice had written over the past year. She was still very much in love with him, missed him terribly, and warned him again and again to "please be safe, my darling Dudley." To make matters worse, the confrontation with Fritz over money had only escalated once they were gathered on the boat, where the boys seemed to assume he would pick up more than his share of the bar bills. Feeling like the team's cash cow, Dudley approached the men and asked to be written a formal receipt for the money he had already advanced. On April 3 Fritz wrote the chit on behalf of the team, adding a bit of facetious edge:

My dear Dudley,

The books of the Expedition, as they appear today, show advances from you totaling $1,300.57.* It is mutually agreed by the other members of the Expedition, that this sum shall be repaid you, from the Treasury of the Expedition, as soon as my subscription is paid in, which will probably be by the middle of the summer.

It is understood that this account is not final, and that suitable adjustment will be made later, if necessary.

Believe me always,

Very sincerely yours,

F. H. Wiessner, Leader

Dudley sent the note to Henry Meyer asking him to put it in the safe. Although somewhat satisfied, he stepped back from the financial transactions, and Fritz was forced to go to Cromwell and Cranmer, his two other wealthy members, to spend money the expedition didn't have.

Dudley was beginning to worry about the expedition as a whole. Not only was Wiessner's leadership weak on details and organization, but the team evidently lacked strength and experience. Fritz had assured Dudley that not only would Bestor Robinson be part of the team, but that Alfred Lindley and possibly Sterling Hendricks, both seasoned climbers, would be also. But those qualified men had bailed out of the trip and now, as Dudley looked at the young, almost sophomoric Dartmouth boys, the older and stiffly arrogant Tony Cromwell, and the autocratic Wiessner, he could only hope they would come together as a team.

On the boat with them was Dr. Hjalmar Schacht, a "vacationing"

---

* $19,509 today. It's no wonder Dudley was getting nervous.

Nazi financier whom Fritz had known in Germany. Schacht was later to be credited with having designed the rearmament of Germany after its financial collapse following World War I, eventually enabling it to wage World War II. From 1933 until January 1939 he had been president of the Reichsbank, and was now traveling as Hitler's minister without portfolio while still receiving his full salary from the Nazi government. He spent untold hours and dollars entertaining the Americans with stories and champagne, and most were charmed by him, particularly Fritz and Jack. Dudley, however, found him a "smooth article" with "a weak chin," and, knowing that the British were watching him carefully, he questioned what Schacht's actual business on the boat and in India might be.

Given that the team presented a dashing and handsome picture of adventure, wealth, and daring, women found them irresistible. The men befriended several of the prettiest ones, who laughed and pursed their fashionable red lips at Dudley's camera while posing along the ship's rail. One of them, a beautiful young German named Susanna Dreher, spent much of her time aboard ship torturing the randy young college boys. An attractive American, Mrs. Dorothy Dunn, also impressed the men with her long black hair, flashing blue eyes, and intelligence.

While Jack walked Dot Dunn up and down the palm court promenade and Dudley talked politics with her in the lounge, George and Chap had eyes only for Susie Dreher. George shamelessly flirted with the girl, incessantly trying to lure her away from her mother and into any number of compromising positions, but it was laconic, shy Chap who tantalized her with his reserve.

Chap was a born gentleman who would later woo his wife, Betty, by being the first man she ever dated who didn't "jump all over" her. Instead, Chap would arrive at her house on time, open and close every door in her path, hold her firmly but respectfully on the dance floor, and then walk her back up the porch to her door, shake her hand, and say goodnight at the end of the evening. His boyish good looks and almost apologetic reserve were catnip to attractive women who had tired of more aggressive suitors.

In the end, George's relentless hounding of Susie succeeded. On their last night on the ship and after many glasses of champagne, George headed to the pool for a nocturnal dip. As he went by Susie's window he yodeled for her to join him, which she did. After some playful splashing in the pool under a waning moon, they sat on the deck "bundled in my big bathrobe" doing "one thing or another" until four in the morning.

When the men disembarked in Bombay the next day, George was "confronted by a paradox of emotions" at leaving behind Susie and, he admitted, the comforts of the ship. Susie and Dorothy Dunn joined the team for a lavish farewell lunch at the Taj Mahal Hotel, after which George and Jack walked the women back to the pier and stood as the *Biancamano* headed out of port for Singapore. George watched long after he could no longer see Susie's white handkerchief waving from the deck, and then he and Jack walked back to the hotel. He was smitten and mused what an "awful blow to the family if I came home a married man." Still, he wrote, "reason and the heart wind separate paths."*

In Bombay the team walked the hot, dusty streets, marveling at the beggars who slept "littered all over the sidewalks," the cacophony of tropical birds and honking horns, and the leisure of having servants draw their baths and serve them hot tea in bed. While there, they provisioned themselves with the last of their gear: hemp

---

* George never saw Susie again, but years later when his only daughter, Susan, learned of Susie's existence, she wondered if her father's long-ago shipboard romance had been the source of her name.

rope, foodstuffs they wouldn't be able to get in the remote villages of northern India, and lightweight cookpots called *dekshis*. Also on the list were cheap glacier goggles to protect the scores of porters who would carry the team's tonnage into base camp against snow blindness on the glacier. At every stop, with money already an enormous concern for Fritz, many important supplies were either eliminated or reduced. While the goggles were inexpensive they were not free, and if corners were to be cut, the porters would be the first to feel the blade.

After exclaiming at the enervating 130-degree heat, which felt at once clammy and dusty, the men boarded the Frontier Mail train for the two-and-a-half-day, 1,000-mile journey north. With the carriage windows open to the heat, dust, and stench, after a few hours on the rackety train the men were caked in a layer of grime and dirt they felt as grit in their teeth. Mile after mile, station after station, they made their way north. Some stations teemed with monkeys which jumped through the trees as the train coasted into the depot; in others, shrouded women and girls approached the train and sold food to the passengers through the windows. From the scorching lowlands which Jack thought resembled America's desert Southwest, through the tree-lined streets of Delhi, they eventually saw the city of Rawalpindi come into view.

Filled with the clamor of mules, horses, goats, sheep, dogs, rickshaws, taxi horns, and men wearing turbans, long robes, and baggy pants, Rawalpindi was bursting with the smells and noise of Far East commerce. Several times the men had to jump out of the way of wildly ornate horse-drawn carts, some of the last remnants of the jeweled elephant trains which carried the Moghul emperors from Delhi to their summer palace in Srinagar. Now, rather than emperors and jewels, the carts were piled high with grain, fruit, and live chickens and goats, and were adorned with garish paint and shiny trinkets. Stepping carefully over the piles of excrement and open sewers, the travel-weary team made their way through the mayhem to their hotel, where the tea was hot and the bathwater warm enough to shave with for the first time since Bombay. For breakfast they had a feast of cereal, fish, liver, potatoes, ham, eggs, and fruit, which barely held them until lunch because of their hard work packing and weighing scores of loads for the porters. Dudley and Jack organized the foodstuffs while Fritz "fussed" with the duffel bags. As they worked, Tony strutted about, officiously checking his clipboard, clucking and warning the men that they couldn't possibly get the loads packed in time for the freight train's departure that afternoon to Srinagar. Dudley exchanged annoyed looks with the other men, all of whom ignored Tony and continued packing. When they finished their job with time to spare, they stifled the urge to say "Told you so!" as they loaded the crates. At first light in the morning, they followed the freight to Srinagar, the capital of the Vale of Kashmir.

The team traveled in two decrepit station wagons, a Chevrolet and an Oldsmobile, the drivers of which had to tweak and fiddle with the engines to keep them running on the long drive north. They passed through irrigated orchards of banana, plum, orange, apricot, and peach trees, above which every inch of available mountainside was terraced with fields of rice and other grains. Averaging only 20 miles per hour, they took nearly eleven hours to make the 200-mile drive along rutted roads and through flooded rivers. For the men, Srinagar was literally the end of the road. From there they would be trekking the 330 miles to base camp on foot.

In Srinagar, they stayed at the villa of Major Kenneth Hadow, a cheerful representative of the fading British colonial rule, whose great-uncle had perished on the Matterhorn in 1865. Hadow was a fan of both mountains and Americans, and his hospitality was legendary among explorers, cartographers, photographers, and mountaineers who traveled through the area over the years. He showed the men to a private guesthouse in which they each had their own room and specially hired servants to attend to their every need. Jack, who was not used to such pampering, felt as royal as a king and Dudley, who was accustomed to it, agreed that he had rarely felt so well cared for.

As the men basked in Hadow's hospitality, they each picked up a pen and tried to capture the first two weeks of the trip in their journals and letters home. While Dudley wrote to Alice, Gwen, and Clifford of the hot, crowded ship and boisterous Bombay, Jack detailed his trip from the train station in White River Junction, Vermont, to the foothills of the Himalayas, taking particular note of the meeting with Fritz on the *Biancamano*. He wrote that he couldn't quite forget "Fritz's look of disappointment at finding insignificant Jack filling Bestor Robinson's boots. Ah well, there I was, and who the hell cares what 'Baby Face'* thinks anyway?" It was an odd statement, given that Fritz liked Jack and had worked hard for his inclusion and that, until the expedition, Jack had admired and liked Fritz. Whatever Jack was feeling sitting by Hadow's fireplace in Srinagar, either insecurity and embarrassment because he couldn't pay his full expedition fee or perhaps resentment because Fritz wasn't treating him as the team's top dog as he had for some reason expected as his due, it's evident that, only a few weeks into the trip, the dynamic of the team was shaky and Fritz's leadership had already begun to unravel.

As the men looked toward their assault on K2, they knew they had untold amounts of hard work ahead of them and a limited window in which to get it done. Learning from what the early explorers

---

* The team called Fritz "Baby Face"—a term of endearment—because of his round, youthful features. He became known as Bara Sahib among the porters.

had discovered of the region, Charlie Houston and now Wiessner knew they had only four months in which to reach the mountain, climb to the summit, descend back to base camp, and trek back out to civilization, before catastrophic amounts of snowfall and frigid temperatures would stop the team in its tracks. Teams must wait for the worst of the snow to melt before they can get close to the mountain and, once there, they have only two months before winter returns in mid- to late August.

In preparation for the unrelenting labor ahead, Fritz had arranged for the men to spend a week acclimatizing and skiing at the Ski Club of India's Khillanmarg hut overlooking the vale. It sat a day's hike above the mountain village of Gulmarg, a favorite resort for Western diplomats and military brass who often left their wives (and girlfriends) unattended while they returned to their offices in Bombay and Karachi. Curiously, he also invited two young British women, Rosi Briscoe and Fiona Williams, to join the team at the hut. While George Sheldon noted that they were "not too interesting and they have a sense of humor like a lemon," Dudley wrote to Alice that he feared "two girls amongst six men is bound to cause demoralization" and distract them physically and psychologically from their preparations for the physical rigors ahead. The only member on the team to have seen the horrors and demands of warfare up close, Dudley was all too aware that the battle they faced ahead of them in the mountains could be just as life-threatening. While he didn't question Fritz about his decision to invite the young women, Dudley was concerned about the man's judgment.

The team's training took on a competitive edge once the men hit the slopes. After climbing on their skis from the hut at 10,000 feet to the summits 3,000 and 4,000 feet above them, they raced each other down, each boasting of his exploits and deriding the others' achievements. Jack noted each time Chap fell; Sheldon took particular delight in detailing Fritz's missteps; and both men remarked that Dudley usually steamed ahead of the group and then raced down like "a rocket," zooming past them all. While Jack was an accomplished skier and expected to do well, Dudley surprised them not only with his strength and speed on the rough and challenging slopes but also with his seeming indifference to the thinner air at 14,000 feet.

Dudley was pleased that the long, hot, dusty journey to the foothills of the Himalayas was over and that he felt better and in finer shape than he had expected he would. The skiing was some of the best he'd ever had, although the younger men were often careless; if not for some fast maneuvering on his part, he and Chap would have collided as the boy skied out of control down the steep slope straight toward him. Sounding rather avuncular, he scolded Chap after the near-collision. Chap tipped his hat in apology as he continued down to the hut. Again, as Dudley watched in concern, Chap gathered too much speed on his already tired legs in the deep snow, fell, somersaulted four or five times down a hundred feet, and finally came to rest, miraculously in one piece. He then climbed back up for his poles, shook himself off, and skied slowly down to the hut, carefully turning the skis with legs that now shook with fatigue.

Each day ended with an enormous dinner, a parlor game called Up Jenkins, which involved two teams passing a hidden coin beneath the table, and a round or two of chess, although the men were learning that Fritz was not only a terrible chess player, he was a worse loser and took most of the fun out of it for them. Often, as if they couldn't quite help themselves, the Dartmouth boys would have a water fight, exhausting themselves in the thin air and soaking their already damp clothes. Some nights, Jack,

Fritz, Chap, and the two English girls would argue politics and religion while Dudley, Tony, and George read books and wrote letters home.

The days began with the servants softly murmuring "Chai ready, sahib," as they handed each man his tea in bed. After a relaxed breakfast, the men would put a coat of wax on their long wooden skis, adjust their leather and steel bindings, gather their gear, and climb a different mountain, gazing in amazement at the scenery around them as they ascended. As they reached the summit, the landscape on the other side would reveal itself: seas of white foot-hills capped by towering rocky, snow-covered peaks, mountain lakes, and, in the distance to the northwest, their first glimpse of an 8,000-meter peak, Nanga Parbat. The men stared in silent wonder at its sheer size, 26,660 feet rising almost ominously out of the earth, its complex ridge lines, ice cliffs, hanging glaciers, and rock walls reaching toward the sky. They had never seen anything like it and they weren't sure it was an altogether pleasant sight. *If this is what Nanga Parbat looks like,* many thought, *what the hell are we in for with K2 and another 2,000 feet on top of that?*

The men climbed and skied hard and conditioned their bod-ies well, often taking their pulse as they reached the peaks above Khillanmarg. Except for Jack, who suffered insomnia, one of the classic signs of altitude sickness, none seemed unduly bothered by the climbing with heavy skis or demanding skiing at that altitude. As part of their conditioning, George and Jack bet five dollars that they would both keep their cigarette consumption down to three Lucky Strikes a day until their return to Srinagar in August. (What's remarkable is that they could smoke at all in air which felt increasingly claustrophobic the higher the men got.)

On one of their last mornings at the Khillanmarg hut, Sheldon, whose pen was often as sharp as his wit, was in rare form:

Chota Hazri* at 5:30 am. Everybody pretends to ignore Kargil [one of Hadow's servants] as he pushes you with a pleasant 'good morning.' I'd like to shoot him. But Jack immediately jumps up and throws on his clothes. He then cracks bad jokes which would even be lousy with a beer let alone early in the morning. Then Lhama [another servant] grunts and rolls over. Pop Sahib† and Dudley quietly get up and set about dressing. Then comes the climax of the operation. Baby Face, Half Pint, or Fritz Sahib gets up. Now, Baby Face sleeps with woolies around his neck to keep out the air. He always is way down in the foot end of the bag. But when he gets up; Ah, first there is a movement in the bag and a bald head comes out (this process may be likened to the process of birth), then a pair of shoulders and after a mighty convulsion—the whole man. Immediately it becomes alive and intensively awake (up to this time it might have been an egg). It jumps up, a smile on its face, mighty flexes of muscles. The Leader is up!

Although it had been an invaluable week of conditioning, Dudley couldn't help but notice that the men just weren't coming together as a team. Fritz was a detached ruler, issuing directives and criticisms which the rest of the men largely ignored, often with snickering derision. Jack and George seemed incapable of a day without pranks. Chap was a nice boy, but he was almost impossible to get to know and he went through the day nearly mute in his silent observations of the world. And Tony somehow seemed out of place, having already told Fritz he didn't intend to climb far

* Small breakfast, usually tea and fruit.

† Tony Cromwell, approaching his forty-seventh birthday in September, was the eldest member of the expedition and became "Pop Sahib" to the porters, Sherpas, and fellow teammates alike.

out of base camp. Why then, Dudley wondered, was he here? As Dudley packed his ski clothes and parka, he hoped his worry was just nerves and that everything would move into place as soon as the men started on their trek.

On April 27, the team left the ski hut and returned to Major Hadow's for a final week of equipment staging, team organization, and the obligatory goodbye parties. Unlike British explorers Eric Shipton and Bill Tilman, who favored small, lightweight expeditions where every man carried his own gear plus a share of the team's essential equipment, the 1939 American K2 expedition had four tons of equipment, necessitating first a fleet of ponies and then scores of porters from the Hunza region of Baltistan. For the first two weeks of the march, porters carrying 50 to 55 pounds and ponies carrying 150 pounds would be able to haul the bulk of the team's gear, but once they left the flood plains of the Indus, Shigar, and Braldu rivers and headed into the mountains, they would rely entirely on manpower to carry their loads.

These porters, or "coolies," as they were called by the "sahibs" before the civil rights movement of the 1960s dictated a less racist distinction, have been hired since the days of Alexander the Great to do the white man's heavy lifting on his explorations. Even though they are indispensable in carrying the team's tonnage, these local men and boys are still largely seen as uneducated and often untrustworthy servants. In 1939 the team's month-long trek into the mountain would require a series of porters, each traveling between two and three days from their village, paid pennies a day for their effort, and sent home as another group was hired for the next leg.

Fritz looked over his first group vying for the job. Some were older than his father and many seemed young enough to be his grandson. Fritz walked among the applicants like a horse trader, checking their feet and teeth—if either went bad on the trek, it could mean an expensive and irrevocable delay. While many were barefoot, some had yak-skin boots, others had sandals made from old tires. All of them were filthy in patched pants and long blouse-like shirts, and they draped themselves in tattered blankets against the cold and wore various forms of headgear—hats, shawls, woolen caps, and cut-up blankets—even though the temperature would be close to 130 by midday. Fritz chose his first group of men and then the village elder, like a circus ringleader with a whip, corralled and separated them into "hired" or "not hired" groups, and they dispersed through the dust.

With the porters chosen, the team members laid out their equipment, food, and personal items in a sea of gear on Hadow's lawn in order to pack it into 55-pound loads. As it was slowly unpacked, catalogued, and organized, Dudley discovered a glaring omission: the two-way radios he had instructed Fritz to buy. He had learned first-hand on the open ocean the value of the communication they afforded, but Fritz, hating all things mechanical and desperate to save money and weight wherever he could, had cancelled the order and put the money toward other expenses. Dudley stood looking at Fritz waiting for an explanation, but Fritz waved off his concern with his usual flick of the wrist and told him that they would be using smoke signals instead. Dudley didn't know what to say; the very notion of using smoke signals high on a mountain with gale-force winds was insane. It was, Dudley realized, as foolish as thinking you could use them on a boat in the middle of the ocean. Besides, what in hell were they going to burn? They would be nearly sixty miles from the last tree once they climbed onto the glacier above Askole. Dudley looked to the other men for backup, but he realized that none had ever been in a circumstance where communication could mean the difference between life and death. These boys had never experienced weeks in uncontrolled wilderness. Summers guiding in the Tetons and weekend trips to the Adirondacks do not prepare a man for months at the edge of the world. Fritz had been to the edge of that perilous world on Nanga Parbat, and Dudley couldn't help but wonder, once again, why his decisions seemed often to be based not on sound reasoning but on snap judgment. But it was too late. The radios were back in Europe and the team was thousands of miles into its journey. Dudley walked away from the conversation, but his unease was growing.

Fritz had made the decision early on that his team would attempt the summit without the benefit of supplemental oxygen. Not only was it prohibitively expensive, it was notoriously unreliable; many an expedition had found a number of their tanks empty once they got to the mountain. Stored in heavy, cumbersome steel canisters, bottled oxygen had been used by the British as they struggled to conquer Everest in large, assault-style expeditions, but, mainly because of cost, the underfunded, streamlined American expeditions to the Himalayas had largely gone without. Charlie Houston, leader of the 1938 and 1953 American expeditions to K2, said its weight and cost were the reasons he didn't bring it along on either of his teams. But he also said he didn't consider it "good sportsmanship to use gas," comparing its use to cheating. Besides, having helped organize the first ascent of Nanda Devi, a peak in northern India just shy of the fabled 8,000-meter mark, in 1936, Houston was "quite confident we didn't need it" to reach the summit of K2. However, Houston, a young medical student who would dedicate himself to high-altitude physiology, had brought two canisters of oxygen for medicinal purposes; if a teammate were to get sick at base camp or low on the mountain where the supplemental oxygen was available, he knew it could mean the man's survival.*

Good sportsmanship or not, when used higher on the mountain bottled oxygen exponentially increases a climber's chance of survival by providing the body and brain with rich, condensed oxygen it can't otherwise get at high altitude. Until 2008, when a series of freak avalanches high on K2 killed eleven people, none of the deaths on descent of the mountain had happened to a climber using oxygen; it provides that much life-giving sustenance. When climbers finally don an oxygen mask as they enter the so-called Death Zone above 26,000 feet, they feel a rush of warmth from their nose to their toes as well as a sudden mental clarity, as if the world were coming into sharp focus. But in 1939 no one really knew what would happen at the heights they expected to reach, so bottled oxygen was another advantage Fritz's team would do without as they approached K2.

The list of team gear included pack frames, goosedown sleeping bags with an inner liner of eiderdown, rubber air mattresses, crampons, pitons, carabiners, snow goggles, ice axes, large Logan canvas tents and smaller, two-man Yak tents, Primus stoves and gasoline, aluminum water bottles, canvas duffels, kitchen paraphernalia, climbing ropes, willow wands to mark the route, gasoline lanterns, sewing kits, and "one wash basin." In his personal gear, each man had a pair of skis, at least two sweaters, two pairs of heavy, wool long underwear, two or three turtleneck sweaters, six pairs of wool socks, four pairs of wool mittens, wool hat and balaclava, double-layer windproof parka and trousers (heavy khaki), buckskin and canvas gauntlets, rubber-soled shoes for the long walk in, leather

---

* For all of his good intentions and effort, when they arrived at base camp in 1938, Houston found the canisters were empty. Whether old or merely defective, they were nonetheless useless.

boots with tricouni nails for the mountain, a pair of sneakers, a rain cape, and any assortment of miscellaneous items of each man's choosing. Dudley's list of "extras" which he brought on the trip reflected much about the man: gold monogrammed cufflinks and collar pins, three pairs of mountain boots and three pairs of dress oxfords, golf shoes and bedroom slippers, a herringbone tweed jacket and a Tyrolean sports coat, a tuxedo and a double-breasted Loewy suit custom-made in Vienna, a pair of knickerbockers and a pair of grey flannel dress slacks, a Fair Isle sweater and a linen coat, two mufflers and four pairs of leather dress gloves, twenty silk ties and a Brooks Brothers bathrobe, two dozen handkerchiefs and eighteen shirts, and finally, thirty-five pairs of silk, wool, dress, and casual socks. Needless to say, he was ready for any contingency, from the opera to base camp.

Before leaving Srinagar, they were joined by their last team-mate, Lt. George Trench, who would serve as the British liaison officer assisting their passage through the tribal areas of the wild and lawless Northwest Territories. Tall and lanky bordering on gawky, Trench towered nearly a foot over the rest of the team and had a pinched face, narrow eyes which often squinted through his round glasses, unkempt blond, curly hair, and what Sheldon considered the usual "insipid" mustache of the British. After some amiable joking about there being one too many Georges on the team, Trench agreed to the moniker "Joe" for the summer to keep things simple. It was agreed that while he would help ferry supplies to the low camps on the mountain, he would not climb much above Camp IV, at around 21,000 feet.

Finally, the team's nine Sherpas arrived from Darjeeling. An invaluable addition to any Himalayan expedition, the tireless climbing Sherpas had enabled generations of Western explorers and climbers to reach remote areas and heights on the mountains barely imagined. But, unlike the sahibs, they were there not for the glory of climbing a mountain but to earn a wage. While they were respected and admired for their hard work and ability to carry heavy loads at high altitude, it was strictly a master–servant relationship; they too were often referred to as "coolies." With this power structure firmly in place, the Sherpas had proven on other expeditions that they were often unable and unwilling to assume control or to make crucial decisions on their own. It simply wasn't in their understanding of the dangerous and difficult job ahead: they were servants, hired to work for the sahibs, not to make decisions for them. Thus, the sahibs had to make sure the Sherpas were always under the direction of a consistent and strong leader, lest they too fall victim to the exhaustion and demands of a high-altitude assault.

The 1939 team was extremely fortunate in having not only five of the Sherpas who had been with the 1938 team, but 1938's *sirdar*—head Sherpa—as well, Pasang Kikuli, considered to be the best Darjeeling climber of his day. He had been Charlie Houston's right-hand man in 1938 and had survived the deadly 1937 season on Nanga Parbat, albeit with badly frostbitten feet. As a result, Kikuli had to take special care to avoid prolonged exposure to the highest altitudes because, once frozen, the affected tissue remained susceptible to further injury. When he and the other eight Sherpas posed for their team picture, they looked gravely at the camera, proud and fit in their Western clothes and new climbing boots.*

Unlike the liaison officer for the 1938 team, who was fluent in the local dialects, Joe Trench was not, so Fritz set about finding someone who could act as the team's interpreter with the porters.

---

* Part of the Sherpas' compensation was a climbing package of boots, sleeping bag, and steel-frame pack. Although each piece of gear was a cheaper version of what the sahibs had, it was more and better than they could afford. They valued their gear as much as the rupees they would receive at the end of the expedition.

Hadow recommended Chandra Pandit, a teacher at a local mission school and a member of the nascent Kashmir Climbing Club. Fritz immediately signed the man on, and, at Chandra's suggestion, included one of the school's students, a young man named Amarnath.

On their last night at Hadow's, the team enjoyed a final party in honor of Colonel D. M. Fraser, the Resident of Kashmir, at which Dr. Hjalmar Schacht, Hitler's financier whom they'd seen on the passage over, appeared. Again, Dudley thought him very curious, and thought the British were also a bit confused by his attendance. While Fritz, Dudley, and Tony held court with their diplomatic guests, and Chap spoke in French to Schacht's nephew the entire evening, George and Jack spent the afternoon and then the evening drinking themselves into stupors, eventually passing out in their "monkey suits" until pounding headaches and sour stomachs awoke them in the morning. (When he sobered up, Jack realized that Schacht had "swiped" all of his best photos of Dot Dunn taken on the *Biancamano*.)

Dudley was beginning to feel like the team's unwanted chaperon as he watched them become distracted and exhausted by late nights and too many bottles of champagne. *Why wasn't Fritz corralling their irresponsible behavior?* he thought. "There was too much to do to get this expedition off on the right foot," he wrote Alice, to see it compromised by parties and drunken frat-house pranks. In one, Chappell expelled gas at the same time as the chair collapsed beneath him, splaying him on the ground in a pile of splinters, much to the glee of Jack and George. Again feeling like their disapproving uncle, Dudley sat back and watched their antics, his natural instinct for being a loner only isolating him more.

Finally, after the skiing, the girls, the parties, and the pranks, on May 2 the men shouldered their loads and began their month-long march to base camp. After being driven the short distance to Srinagar's Woyjil Bridge, the men said goodbye to their last mechanical transport for months, and found themselves in some of the harshest, most spectacular and variable landscape on earth: arid desert plains, lush apricot orchards and poppy fields, cannabis growing as thick as azalea bushes, deep valleys blanketed in ethereal mist, thunderous rivers coursing with run-off from the glaciers, bus-sized boulders tumbling through the rapids, narrow canyons, crumbling rock walls, and, all around them, towering snow-capped peaks jutting into the bluest sky any of them had ever seen. In one particularly lovely grove of apricot trees outside a village called Oling Thang where the men camped in an open field, Jack felt "as near to heaven as I will ever be," and quietly sang to the North Star as he lay in his sleeping bag that night. As beautiful as the landscape was, the villages were dirty and impoverished, usually nothing more than a collection of mud huts where goats and people lived together in one smoky, flea-infested room. The scenes had remained largely unchanged since Alexander the Great explored the region in the third century BC: idle men drank tea and smoked their hookahs in open-front shacks, boys with dirty faces watched with curiosity as the light-skinned strangers walked through their village with a foreign sense of purpose, and, far off in the fields, women and girls tended the crops, bent heavy with infants on their backs—and always, everywhere, what George labeled the "wherever the urge calls" sewage system, which left the streets and yards littered with human feces, dead animals, and rotting food. Having marveled at the irrigation systems which for generations had brought the water down from the mountains to nourish the plains hundreds of miles away, the men couldn't get over the filth in which the people lived. *If they could invent these intricate terraced orchards, why couldn't they figure out an outhouse and hot water bath?* The men made sure all of their drinking and cooking water was thoroughly boiled. Because of the filth and lack of medical care—as well as generations of poly-andry* which had spread venereal disease like fleas—the sahibs were approached in each village for treatment of ailments ranging from gangrenous wounds to goiters the size of footballs hanging under chins to abscessed teeth which had been ground nearly to the gums by poor care and food. Usually "prescribing" an aspirin and a bath and giving the villagers a "few coins," the men could do little to help as they walked through.

From village to village, the local men would address them with respect, murmuring "Salaam, sahib," as they passed.† One man shocked George when he gave them a curt "Good afternoon, gen-tlemen," in precise, clipped English. The rare woman they saw was covered head to toe in a *shalwar kameez* and George, ever ready with a cutting observation, remarked that he was "beginning to see why; they are ashamed of their ugly pusses." The men learned fast the taboo of photographing Muslim women and once had to run for cover from a screaming mother who demanded they destroy the film with her and her child's image.

As the men got into their own rhythm on the trail, Jack and George often lagged, taking pictures and making sure none of the porters was skirting off trail to hide portions of his load for later use. With close to thirty exploratory expeditions having traveled through the region over the centuries, the porters from Baltistan had gained a reputation for thievery and, once on the trail, for crippling expeditions by calling strikes in demand of more money. What Jack and George failed to understand was something that

---

* A practice in which a woman is married to several men at the same time, polyandry occurs when a woman marries the eldest son in a family and automatically becomes the wife of all of his brothers.

† Literally, "peace," *salaam* is the Arabic and Urdu version of "Have a good day."

is as true today as it was seventy years ago: poverty in the region is deep and rampant, and when the local porters see the largesse of food and warm clothing they think, *Surely a bag of rice or sugar won't be missed when these men have so much and can easily order more.* Instead, the two Dartmouth men thought the porters "filthy beggars" and had great fun teaching them English profanities. They laughed delightedly each time the "Kashmere [sic] genius" would innocently wave and holler "Fuck you!" thinking he was offering the sahibs a cheerful greeting.

The team's long days began before daylight, when they were awoken by the cacophonous squabbling of the porters who fought to claim the lightest load for the day. Temperatures often reached 140 degrees (there was almost no shade), and the men tried to breathe through their noses because their mouths and throats were painfully parched. Each day ended with the sun disappearing behind a cathedral of peaks which the famed photographer Galen Rowell once called the "throne room of the mountain gods" and painting their summits in gold. Tired as they were, the men each took note of the unspeakable beauty around them before finally closing their eyes, many nights sleeping on the outskirts of villages in polo fields where the game had originated centuries before.

After only a few days, the team rose at 11:45 p.m. in order to traverse the Zoji La,* or pass, before the midday sun made the avalanche danger too great. With the porters chanting a prayer to Allah for safe passage, they climbed 2,500 vertical feet in four miles under a full moon, in the almost ethereal beauty of the whitewashed 20,000-foot peaks on either side of them. Reaching the top of the pass at 11,570 feet, they felt as if they were on the world's highest football field, the moonlight-drenched Zoji La a flat

---

* The Zoji is one of the oldest passes of the fabled Silk Road which connected Kashmir, Ladakh, Baltistan, Tibet, and the Kashgar region of central Asia.

meadow stretched out in front of them, before gradually descending on the other side. Although it was minus 15 degrees Fahrenheit on the pass, they stopped and watched in silence as a total lunar eclipse passed above them.

All the while, Dudley remained a cheerful if quiet teammate and a stoic trekker. Like all of them he suffered shin splints, blisters, and aching muscles, but he faced these aggravations without a lot of drama, soaking his feet in a warm salt-water solution at the end of each day and riding one of the pack ponies when a sprained ankle slowed him down too much. At the end of every day he would massage his sore ankle and shins, and, like the rest of the team, he ate more than he thought possible. He had never been so hungry in his life. He frequently wrote to Alice and Clifford in chatty detail about his adventure. Even though the letters took three to four weeks to reach their destinations, during most of the journey being ferried by runners between the team and Srinagar, the three wrote often to each other throughout the summer. While Clifford and Dudley talked politics, Alice urged Dudley to be careful and Dudley assured her that all was well, even pleasant, though someone had severely misled him into thinking that they would be sleeping in "bungalows every night with porters preparing nice, hot baths every evening." While the Sherpas did indeed set up their tents and blow up their air mattresses, it was hardly the luxury safari he told Alice it was.

One evening while lying in the sand along the banks of the lazy Indus in Skardu, he wrote to Alice in detail about their journey. After he finished, he scooped a handful of sand and poured it into the envelope with the postscript: "PS: This sand is from the Indus. Berg Heil!* Dudley."

---

* "Glory to the Heights!" In short order the German salutation became the expedition's unofficial slogan, with the men using it to close many of their letters home as well as notes to each other on the mountain.

Averaging ten miles a day, the men made steady progress toward the mountain. Most of the mileage they traversed on foot, but with several ponies on hand for loads and the occasionally lame team member, they took turns riding in order to rest their feet and sore legs. One day Sheldon named his "white hag, Rosie" after the girl who had accompanied them to the ski hut, evidently because the horse "greatly resembled" her.

Just as the skiing had become competitive above Srinagar, so became the trekking on the Deosai Plains of northern Baltisan. Each day, Jack and George in particular tried to outrun the other up the trail. With 25- to 35-pound packs and fighting the rigors of altitude acclimatization with every step, the men's egos proved stronger than their common sense, and they ended up suffering headaches and insomnia more severely than their teammates in the ever-thinner air.

Every day, Dudley found himself walking further and further away from the boys. The scenery reminded him of Shangri-La and its silence was so wondrous that he found, when he stayed near the others, the majesty of where he was and what he was doing spoiled by the pranks between the other team members. Their shrieking laughter sounded like hyenas and their persistent game of tag invariably left them in a heap on the rocks, gasping and choking for air with histrionic exaggeration. Dudley wondered why Fritz didn't warn them about wasting so much energy, but he kept his concern to himself and each day would either leave camp early or lag behind, content in his solitary marveling at the new sights around every corner. Because he was often alone during the day, he would set up his Kodak movie camera on his tripod, frame the shot, and then walk through the scene, enabling the viewer to see not only the landscape, but the action of the trek.

On May 17 the team said goodbye to the ponies and crossed the swollen Shigar River at Dassu on boats made of inflated goatskins used as pontoons. It was a wild ride made all the more so by the Muslim oarsmen shouting loud prayers to Allah as they navigated through the torrent. All the loads and men made it without even getting wet.

For the final ninety miles to base camp, the loads would be carried entirely by men. They soon discovered why. Not only had the wide river valley become a narrow gorge, but the only way to cross the raging river was on "rope" bridges actually made of woven twigs. With one rope for the feet and two ropes as handrails, the bridges had existed for centuries. Told that the rope twigs were replaced only after they broke, not proactively, the men watched with dread as the porters and their loads teetered across first. Only inches from the rushing currents beneath, the men's feet and hands swung wildly as they tried to find the perfect balance between the three points of contact. A few lost their balance and flipped the bridge and themselves entirely over, hanging onto the twigs for dear life before righting the whole thing again. When the last porter was across, the men handed their packs off to the Sherpas in order to reduce their imbalance and inched across, clinging to the handrails, their hearts in their throats. Dudley went first so he could film everyone else's traverse. On the other side, he filmed the team and urged each man to wave as he crossed, but only Jack would let go of the rope to do so. For one of the only times the men witnessed on the expedition, Fritz showed real fear when it was his turn, clutching the bridge with white knuckles and grinding his jaw as he inched across. Celebrating their successful crossing that night, Tony made them all rum toddies.

Their last village before the mountain was Askole. It too was a miserable collection of mud huts and fetid streams, but because the area was rich in grain fields, it was actually more prosperous than many of its neighboring villages downriver. The men camped in a dusty field swarming with flies and were constantly watched by the curious "natives" around them. Even though they tried to keep a watchful eye on their gear, food and equipment mysteriously disappeared in the night, and when the team left in the morning George and Jack were glad to be rid of the "robbers" and their squalid village.

In the third week of May, the team left the narrow gorges and entered the wide floodplains of the Braldu River. Instead of rope bridges the men crossed the one- to four-foot-deep glacial streams through the water. The closer to the mouth of the glacier they got, the more frequent and the more frigid the crossings became. Each time they approached a stream they took off their boots and socks, tied the shoelaces together, and slung the boots over their shoulders, and then braved the near-freezing water as they navigated the slippery rocks and low rapids which threatened to pull them off their feet with every cautious step. Still, the men all but ran across, screaming in agony as they danced through the icy torrents, the water feeling like knives stabbing their feet and lower legs. Sometimes the water was so deep their groins were submerged, and after stripping from the waist down the men shrieked with real and theatrical shock at the numbing pain as they waded half-naked through the water, their pants and boots held high over their heads. Reaching the other side, they danced about, slapping themselves on the buttocks and thighs until blood finally tingled back. As excruciating as it was wading through the rivers, it became a rite of passage, and the men performed it gamely and even a bit humorously, each daring the next to strip and scream his way across.

After one particularly long, deep, and painful crossing, the men sat rubbing their legs and feet and drying between their toes as they put their boots back on. Looking back across the stream, they saw Wiessner approach from the other side and take stock of the water. Instead of bending to take off his pants and shoes, he motioned to one of the porters and then, as Dudley and the other men watched with growing disbelief, Wiessner handed off his pack, jumped on the back of the porter, and rode the poor man across the stream, like a damsel in distress faced with a mud puddle. Dudley had seen many a Napoleonic tyrant during his time on the front lines and in the French Foreign Legion, but the younger men were astounded. They were learning that Fritz often acted more like a petty dictator than a leader; between his barking of orders and his deaf ear toward criticism, he was becoming a difficult personality for the young, brash Americans. At the next crossing, Fritz again handed off his pack and hopped onto the unfortunate porter's back to be carried across. This time, the porter teetered on the slick, rocky bottom and, with a great splash, both men fell into the frigid stream. The rest of the team nearly fainted from laughing in the thin air. Fritz emerged from the stream soaking and furious and gave the men a withering look as they slapped their thighs and wiped tears of laughter from their eyes. At the next crossing, Fritz didn't even hesitate; he just kept walking, boots, socks, and all, across the stream, and continued hiking when he got to the other side, all without a word.

After seemingly countless days trekking across this exotic wilderness, the team finally stepped onto the forty-mile-long Baltoro glacier, one of the greatest ice fields outside of the polar regions, and began their last fifty miles to base camp. Using their long, wood-handled ice axes as walking sticks, they navigated over the rocks and around crevasses following the Duke of Abruzzi's hand-drawn map and the notes Charlie Houston had provided. Every day they climbed they gained another 1,000 feet in elevation, the maximum that could be expected of the porters with their 55- to 65-pound loads (after the ponies left them in Dassu, each porter's load increased to avoid having to hire more men). The days grew cooler and the nights downright cold, cold that seeped up from the rocks and ice through their rubber air mattresses and sleeping bags and settled into their bones. They started wearing most of their clothes, their hats, and even gloves to bed. The porters didn't have the luxury of extra clothing so the team distributed tarps which, Jack noted, "held in their warmth and their Balti stench" as they nestled together on the rocks and ice like sardines against the cold.

After their second night on the glacier, the team was waylaid for two days by storms at a rocky outcropping called Urdukas camp. The men felt a bit stir-crazy during the long days and restless nights as their bodies struggled with the increasing altitude.

In any gathering of men, be it an army unit, a college fraternity, or a mountaineering expedition, a repartee often develops where each man is assigned, and sometimes earns, a label: the funny one, the moody one, the quiet one, the difficult one, the controlling one. The 1939 expedition was no exception, particularly given the stark contrast in personalities: Fritz was undoubtedly "the moody boss," Jack "the sharp-tongued wit," George "the light-hearted party man," Chap "the quiet and wise divinity student," Tony "the fussy old man," and, finally, Dudley "the reserved good egg." As they got to know one another and learned how far each could be pushed with jokes, ribbing, and public humiliation, it was quickly determined that Fritz's ability to laugh at himself was limited to a grunt of acknowledgment, while Jack's tendency to jab and deride someone until their ribs were bloody and their feelings raw was endless. The men were finding that Jack was somewhat of a bully, quick to ridicule but loath to confront. While Chap and George's personalities and the fact that they knew each other from Dartmouth provided comic relief after Jack's acerbic attacks, Dudley remained aloof from most of the immature banter. Quick repartee and verbal volleying were not his style, so he simply withdrew. While his money had made the other men's travel more enjoyable and some of their equipment possible, it probably also caused a lot of resentment, particularly from Jack, who had the least resources of any of them. As is often the case with resentment, it can surface as an attack. Then, when altitude is thrown into the mix, teams quickly become powder kegs of emotion, ambition, bravado, and humiliation. In short, expeditions can get ugly, in large part because high altitude often causes the same physical and emotional reactions as too much alcohol. While Jack had all the team members on a daily dose of vitamins, minerals, and yeast, he thought that perhaps a "temperance pill" might also be in order, given the team's early personality conflicts.*

As the 1939 team got closer to K2, its members were already feeling uneasy. George complained that the Sherpas were as bad as "natives" and couldn't make a decision to save their lives. Jack was not only being eaten alive by fleas, he was already suffering many of the classic symptoms of altitude sickness: headaches, insomnia, and a flu-like ache in his shoulders. And Dudley was becoming increasingly bothered by Fritz and Tony's talk about the team being broke and about their use of his films and photographs once back

---

* After two expeditions to K2 and chronicling countless examples of bad base camp behavior from high-altitude climbers, the author has developed a theory. When the body detects even the slightest reduction in sufficient oxygen, the brain starts pumping a flood of different hormones, among them estrogen, one of the strongest life-sustaining hormones. That much is fact. Now, here comes the theory: Every woman has at least a small amount of testosterone and every man has a small amount of estrogen. Therefore, when men go to high altitudes perhaps they endure their first onset of estrogen-induced emotionality, or PMS. While the theory is entirely the author's, medical and high-altitude experts became fascinated with the hypothesis and NASA is taking it into consideration as it designs the SpaceLab for extended exploration through the solar system.

in civilization. With the expedition's debt high (and the Urdukas delay potentially costing each of them another $100*), a few on the team were planning lectures and articles to help offset the team's debt, not only to Dudley but to the American Alpine Club for Jack's reduced fare. Some of the men apparently assumed they would have free access to the film that Dudley had bought and was now shooting on the expedition. Always getting the best of everything, from his commissioned yachts to his monogrammed Brooks Brothers shirts, Dudley had brought two top-of-the-line Leica cameras, a Zeiss Ikon box camera, and a Kodak 16mm movie camera, one of the first models to shoot color film. After their second day marooned at Urdukas, when mail runners took a load of letters back to Srinagar, Dudley sent several rolls of exposed film to his secretary, Henry Meyer, and included vehement instructions in the letter:

> Under no circumstances whatsoever allow any person to borrow these films from the office. I do not care who the person may be—the American Alpine Club, the leader of this expedition, or any member of it. I do not care what excuses they may make— even if they say that they have written permission from me to take them. <u>DO NOT let these films go out of the office. DO NOT let anyone have them.</u>
>
> I have secured these pictures myself at much expense, hard work, and risk and I want them untouched till I return.

This was harsh language indeed for Dudley, particularly as he gave Henry no explanation as to why he was so concerned about the film getting into other hands. But with George, Jack, Tony, and

* $1,500 today.

Chap taking their own pictures, the only member left about whom Dudley could have been concerned was Fritz, the man who hated all things mechanical and who was never seen with a camera or even taking a single picture by any of his family or climbing partners in his entire life. Dudley, who already felt used by Fritz and perhaps the team, was not about to give the leader carte blanche with his photos or movie films.

After the storms cleared out of Urdukas the team continued up the glacier toward K2. As they got deeper into the Baltoro glacier valley, over forty 20,000- to 25,000-foot mountains rose around them, each more spectacular than the last. While Dudley, George, and Jack shot countless pictures, each admitted that there wasn't a camera on earth that could capture the magnificence of these peaks and that their true beauty would live only in the men's memory.

Three days up the glacier they neared Concordia, the confluence of the Baltoro and the Godwin–Austen glaciers, which, at 15,500 feet, sits higher in altitude than any point in the lower forty-eight states. There they spotted odd and fascinating ice formations. Getting close, the men again pulled out their cameras, trying to capture their beauty and solve their mystery as they clicked image after image.

Shaped like enormous frozen ships at full sail, these formations rose anywhere from 20 to 150 feet in the air, the light shimmering off their smooth blue-white opalescence as if from a giant gemstone. Jack, putting his mountain knowledge to the test, surmised they were formed by the pressure of the glacial movement pushing huge chunks into the sky which then melted into enormous, sail-like cones under the hot sun. George doubted the pressure theory but, not having any better explanation, he and the rest of the team let Jack have his geological guesswork as they climbed to the tops of the towers to take one another's pictures.

As the men ticked off the last of their 330 miles they realized that except for the expected tired bones and fleas, they had traveled well. Finally, on May 30, the team rounded the last bend at the end of the Baltoro glacier and looked left.

There she stood, K2, still another ten miles down the Godwin–Austen Glacier, 28,250 feet rising out of the earth like a pyramid out of the desert—alone, majestic, and utterly in command of the lower peaks and glaciers at her feet. Nearly one thousand square miles of rock, ice, snow, avalanche gullies, hanging glaciers, crevasses, and constant wind, K2 sat before them as terrifying and spectacular as anything they had ever seen.

The men stood looking at the mountain as many explorers had before them—in silence as its power reverberated through their bellies. When they could speak, it was in hushed phrases: *Christ, just look at it,* and, *It's unbelievable.* A few of the men later admitted to thinking, *What the hell am I doing here imagining I can climb that? Even the sight of it terrifies me.*

In his journal, George wrote almost callously what he thought they were in for: "A trip like this, I believe, changes boys to men—they either come through or they don't, and if they don't, it is too damn bad. But if they do, they'll be men. We shall see."

On their last day of the trek, the lack of glacier goggles became a critical issue, as one porter after another fell to the snow holding his eyes and moaning in pain. Snow blindness occurs when the cornea and conjunctiva are burned by prolonged exposure to reflected light off the ice and snow. Like the severe sunburn it is, snow blindness inflames the eyes, can even swell them shut, and feels as if acid were being poured into them. The only cure is to cover the eyes completely, protecting them from all light with cool, damp cloths, while waiting for the inflammation and pain to subside.

The porters sat on the rocks, refusing to move another inch without glasses. With Fritz, Tony, and Chap far ahead, Jack, George, and Dudley set about cobbling together some makeshift eye protection out of cardboard, strips of polarized celluloid from a pair of Jack's extra sunglasses, and string. They cut rectangles out of the cardboard, then narrow slits through which the porters could see, covering the slits with celluloid and then strapping these "glasses" to the porters' heads. With base camp only a few hours further, the porters who could still see roped the blind men together and led them the final miles up the glacier. But five of the porters had pain so severe they could only lie writhing on the rocks. George scolded them to "Get up and get moving!" not quite understanding the degree of their anguish. Finally each man was given an aspirin and a cigarette, had his load taken from him, and was sent back to Askole. Then, burdened with double loads and a chain of battle-weary porters, the last members of the 1939 American expedition to K2 limped into base camp.

It was May 31. After nearly three months getting there, the team established itself on the cold, barren strip of undulating rock and ice at the base of the great K2. After 330 miles they now had "only" 12,000 vertical feet to their goal: the summit.

Chapter 6

The Climb

> *The struggle of man against man produces jealousy, deceit,*
> *frustration, bitterness, hate. The struggle of man against the*
> *mountains is different . . . Man then bows before something*
> *that is bigger than he. When he does that, he finds serenity*
> *and humility and dignity too.*
>
> —WILLIAM O. DOUGLAS

Climbing through the ice fall above base camp.
(Courtesy of the George C. Sheldon Family)

Eventually K2 would become known as the Savage Mountain, for its unrelenting list of victims. But even in 1939, before a single man had climbed or been lost on the mountain, the mountain's shape, size, weather, and remoteness reflected a savagery. As did its name: while other 8,000-meter peaks have lyrical names bestowed by local populations living at their base—Kangchenjunga, Cho Oyu, Shisha Pangma, and Chomolungma (the Tibetan name for Mount Everest, which is itself an elegant if colonialist name)—K2 has the bare, almost ruthless mark of its first official cartographer.

In 1856, T. G. Montgomerie was mapping the region for the Great Trigonometric Survey of India and saw two prominent peaks to the north and west. Sitting atop a hill in the Vale of Kashmir, Montgomerie pulled out his sketchbook and pencil and made a rough outline of the peaks, marking them K-1 and K-2, "K" for the Karakoram Range in which they sat. *Kara*, meaning black, and *koram*, meaning loose gravel, Karakoram aptly describes the volcanic rubble that covers the glaciers at the base of the mountains. Later, when Montgomerie tried to find a local name for the mountains, he found that K-1 was known as Masherbrum. K-2 however was so remote that although each village had its own name for the great peak—Chogori, Lanfafahad, Dapsang, Lamba Pahar—not one name was widely recognized. Rather than trying to decide which village's name would become the official one, he simply left it as K-2 for the time being, thinking its proper name would reveal itself in time. Perhaps because the name so simply reflects the mountain's harsh, cold, geometric presence, K2 has stuck. Now, over 150 years later, it is hard to imagine that any name could fit the mountain as well as the cartographer's austere notation.

By the early 1900s, over thirty expeditions had explored the area, but only three had approached the mountain with the intent of climbing it: Oscar Eckenstein's in 1902, which had among its climbers Aleister Crowley, a fascinating, devil-worshipping character who went by the moniker "666 The Beast";* the Duke of Abruzzi's expedition in 1909, which reached 21,870 feet; and Charlie Houston's 1938 team, which reached 26,500 feet. It wasn't until Houston's so-called American Cowboys came so tantalizingly close to the summit that the world realized that not only could the mountain be conquered, it could be done by a relatively inexperienced team (only two of Houston's men had been tested at altitudes above 20,000 feet) and without a battalion of support or supplemental oxygen on its upper reaches.

Still, even the somewhat bare-bones assault of Houston's team depended on tons of equipment and a Herculean amount of work to get where they did on the mountain. Learning from Houston's plan, Wiessner's designed attack on the mountain was first to place ropes through the most treacherous sections of the 12,000-foot ascent from base to summit, thereby providing climbers with a measure of safety as they ascended and descended the mountain. Then they would build a series of nine or ten high camps roughly every 750 to 1,000 feet up the mountain, at which they would erect tents and stock them with food, extra sleeping bags, stoves, and fuel. Finally, through carrying loads from base camp to the lower camps, each climber would condition his own body for the ravages of the climb and the thin air above. Unlike the 14,000-foot mountains scattered throughout Europe and America, which can be climbed in a day, the Himalayas demand months of preparation, planning, conditioning, building, and then waiting as violent weather rolls through the mountains, often pushed without

---

* Crowley would be one of the first high-altitude explorers to properly identify cerebral edema as one of the maladies afflicting climbers above 20,000 feet.

warning to hurricane force through the narrow valleys and fueled by monsoon rains from the Indian Ocean.*

All in all, high-altitude climbing is a test of body, mind, and will, in almost equal measures, and the 1939 team's challenge was no different. Using only rough sketches of the Abruzzi Ridge, identified by both the duke and Houston as the mountain's most climbable route, and several wide-scale photographs of K2 provided by Vittorio Sella, Fritz Wiessner and his team set about the arduous, weeks-long work of getting the camps set up on the mountain in order to support the men who would eventually attempt to reach the untouched summit. While Fritz didn't have his desired team of talented climbers, he nonetheless arrived at the mountain with four strong and able men. Unbeknownst to him, half of his team would soon be out of the running, one due to illness and the other to fear.

WHEN THE 1939 team finally put down their packs and chose the spot where their base camp tents would sit for the next two months, Jack looked up at the mountain and the world of ice and rocks around him and, instead of feeling like a conquering hero, he felt like a fraud. All he could think was, "We're fucked. We are totally fucked." The mountain was so much more than he could possibly have imagined. Looking around him at his teammates, he thought that none of them, certainly not himself nor the two other Dartmouth boys, and by the looks of them not the silver-spoon-fed Dudley Wolfe nor the mincing Tony Cromwell, had the experience for anything even half this size. As he busied himself with the work

---

* While it is often thought that the mountains of northern India (now Pakistan) are too far from the Indian Ocean to suffer monsoon-like amounts of moisture, for over one hundred years expeditions have reported storms of seven to ten days with snow totals measured in feet, not inches. In short, monsoon weather.

of setting up camp, a chilling thought kept creeping into his head and wouldn't leave: "I am going to die here."

In the morning, he faced the fear of someone else dying: his friend Chap Cranmer.

On the last day of their 330-mile trek into base camp, a porter had dropped a tarpaulin into a crevasse and, after the porter had failed to find it, Fritz had lowered Chap down to retrieve it. After searching for the tarp for well over an hour in the dark, wet caverns, he finally found it and was pulled to the surface, soaking wet and shaking uncontrollably. For whatever reason, Chap had worn shorts for the entire trek, even though his thin legs often turned an unsettling purple from the sun and the cold. Now, standing on the glacier in soaking wet cotton shorts and shirt, he was dangerously chilled. In the morning he said he didn't feel well and by noon he was close to death. Thick phlegm choked his lungs, vomiting and diarrhea quickly stripped his body of liquids and nutrients, and a high fever put him in a moaning delirium. With Fritz and Tony having left on a reconnaissance trip to scout the Northeast Ridge and Joe Trench unable or unwilling to assist, that left Dudley, George, and Jack to take turns in the fetid tent, making sure that Chap was breathing and cleaning up after his explosions of excrement and vomit. Chap's "clumsy nurses" all watched as the pile of rank sleeping bags continued to grow by the side of the tent. Soon they would run out entirely if they didn't start washing those that had been fouled.

Through it all, Jack was in charge. At one point Chap began vomiting cupfuls of frothy liquid before the phlegm became so thick that he could scarcely breathe at all, and for two hours Jack gave him mouth-to-mouth resuscitation to keep him alive. Other times he would rock Chap gently for hours, keeping the fluid moving through and out of his lungs. Whether Fritz had been unable or unwilling to hire a doctor to accompany the team is unknown, but in the absence of professional care Jack became the team's physician. There was also an assumption that given his discounted fee, he would in effect "earn his daily bread" by performing extra duties.* But it was a burden borne heavily by Jack, particularly as Chap's illness went from grave to life-and-death. As night turned to day and then to night again, Jack sat vigil, holding a pail under Chap's chin as he choked up cupfuls of viscous sputum and vomit, cleaned up when Chap eliminated streams of thick diarrhea into the sleeping bags, and continuously refilled tea bottles with hot water which he tucked around Chap to relieve some of his convulsive shivering. Dudley and George relieved Jack when they could, but because Chap was close to death, Jack was needed by his side nearly the entire time. He would later remark, "In all my years of medical practice, I never had a patient as sick as my first." For his part, Chap muttered through his delirium that he felt as if he had only a "one in three chance" of pulling through. Even if he did, Jack feared, the pneumonia and dysentery† had critically weakened him and it was doubtful he would ever be able to climb above base camp. He had also developed a peculiar odor, beyond the obvious effluvium of sickness, which Jack had no answer for although he hoped it wasn't the smell of death.

Through all of Chap's round-the-clock care, Jack became physically and emotionally undermined and his headaches, insomnia, and general ennui got worse. Given what he had been through,

---

* Jack Durrance, diary entry, June 19, 1939.

† Years later, Chap would be diagnosed with celiac sprue, a genetic disorder that sets off an autoimmune response when certain types of gluten are eaten, resulting in damage to the small intestine. This, in turn, causes the small intestine to lose its ability to absorb the nutrients found in food, leading to malnutrition and a variety of other complications. Given the wheat-heavy diet on the expedition, Chap would continually fight sickness. As a result of his chronic malnutrition, both before and on the expedition, at five feet nine inches Chap's weight fluctuated from a high of 140 down to a low of 110 pounds.

plus the 16,500-foot altitude of base camp, it's scarcely surprising.

Meanwhile, their volunteer translator, Chandra, had been felled by mountain sickness and rolled about in his tent moaning and crying with a headache and nausea. Joe Trench, hired to be the locals' liaison and advocate, sardonically commented, "There is nothing quite so sick as a native who thinks he is." Several days later Chandra adjusted to the altitude but, like many on the team, he never fully recovered and he and the student from the school in Srinagar, Amarnath, often were more trouble than they were worth, as well as being terrific gossips. After several days of demanding more food and threatening legal action against the cook if he didn't get it, Amarnath was sent packing and left base camp with the next set of mail runners.

Chap finally began to come around, and although he was still very weak his fever had come down from its high of 103 and he was able to take in fluids, although he repeatedly "blew"* them all over the tent. A fine nurse as well as a promising doctor, Jack brought a wash basin of warm, soapy water to Chap's bedside and gave him a sponge bath and then brushed his foul teeth and combed his hair. Chap felt almost human again.

With Fritz and Tony still on their recon of the Northwest and Abruzzi ridges, an increasingly lazy Joe Trench making excuses about having to handle paperwork, and Jack still tending to Chap, it was left to Dudley and George to properly establish base camp. First they moved the tents they had hastily erected upon arrival to better positions on the uneven rocks and further from the ever-threatening rockfall and avalanche-prone gullies. Then, with a much-improved Chap sitting in the sun in a camp chair wrapped in a sleeping bag, Dudley and George set about digging an ice

---

* George Sheldon, diary entry, June 3, 1939.

house into the side of the glacier near the mess tent for the perish-able food. As they dug, Jack yelled over to them not to waste too much time and energy building what he called an "unimportant ice chest." Bruised by his disdain for their work but excited by their progress, Dudley and George kept on. It was hard work, made all the more exhausting by a blazing sun and temperatures close to 95 degrees. Somehow, none of them had thought base camp would be anything but a cold, icy place. But here it was, hotter than any beach they'd ever been on, and yet they were unable to take off their wool shirts and insulated pants for fear of blistering sunburn. Worn out by the stultifying midday heat, they were stunned by the sudden drop in temperature into the thirties when the sun disap-peared behind the mountains to the west.

In the mornings, they broke the ice which had formed on their wash bucket in order to splash their faces. They chewed at their semi-frozen tubes of toothpaste, breaking up the slushy paste, suck-ing it out of the tube, and spitting it on the brush so that they could clean their teeth. Base camp felt as foreign and hostile as the surface of the moon.

After lunch on the third day, the men lifted Chap, who was still not walking, into the sun and then pulled their own chairs outside the mess tent and sat drinking tea. Excusing himself to arrange his climbing gear, Dudley retired to his tent. As Jack, Chap, George, and Joe basked in the sun, they saw Dudley's feet poke out of his tent door wearing black velvet bedroom slippers.

Dudley's three cameras, professional lenses, filters, tripods, and films, his nautical field glasses, state-of-the-art barometer and altimeter, endless supply of beautiful clothes and silk handker-chiefs, were certainly remarked on by his teammates, but somehow his extravagances were hard to dislike because he himself was so likeable. He was unfailingly generous. He had upgraded all of the men's *Biancamano* tickets to first class and bought more rounds of drinks and dinners than all the other men combined. He also could be a hell of a lot of fun. Although for the most part a shy and retiring man, he would sometimes break into song, regaling the men in what George called a "pleasant but untrained voice" with tunes he'd learned from foul-mouthed sea captains, adolescent prep school boys, and wounded troops on the front lines in Italy. His stories were peppered with fabulous anecdotes of trench warfare, rogue waves off the Grand Banks, and the secret ceremonies of a Harvard Final Club—perfect entertainment for the otherwise mundane and utterly male nights at base camp. In an environment where, according to high-altitude climbers who have suffered many months-long expeditions, all conversation eventually devolves into "food, shit, and sex—what goes in, what comes out, and what goes in and out," Dud provided an element of class and humor. Still, the slippers raised eyebrows to a new notch.

When Fritz and Tony finally returned to base camp from their recon of the Northeast Ridge, George and Dudley rushed to meet them on the glacier with the news of Chap's illness and (much to Jack's annoyance) of their parts in the doctoring.

Fritz shook his head in frustration. He considered Chap his "best man" on the team, and it now looked as if he might be out of the climb before a single high camp had been established. But Fritz still had hope that Chap would regain his strength. The year before, Charlie Houston had been forced to stay in Askole with his teammate Paul Petzoldt, who had suddenly become delirious with high fever and crippling back pain.* While the rest of the 1938 team had continued on toward base camp, Charlie tended to Petzoldt, not knowing if he would live or die. Petzoldt had not

---

* Houston later diagnosed Petzoldt's illness as the mosquito-borne dengue fever.

only recovered, he had climbed to 26,500 feet on the mountain, higher than any member of the team. But unlike Petzoldt, a feisty Wyoming mountain guide with a reputation for tough and brawny machismo, Chap never got back his strength or, apparently, his interest in climbing the mountain, and instead was content to lounge in base camp for the duration of the summer.

Fritz's team was effectively down to four: Jack Durrance, George Sheldon, Dudley Wolfe, and Fritz himself, with Tony Cromwell and Joe Trench only helping to supply the low camps. Just two of the men, Wiessner and Durrance, had any real mountaineering experience as guides, not clients, and only Fritz had been tested above 15,000 feet. But even with his experience on Nanga Parbat, Fritz was uncomfortable, even fearful, of steep ice faces, much preferring the more stable and predictable surface of rock.

Nonetheless, his grossly inexperienced team, which had just become critically weakened with the loss of Chap, had to begin its work to climb the formidable mountain.

By June 5 Chap was well enough to take care of his own bodily functions. The team left him with Noor, their base camp cook, and started carrying loads of gear to the base of the mountain. The plan was a simple if arduous one. The team would climb up the mountain to where last year's team had found suitable space for the high camps—not always easy to find on the steep, rocky ridge. There they would carve out tent platforms in the ice and snow, erect a tent, bring up supplies from the camp below, and then move up to where the next camp would be built. From camp to camp, the team would build a supply chain up and, more important, down the mountain. As necessary as the camps were for the ascending team, they would be crucial for those descending, particularly if the summit had been reached. By establishing a veritable lifeline of food, fuel, stoves, tents, and sleeping bags, the team would be able to descend the mountain without the added weight of supplies. Given what their exhaustion was going to be, every ounce not carried in their rucksacks was an ounce of energy in their bodies which could mean the difference between survival and death.

In order to avoid the worst of the heat as well as the threat of avalanches sweeping down both K2 and its 8,000-meter neighbor, Broad Peak, and across the glacier where they would be walking, the team rose in the predawn chill, packed food and equipment into 50-pound loads for the Sherpas and 35-pound loads for the sahibs, and trudged the six miles up the glacier to the base of the Abruzzi Ridge. While most of the going was straightforward, as the men neared the base of the ridge, where the glacier turned a sharp corner, they encountered a mile-long field of house-sized blocks of ice. Much like rapids in a river, these ice falls form where the glacier drops sharply in elevation and where it narrows or bends around the base of the mountains, thus constricting the flow of frozen water and buckling and breaking it into blocks. Always changing and constantly shifting, ice falls can be one of the most dangerous sections of a mountain to climb. (Some consider the ice fall on Everest to be the mountain's deadliest mile.) Finding their way through its often circuitous caverns, Fritz and the team finally established what they hoped was a safe route for their frequent trips between base camp and Camp I.

Returning from carrying a load to Camp I, Jack and George got into one of their competitive races, even though they were at 18,000 feet. Predictably, when George sped up, he forced Jack and Fritz to match the breakneck speed and, once at base camp, all three men felt the ill effects of "jogging" at altitude. Fritz sharply chastised the men, George in particular, for their little stunt.

As Dudley crawled into his tent that night and lay in his sleeping bag, he realized with some sadness and alarm that the team was not coming together as he had hoped. He had worried both on the boat and again at the ski hut in Gulmarg that the boys seemed ill-prepared, both physically and mentally, for the task at hand. Today's game of tag on the glacier only squandered their already compromised energies. He was glad Fritz had finally said something, although he doubted they took it seriously—they had made schoolboy faces behind Fritz's back after his rebuke. Dudley often felt he was in the middle of a fraternity house prank rather than a Himalayan expedition. But he would have to put that out of his mind. He was here to climb the mountain, and so was Fritz. If necessary, they would do it without the others.

The next day, as the team was returning from another carry through an ice couloir below Camp I, Fritz suddenly disappeared ahead of them down the route without a word. The Sherpas took over the lead and helped the less experienced sahibs navigate the icy section. After they all made it back safely, Jack approached Fritz and asked what that was all about.

"It was a test," Fritz said sharply. "To see how you all did without me."

Jack looked at him with alarm. Testing the men with a potentially dangerous stunt was even more brazen than Jack had thought Fritz to be. Never eager for a showdown, Jack walked away without challenging Fritz, but, like Dudley, his apprehension grew every day.

On June 7 Dudley, the team, and the eight Sherpas* carried

---

* On approach march, their ninth Sherpa, Pemba Kitar, had taken ill with pneumonia and was sent back to Skardu to recover and return with a doctor's note assuring that he was fit for work. He returned on June 28, but he was still weak and without a note. He left for good two days later. The team was therefore down to eight climbing Sherpas.

their third load of food and gear (including one thousand ciga-
rettes) from base camp to Camp I. There, Jack, Dudley, and George
drew straws to see which of them would accompany Fritz on a
reconnaissance climb and load carry to where their Camp II would
be situated. Jack won and started out with Fritz. Soon, he felt like
crying out loud in pain as he struggled with his heavy pack in the
thin air. After finding a suitable spot for Camp II, they dumped
their pack loads and retreated back to Camp I, where the rest of
the men waited. When they all returned to base camp the following night they felt the satisfaction of their hard work. Climbing
into their sleeping bags with a pipe and a book after dinner and
wearing layers of clothes and gloves on their hands against the
bitter nights, the men relished their exhaustion. But as they tried
to settle into deep sleep, they were frustrated by it being a series of
naps rather than solid slumber. Not only was the altitude causing
headaches, dizziness, light nausea, and insomnia as their bodies
adjusted to the thin air, but they were frequently awakened by the
glacier beneath their heads. Its constant movement caused it to
buckle, crack, groan, pop, and snap with such violence and volume
the men feared it would open up and swallow them, tents and all.
It reminded some of them of skating on a partially frozen pond
and hearing and feeling the vacuous booms as the ice cracked and
moved beneath them. Disconcerting at best, terrifying at worst,
the glacier's noisy shifting was a natural occurrence but difficult to
sleep through, particularly when the great echoing explosions of
ice beneath them could be felt through every inch of their bodies
stretched out in their sleeping bags.

For Jack, the days on the ice weren't much better. His only winter experience in the mountains had been on skis, not in hobnailed
boots, and he was nervous with every step as he negotiated over the
crevasses on the daily trips to Camp I. Shaking his head to clear

it of the dull ache and fuzziness that had begun to plague him, he tried to learn as fast as he could about glacier technique. The groaning, cracking, almost belching world of ice was foreign to him, and he didn't much like it. At one point, Fritz and he doubled the safety rope between them and ventured out to the middle of the glacier, testing its strength and scouting for hidden crevasses into which the men might disappear without warning. Once back on the thicker edge of the glacier nearer the mountain, Jack was enormously relieved and hoped he wouldn't have to repeat the mission. From his first moments at base camp, he had started to fear that he wouldn't survive this unpredictable, frightening landscape. He knew it was crazy and premonitions had never been his style, but regardless, he couldn't shake the feeling that he wouldn't live through the summer and this world of capricious, almost evil ice which he now called home.

After only a few days working to cache gear low on the mountain, the already weak organization of the team began to deteriorate further. Rather than packing loads and helping keep the mess tent orderly on their rest days at base camp, most of them would nap and read (*War and Peace* in George's case, *Betrayal in Central Europe* in Dudley's). Jack was left to do a lot of the grunt work and his resentment flourished. Time and again he found himself the only one cleaning up after meals or preparing loads, as well as tending to the medical needs of the Sherpas, his other teammates, and the ever-ailing Chandra. Joe Trench in particular irked him. The British officer had proven to be not only lazy and complaining, he had developed a "sahib attitude" toward Jack, ordering him around like his "Indian servant." Adding to Jack's and the team's frustration with Joe was the fact that although he was supposed to be their liaison to the local porters, he hadn't bothered to learn their language. He was, in Jack's thinking, a "total waste of baggage" and a clumsy, even dangerous, load on the mountain—one which Jack was forced to lead up and down the rope when they carried loads to Camps I and II.

On June 9, before the first light of morning appeared, the men at base camp awoke to the hiss of the stove being started as Noor began breakfast for the team. Nearby, Dudley sat up in his tent and lit his lantern, careful to avoid touching the sides of the tent which had gathered condensation overnight and, if bumped, would rain down on him. All of his clothes and gear sat in neat piles. Today was it. He and Fritz, and hopefully George and Jack, would climb from base to Camp I and then continue on to establish Camp II. With Camp I fully stocked it was now their job to move themselves and the supplies farther up the mountain.

Like most climbers at base camp, Dudley wore his long underwear day and night except to occasionally give himself what his buddies in the war had called a "French whore's bath"—quickly swabbing his armpits and groin with soap and water. Still seated in his sleeping bag, he pulled on a plaid wool shirt over the long underwear, then his heavy Irish knit sweater, and on top of it, his fleece-lined anorak. Next, he pulled on a pair of thin wool socks and over them a pair of his heavy ski socks. Finally, he reached for his double-layer khaki pants and scooted into them, half sitting and half lying on the sleeping bag. Fully dressed, he kneeled on the air mattress and began carefully folding and rolling the sleeping bag as small as he could before tying it tight with a leather strap. Sitting back, he picked up his heavy, leather climbing boots, and, even though he had sharpened them the night before, made sure the hobnails had a good edge. He then looked at the gear he would take high on the mountain. Each man could only take what he could carry himself; the Sherpas would not be able to carry any of the sahibs' personal gear. Leaving his two larger cameras and his movie camera, Dudley put his smaller Leica and a few rolls of film near his rucksack. Quickly but carefully he chose the personal items he would take: toothbrush, small tube of paste, half a cake of soap, metal file to sharpen his hobnails and crampons, small leather journal, pencil, pocket knife, stainless steel match case, and one needle and a spool of heavy black thread from his sewing kit. Then his climbing equipment: crampons, goggles, and windproof double-layer parka and trousers. He would live in the clothes on his back, but took an extra wool shirt and a pair of socks, just in case. He had traveled the world with trunks of clothing and accessories; this time, everything he needed would be on his own back.

He put the gear into the rucksack, mindful of what he might need during the day's climb, which he put in last. He tied his sleeping bag to the pack and put on his boots and knee-high gaiters, adjusting the leather foot straps so they weren't touching a hobnail. He took one last look around the tent to make sure he hadn't forgotten anything. Satisfied, he untied the tent flap, turned and blew out the lantern, climbed out backwards on all fours, and reached back in for the rucksack. Standing straight, he slung the rucksack onto his back, put on his leather and canvas gauntlets, and reached for his ice axe, which was stuck upright in the snow by the tent. He was ready to climb K2.

As the team made its slow progress up the rock and ice slopes, Fritz soon realized he had no one else on the team he could trust to establish the route and anchor the safety rope through the steepest sections. None had the experience or technical ability. He had to assume the entire responsibility. As the history of K2 became written in the years to come, Fritz's feat in leading and anchoring all but a few of the rope lengths on the mountain is unparalleled. With so much exhausting work ahead of him, Fritz tried to delegate logistical responsibility to his deputy, Tony, giving him a list of directives and instructions that in his absence were to be carried out lower on the mountain: what supplies were to be carried to what camps and when, which of the Sherpas could be trusted with which loads, and so on. But Tony immediately balked, and, while Fritz and Dudley were exploring what was above them on the mountain, he did none of the work Fritz had requested. When Fritz and Dudley descended back to Camp I from their reconnaissance a few days later, they found the entire team lolling about napping and resting. The large Logan tent was a chaos of gear and garbage, no dinner was prepared, no loads readied, and no evident movement had been made toward actually climbing the mountain. Unleashing his infamous temper, Fritz put the blame squarely on Tony, accusing him of insubordination, laziness, and ineptitude. As was his style, after his tantrum Fritz assumed that since he was no longer angry, no one else was either, and that they all went to bed that night "friends." But Tony was mortified and outraged by Fritz's attack and decided then and there that he was finished on the mountain, with the expedition, and, in particular, with Fritz. Unknowingly, Wiessner had lost another foot soldier. He had also lost, in every sense of the word, a team player.

Adding to this troubled mix was Jack's chronic list of physical maladies, from toothaches to headaches to cold feet to "feeling like shit—winded and despondent," to sharing Tony's frustration with their autocratic and often absent warlord. As Jack's inability to climb grew more evident, his outlook became darker. Adding to his misery and frustration was his lack of good climbing boots. Having left America with only three days' notice, he had had to order climbing boots in Europe and now awaited their delivery at base camp. In the meantime, his feet froze in thin leather ski boots designed for day trips on the mountains of New England, not the Himalayas.

Finally, George Sheldon's inexperience and immaturity began to be a real problem. Fritz knew when he signed Sheldon onto the team that the college junior was young and had never done much climbing outside of a Dartmouth club event, but he had hoped that George's youth and energy would serve their efforts on K2. Instead, Sheldon had proven to be a brash prankster who, like Jack, enjoyed his alcohol a bit too much, something the austere Fritz found worrisome. Now, as they were getting their teeth into the climb, Fritz saw that George was also unpredictable, as if he simply lacked the will to focus on the task at hand. As he watched George continue to struggle with the rope in one hand and his ice axe in the other, frequently getting tangled into a dangerous knot, Fritz wondered how he was ever going to get this boy up, never mind off, the mountain. It was not unwarranted criticism; George himself agreed with Fritz's loud and frequent harangues about how careless and unfocused he was. While George couldn't put his finger on exactly why his head wasn't into the climb, he did very little to get it there, and, like a homesick child at summer camp, he started counting the days until the team would depart for home. With sleep increasingly difficult at altitude, he was also self-medicating with phenobarbital, a sleeping aid which suppresses breathing—exactly what he shouldn't have been doing.

One of the body's primary reactions to the loss of oxygen in the atmosphere is to breathe more rapidly to obtain the same amount of oxygen; this in turn causes a reduction in carbon dioxide in the blood. Because a buildup of CO_2 is a stronger indicator to the body that it is time to breathe than is a reduction of oxygen, a balancing act arises between the two triggers. When awake, a person can consciously breathe when necessary, but asleep, the lack of a CO_2 trigger can cause a person to stop breathing for up to fifteen seconds at a time, eventually waking in a choking gasp for breath.

Finally, as if the sleep apnea weren't bothersome enough, the kidneys excrete more fluid during acclimatization, so that a frequent need to urinate during the night also prevents a person from getting sound, restful sleep. All in all, George was not a happy man.

Meanwhile, Dudley was going strong. It was as if all his years of quiet focus on straightforward goals—whether points on a map thousands of miles away across an ocean or wounded soldiers who needed to be taken from a trench to a dressing station—had finally come together and enabled him to thrive in the harsh environs. Climbing a mountain, even a Himalayan giant like K2, was a very clear goal to Dudley when looked at through his objective lens: *Here is the mountain, here are the obstacles, and this is what I have to do to get there.* He had trained, he had studied other expeditions, and he had obtained the best equipment. Now all he had to do was put his nose into the wind and go. And he did, with the slow determination that was his style. At one point, as he rested on the rope, he looked toward the Northeast Ridge and saw a tremendous avalanche break loose from its upper reaches and roar down the slope, gathering fury and width as it reached terminal velocity thundering down the mountain. Traveling at close to 150 miles per hour, it hit the glacier with such force that it filled the valley with a 3,000-foot cloud of snow, dusting the lower mountain with a fresh coat of powder. Dudley looked above him at the rocky ridge and was suddenly very glad they weren't attempting the less difficult but far more avalanche-prone slopes on either side of the Abruzzi.

Above Camp II, where the terrain grew steeper and icier, Dudley's already deliberate pace slowed to inches, rather than feet, per minute. When their heavy steel crampons became too awkward to use on the mixed terrain of rock and ice, Dudley and the team relied on nails pounded into the soles of their leather hiking boots for traction, like an early version of studded snow tires. But the Sherpas, with the exception of the one or two who would be on the summit team, had not been issued the expensive crampons, so when the team encountered slopes so smooth they appeared polished, Fritz had to cut steps into the ice with his axe. Unfortunately, the steps did little to tame the precarious slickness of the ice, and the pace of the climb slowed to a crawl.

One day, with Jack, Tony, and Dudley on the same rope, the frustration over Dudley's slow and awkward climbing became more than Jack and Tony could bear, and in Camp II that night, both angrily accused Dudley of poor climbing and said that he had no business being on the mountain. Tony, still smarting from Fritz's criticism of his deputy leadership, seemed eager to have someone else to blame for their slow progress. Dudley fired back, saying he had done his fair share of work, carried just as many loads, and if indeed he was slow on the rope through dangerous sections, it was for good reason; it was difficult climbing and he was not going to sacrifice prudence for their impatience. He was here to climb this mountain whether Jack or Tony or anybody else liked it. Besides, he charged, looking at Jack, it seemed to him that he was the only one actually climbing this mountain, while Jack was the one constantly complaining about his physical ailments and bad boots.

It was not a point Jack could argue, particularly after a recent load carry in which he was forced to crawl on all fours, dragging his belly over the rocks imagining he looked like the Little Engine That Could, puffing "I think I can, I think I can" as he pulled himself up the mountain.

Later, some would speculate that Dudley and Fritz had made an almost client–guide arrangement, whereby Fritz would get Dudley to the summit in exchange for the wealthy man's greater financial investment in the team. But, given Dudley's concerns about money and his feelings of being taken advantage of by Fritz and some of the other men on the team, that scenario seems implausible. What does seem possible is that Fritz and Jack had an agreement whereby Jack took on more work, given his discounted fee. Agreement or no, Jack resented the extra labor and was jealous of Dudley's physical success on the mountain while also being truly worried that the older, slower man was going to get in trouble the higher he went.

Even though Jack was intimidated by the mountain and its demands, as well as his own physical limitations at altitude, he nonetheless pulled Fritz aside and again urged him not to take Dudley any higher on the mountain. He told Fritz that no one without the skills and experience to descend alone should be allowed to climb into what would become a trap.

Fritz would hear none of it. He pointed his finger in Jack's face and said, "You listen to me, Jack! I tell you, if we get up, we shall all be the most famous alpinists in the world!"

Jack looked at him and thought, *I have a fanatic on my hands.*

The conversation was over. Jack backed down.

The next day, Dudley talked to Fritz about the confrontation. While he had heard Jack's concerns about his preparedness for the mountain above them, he couldn't help but marvel at how the others seemed to spend their days grumbling and complaining about nearly every aspect of the arduous expedition: the food, the weather, the rest of the team, and most of all, the mountain. They seemed unprepared for the full challenge of a Himalayan mountain and demoralized by its sheer size and relentless demands. Perhaps because he was older and literally battle-tested, Dudley had remained unflinching in the face of K2's daunting presence looming above them and instead focused on the immediate piece of mountain at his feet. He also realized how similar climbing was to sailing; at its best, mountaineering taught a man to live in the environment and, like the killer storms off the coast of Ireland, the harsh challenges of K2 were something he relished.

Still, the public rebuke of his climbing worried him. He did not want to be a burden to the team or an embarrassment to himself. He particularly didn't want to endanger anyone, himself included. The next day, he took even more care with every step, making sure to watch and learn from Fritz's moves.

While Jack found Dudley's slow technique bothersome, one of K2's legendary hazards positively terrified him: rockfall. K2 is a mountain of volcanic rubble covered with layers of ice and crumbling rocks which shed constantly, particularly as the sun melts them out of the surface layers. A whirring hum was the men's only warning before rocks of all sizes showered around them with terrifying randomness. Some came within inches, some flew past and exploded on the slopes below, others nicked at their packs and bruised their legs. Charlie Houston's 1938 team likened it to trying to climb a slate roof piled high with rocks. For many, the intermittent rockfalls were the most petrifying aspect of the entire climb because they came with no warning and there was almost nothing one could do to avoid a rock traveling at terminal velocity. In essence, it was the world's highest crap shoot and Jack didn't like his odds.

ON JUNE 20, only two weeks into the climb, Dudley, Fritz, and George, whom Fritz still hoped would shape up and become a strong member of the team, made a carry from Camp II to Camp IV at 21,500 feet, where they waited for Jack and several Sherpas to follow the next day. Instead, a storm blew in, keeping Jack and the others low on the mountain while trapping the three of them in a tiny tent as the blizzard and hurricane-force winds soon made even leaving the tent suicidal.

K2's wind is legendary, and while all of the famed 8,000-meter peaks regularly suffer violent wind, K2's is nearly constant. Climbers who have survived the mountain talk of how it penetrates everything—tents, sleeping bags, and clothes—and even months after they have returned from the mountain, they can still feel the chill of that wind.

Day after day the storm battered the men at Camp IV, sounding like a freight train coming through a tunnel at full power, its wind gusts flattening the tent so that the men had to push their backs into the fabric to keep it aloft and take some of the pressure off the poles before they snapped in half. Fearing that a sudden gust would pick up the tent and blow them into Tibet, the men sat and lay in the cramped quarters, trying not to lose their minds. With their heavy books left behind in base camp, boredom forced them to read aloud the labels on their cans of food. After they had exhausted that activity, they fell silent again, staring at the bucking and straining tent around them.

Two days later, Dudley picked up his journal and saw the date printed on the page: June 22. On the other side of the world Harvard was hosting his class's tenth reunion and here he was, hoping to survive hurricane winds and subzero temperatures while sitting 21,000 feet up a Himalayan peak. The red and white tents in the Yard that he visualized, the Radcliffe women in their straw hats and white gloves, the Harvard men in top hats and tails, and the robed commencement speaker intoning from the steps of the Harvard Chapel couldn't have made a starker contrast to the tiny tent perilously perched on K2.

Dudley did his best to keep Fritz and George entertained with songs and stories, describing in great detail the yacht cruise he would take them on to tropical paradises, but his audience was often unreceptive and he too would grow quiet again, mesmerized as he watched the sides of the tent flexing and releasing in the wind, which reminded him of the *Highland Light* when she was at full sail. All the while, he massaged his feet hoping to ward off frostbite; he had felt the first nip a few days before and knew that the only cure at this altitude was warmth and circulation. He had to keep the blood moving through his toes.

Next to him, Fritz tried to keep focused on the task at hand: climbing the mountain. He wrote a long note for Tony at base, detailing the team's actions for when the weather cleared, instructing that the porters for the march out should be ordered for arrival in base camp on July 17. If the weather didn't cooperate, then the team would have to split, with twenty porters and a Sherpa and a sahib (if one was available) leading the first half out on the 17th, and those still on the mountain following toward the end of the month.

As he wrote, he watched the tent bucking against the wind and worried about the strength of the fabric, knowing that even a small tear would allow the wind to shred the tent in minutes. He thought the constant "bang, bang, bang" of the tent sounded like claps of thunder. Even after years of mountain expeditions, this was the most terrifying storm of his life and he huddled against its fury, waiting for the next gust to rip the tent open and blow them off the mountain. God knows it had happened before on Himalayan peaks. He just wished the god-awful racket would stop. He suddenly understood shell shock and why boys came home from the battlefield with dull eyes that stared off into space. He now knew why they lost their minds; the brain can process only so much noise before it shuts down, and he felt like he was about to lose his mind.

Nearby, George was also flirting with insanity. All he wanted to do was run—get out of the tent and just start running. He knew it was a crazy notion and that even trying to stand on the steep, wind-blown ice in this furor would mean instant death. The wind felt like a solid wall of force. But if it didn't end soon, and if he didn't stretch his legs and get some blood moving through his body, he would become a raving maniac. He could barely feel his toes. They went from painfully cold to numb and he didn't know which he preferred; at least when they hurt he knew there was blood flowing. Now they were numb, and he knew that meant the blood had gone from freezing to frozen in his veins. If they didn't thaw soon, the tissue would die. He spent his already sleepless nights trying to massage blood into his toes as the thought of losing them to frostbite terrified him. Compounding his miseries was the Primus stove which leaked gasoline fumes and added dizziness and nausea to his now constant headache.

"Jesus, what happens if it never stops?" he wrote miserably, as terror and boredom alternated through his thoughts. Camp IV was proving to be his Waterloo. "My attitude about K2," he wrote, "is to get the hell out of here."

Day after day, the storm raged on and tempers reached their limits. On the 28th Dudley and Fritz began arguing about their options, screaming all day at each other over the din, as George huddled nearby scribbling in his journal. Throughout the storm, all three suffered coughing jags, a common malady at high altitude, which left them gasping for air in the tiny tent.

Below them at Camp II, Jack and Tony were increasingly anxious for their safety. With everyone trapped where they were on the mountain by the 100-mile-per-hour winds, there was nothing to do but worry, write in their journals, and read aloud to each other. Jack read Goethe to Tony and Tony read Tennyson to Jack. Jack also wrote a letter to his father asking for money as the "expedition [is] getting poor." Fritz had been imploring Jack to write his father, a school principal turned real estate broker, for funds; the coffers were close to empty.

On June 29 the storm finally subsided enough for the men at Camp IV to stand outside. It was the first time they had done so in eight days and they all stretched carefully. The three men suffered from frostbitten feet and stumbled about as blood started to flow through the frozen tissue. Looking over at George, Dudley could see that they'd lost him from the climb. The storm, boredom, fear, crippling inaction, and painful frostbite had broken the young man's spirit and strength. Although Fritz thought that all George needed was a good rest in order to resume the climb, Dudley had seen that dead look in men's eyes on the front lines when they had simply had enough and would rather risk court martial or death than fight one more day. For George the war was over, the expedition finished.

At Camp II the boredom and inaction also took its toll, especially on Jack. He now endured near-chronic insomnia, migraines, nausea, dizziness, and depression—all classic symptoms of high-altitude sickness. While he continued to organize the ferrying of the team's supplies up the mountain, none of those loads seem to make it out of camp, in large part because he was unable to lead the Sherpas. This was a bitter defeat, made somehow worse by watching the older, less experienced Wolfe move ever higher on the mountain.

After the storm, as Jack watched George Sheldon descend to Camp II, he looked up the mountain for a second figure in retreat, expecting to see that Dudley too had had enough. But George was alone and when he reached camp told Jack, *Nope, Dudley is feeling great and continuing up*, although his feet had also been frostbitten during their eight-day ordeal. Jack and Tony were outraged to hear this. Even though Dudley was doing well, they thought he had no business climbing any higher and, on July 1, they sent a note to Fritz saying as much. Dudley had proven himself adequate to follow on Fritz's rope, they said, but for him to go any farther would be unnecessarily dangerous.

The warning again fell on deaf ears. Between Tony's ill will, Joe's laziness, and Jack's inability and—in Fritz's mind—increasing unwillingness to work higher on the mountain, it sounded like sour grapes to him. When Fritz shared the note with Dudley, Dudley again asked, *Who are they to criticize me when they can barely make it out of Camp II?*

In response, Fritz sent a note of his own, beginning, "Dear Jack and Tony, I am very disappointed in you." He admonished the men to get off their asses and start bringing loads up the mountain. Feeling totally abandoned by Fritz and merely working as his "puppets," Jack, Tony, Joe, and now George, who had remained at Camp II nursing his swollen feet, railed against the leader and his expedition, which they felt was increasingly a one-man show. But the note did serve its purpose; it nudged them toward a semblance of action. That afternoon they finally prepared themselves and loads for a carry to Camp IV. Unfortunately, weather again intervened and in the morning, when Tony looked out the tent flap at a foot of new snow, he announced that he for one was not moving from his sleeping bag. With insomnia and ennui now chronic problems for Jack, he too was unable to motivate himself and he simply zipped the bag closer around his neck and went back to sleep. Nearby, Joe and George barely stirred.

A few days later, when George's feet had recovered enough for him to put weight on them, he left Camp II and made his last trip down to base camp, where he reunited with Chap over almost an entire bottle of Tony's rum. With the weather clear, Jack and Tony also left Camp II, finally headed up to Camp IV with a load.

But as was so often the case, after a late start and slow climbing through deep snow and clinging to frozen ropes, they barely made the equipment dump at Camp III (at 20,700 feet) before they had to turn around in the retreating light. On their descent, Tony slipped in an icy couloir and began falling, gathering speed as he careened out of control down the steep slope. Fortunately, Jack worked quickly and was able to anchor the rope around a rock and stop Tony's fall before he pulled them both off the mountain.

Over the next few days, storms and a general enervation once again kept the men at Camp II, with Tony complaining about a pain in his side and Jack plugging his ears to shut out the Sherpas' "incessant monkey chatter." One day bled into another and still Jack and Tony remained at Camp II. Soon Joe returned from base camp with a load of mail and a fresh supply of Sherpas, but Jack and Tony did not leave camp.

Meanwhile, Fritz, Dudley, and two Sherpas, Tendrup and Kikuli, steadily pushed up the mountain, first tackling one of K2's most famous obstacles: an 80-foot chimney of rock pioneered the year before by Bill House, who had climbed it without a rope or any fixed protection. This was then the world's highest known free ascent of a rock wall and to this day remains one of the greatest climbing achievements in history. The notorious House's Chimney is a steep, narrow gully of crumbling rock and ice. Even after a safety rope was finally anchored to the rock after House's ascent, because there are almost no footholds, the 1938 and 1939 climbers pulled themselves up with arm strength. As a result, the packs were brought up separately so as to reduce the weight on the rope and the arms. Today there is a steel ladder permanently affixed to the wall.

After taking most of the day to set the safety rope in the chimney and pull their gear up after them, Fritz, Dudley, and the two

Benjamin Franklin Smith, circa 1909. *(Courtesy of the Dudley F. Rochester and Dudley F. Wolfe Family)*

Dudley, far left, with his siblings and mother, 1900. *(Courtesy of the Dudley F. Rochester and Dudley F. Wolfe Family)*

Dudley, far left, at the Hackley Hall School, circa 1904. *(Courtesy of the Dudley F. Rochester and Dudley F. Wolfe Family)*

Dudley, second from right, front row, with Phillips Academy football team, circa 1914. *(Courtesy of the Dudley F. Rochester and Dudley F. Wolfe Family)*

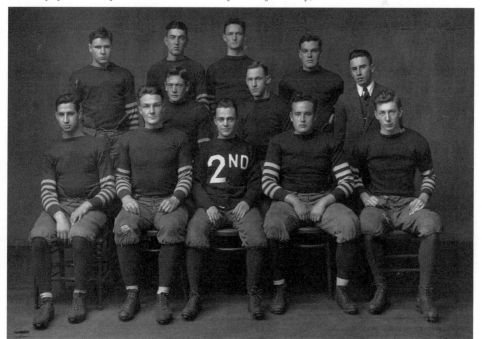

Dudley, rear right, and Grafton, front right, with two summer employees in BF Smith's Old Orchard, Maine, tourist business. *(Courtesy of the Dudley F. Rochester and Dudley F. Wolfe Family)*

Dudley, Mabel, and unidentified friend, circa 1919. *(Courtesy of the Dudley F. Rochester and Dudley F. Wolfe Family)*

Dudley at Hannes Schneider's Ski School, Tyrol, Austria, 1933. *(Courtesy of the Dudley F. Rochester and Dudley F. Wolfe Family)*

Dudley and Alice motoring through Europe in his 1938 Buick Phaeton. *(Courtesy of the Dudley F. Rochester and Dudley F. Wolfe Family)*

Fritz H. Wiessner. *(Courtesy of the George C. Sheldon Family)*

Vittorio Sella, Jack Durrance, Fritz Wiessner, and Dudley Wolfe, March 19, 1939. *(Courtesy of the George C. Sheldon Family)*

Cromwell, Wolfe, Sheldon, Wiessner, and Cranmer aboard the *Biancamano*. *(Courtesy of the George C. Sheldon Family)*

Conte Biancamano Dining Room. *(Courtesy of Serge Guyot)*

Cranmer and Susie aboard the *Biancamano.*
(Courtesy of the George C. Sheldon Family)

Dudley skiing above Srinagar. *(Courtesy of the George C. Sheldon Family)*

Wiessner, center, choosing porters near Srinagar. *(Courtesy of the George C. Sheldon Family)*

Dudley soaking his feet on the approach march. *(Courtesy of the George C. Sheldon Family)*

Team at Urdukas Camp, back row left to right, Durrance, Trench, Cromwell, Wiessner, Amarnath, Chandra, Cranmer, Wolfe, Sheldon, with sherpas sitting in front. *(Courtesy of the George C. Sheldon Family)*

Cranmer crossing a glacial stream. *(Courtesy of the George C. Sheldon Family)*

Team approaches Concordia with G IV looming on the horizon. *(Courtesy of the George C. Sheldon Family)*

Cranmer gets his first look at K2 from Concordia. *(Courtesy of the George C. Sheldon Family)*

Dudley below Broad Peak on the last day of the trek into base camp. *(Courtesy of the George C. Sheldon Family)*

Base camp. *(Courtesy of the Cranmer Collection)*

Kikuli and Durrance at Camp II. *(Courtesy of the George C. Sheldon Family)*

Pasang Kikuli. *(Courtesy of the George C. Sheldon Family)*

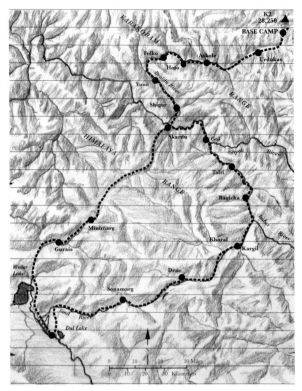

Route of the 1939 K2 Expedition
trek from Srinagar to base camp.
(Courtesy of Dee Molenaar)

K2, the route, the high camps,
and Wiessner's high point, 1939.
(Courtesy of Dee Molenaar)

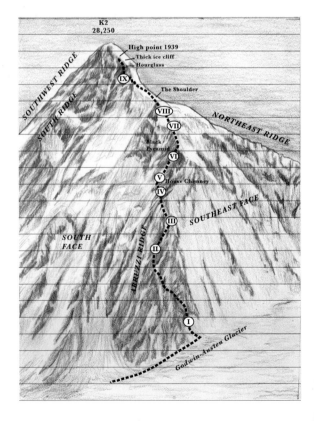

Sherpas established Camp V at 22,000 feet on July 1. Once the camp was built, Fritz, Kikuli, and Tendrup continued up, leaving Dudley to help the Sherpas bring supplies up through the chimney. While Fritz was disappointed that only Dudley seemed willing and able to climb the mountain, he was pleased with the strength and experience of his Sherpas. Kikuli was proving to be as talented and loyal as his reputation indicated, and although Tendrup often needed prodding to quicken his pace on the mountain, the younger Sherpa was also a strong and able climber on the demanding slopes.

For the next week, Dudley contented himself alone at Camp V, cooking and cleaning up from his meals, writing in his journal, and endlessly watching the mountain. At any time of day or night, the sharp crack of an avalanche cutting loose from the slopes above would herald the thunderous torrent to come. Luckily, the tents were in a relatively safe alcove so the freight train of snow, rocks, and ice moving upward of 150 miles per hour would rain down all around him but not on him. Once the initial terror of being swept away passed, it was like standing under a waterfall.

Above him, Fritz, Kikuli, and Tendrup established Camp VI at 23,400 feet on July 5, and the next day they hauled 45-pound loads up to what would become Camp VII at 24,700 feet. Every day they climbed and awaited food, equipment, and fresh men from below, but none came. Frustrated and angry at the "setback" of having to descend rather than continue up toward the summit, Fritz and the Sherpas finally went down to Camp V, where they found Dudley still alone and his supplies running low.

Fritz couldn't believe it. Here he was climbing and establishing camps, practically alone, while his foot soldiers lounged at Camp II. Why, he wondered, weren't they able to push through the exhaustion and the pain of frostbitten feet the way he was?

Why couldn't they embrace the difficulty of the task at hand and just do their jobs? Wasn't he climbing in deep snow? Wasn't he suffering headaches and swollen feet? Were they boys or were they men? While wishing he could, Fritz knew he wouldn't be able to climb the mountain alone and "finish it single-handedly," so on July 9 he descended to Camp II to demand an explanation from Jack and Tony. Once again leaving Dudley in camp, he took Kikuli and Tendrup with him so that they could carry more loads to the high camps.

"Lo and behold," Jack wrote, "Fritz came forth from the hanging fogs of K2 . . . looking somewhat worn since I saw him last 18 days ago."

Eighteen days. It is an eternity on a mountain, particularly when you are left without a leader, foundering in boredom and ennui, and not knowing what is happening above. The men greeted each other and Fritz explained in great, enthusiastic detail how he had pushed all the way to Camp VII. While Jack was energized by Fritz's speech, Tony announced sullenly that the day of departure from base camp was set for July 24 and that he had already called for the porters to come and take them out.

Fritz couldn't believe his ears! How dare they make the decision without any consultation with him and Dudley? Tony tried to remind Fritz of the note he had sent Tony at base camp about splitting the team if the weather slowed their progress, but Fritz continued to rage. Tony looked down at his feet and almost petulantly reminded Fritz that it was difficult to consult him when he hadn't been seen in nearly three weeks.

Fritz ignored the comment and continued his harangue, assuring them how close he—they—were to victory. While Tony finally agreed to carry a load to Camp IV, he said he would go no further than that on the mountain. But Jack was revitalized by Fritz's purpose and energy. It felt like a shot in the arm and he was suddenly envisioning himself on the summit; his European climbing boots had at last been delivered to the mountain and, once the weather gave them a window, Fritz assured him, they would go for the top together.

With Fritz breaking trail through the new snow that had fallen overnight, Jack, Tony, and Joe left Camp II in the morning and headed up the mountain. The going was slow and the rope between Joe and Jack frequently became taut as Joe stopped and gazed off into the distance, as if he were sitting on a park bench watching the clouds roll by. Increasingly incoherent, Joe had clearly reached the end of his climb and perhaps was showing the first signs of cerebral edema. In all fairness to the man, liaison and transport officers are rarely climbers, and the fact that Fritz needed and expected him to be part of the support team on the mountain said a lot more about Fritz's management than it did about Joe's lack of team spirit or climbing acumen.

Meanwhile, Dudley had been waiting at Camp V for nearly a week. It had begun well, but each day he felt himself growing weaker. He needed to keep moving, but he had to wait for Fritz; this was not a mountain he could climb alone. Every day he sat vigil at the top of House's Chimney waiting to help with loads as they came up. But none had. Finally, on July 10, two Sherpas, Tendrup and Sonam, appeared from below and started up the chimney, calling to "Wolfe Sahib!" that they had mail for him. Dudley waved to the men with excitement but then watched in alarm as neither took the time to tie into the rope that had been anchored at the top of the chimney and instead started to climb without any protection. The chimney was the steepest section of the mountain; knowing Sonam was young and inexperienced, Dudley immediately felt apprehensive as he watched the two men inch up the narrow rock. Suddenly, Sonam's feet slipped from under him and Dudley, horrified, watched as he fell twenty feet down the chimney, bounced off the rock and then slid down the steep slope beneath. Powerless to help, Dudley yelled to Kikuli, Sonam's brother, who was lower on the slope. Kikuli ran as best he could over the uneven rocks and icy slope toward his brother as Sonam rolled and tumbled hundreds of feet down a scree slope. Finally, Kikuli was able to grab onto Sonam at the edge of a cliff before the young man fell to the glacier 6,000 feet below. Dudley tied into the rope and clambered down through the chimney to help and to make sure that Sonam was all right. Badly bruised, Sonam was alive, but seeing blood trickling out of his ear Dudley thought the man might have suffered a concussion. He doubted whether Sonam would be able to climb any further on the mountain. Climbing back to Camp V after the accident, Dudley spent another night alone.

The close call with Sonam had actually done Dudley some good. After days of sitting and waiting, the adrenaline of Sonam's fall and his own trip down and back through the chimney had revitalized him for the summit bid. He eagerly waited for Fritz and the others to appear so that they could resume the climb.

The next day, Dudley again descended to Camp IV to check in on Sonam. Assured that he was okay, Dudley looked up to see Fritz and Tony appear at the edge of the slope. They soon lumbered into camp.

Tony stretched his hand out to Dudley. He had not seen the "K2 Hermit," as he and Jack were calling Dudley, since the first week of June.

"Dudley! How are you?" Tony asked.

"Fine, but it's been pretty rough," he admitted. "There's been a lot of waiting alone in the camps."

Tony nodded his head. High-altitude mountaineering involves a lot of "hurry up and wait." A climber has to have the patience of Job.

Seeing that the weather might again turn sour, Tony decided to head back to Camp II in the morning. He had told Fritz that Camp IV was as high as he was going to climb, and here he was. Looking around, he realized that once Jack and Joe finally reached them they'd have more men than tent space for the night.

"Don't worry," Dudley volunteered, "I'll head back up to V. It's just on the other side of the chimney."

After saying goodbye, Tony and Fritz settled into their tent and Dudley climbed the demanding 80-foot chimney to Camp V, once again alone.

Although Dudley had been used to having paid guides in Europe and Canada who prepared and cleaned up after his meals, he quickly realized that once on a Himalayan mountain such luxuries were simply not available, so he familiarized himself with the quirky Primus stove. The long days alone were tough enough; not having enough water and food was painful. So every day he would painstakingly lay out all the necessary tools for dinner: stove, canister of gasoline, pot filled with snow on the burner with a larger bucket of fresh snow outside the tent to replenish the pot as the light, airy snow quickly melted, soup packets and dried meats and vegetables he planned to cook, and finally the matches. Carefully positioning the stove near the door of the tent so that there was ventilation but not enough wind to make sustaining the flame impossible, Dudley would sit cross-legged and bend over it before striking the first match. If he were lucky, the first match took. Usually he was not and it took several to get and then keep the notoriously tricky stove lit. Years later, K2 summiter and renowned high-altitude specialist Louis Reichardt would comment that it was a miracle any of the early climbers were able to keep hydrated, given how horrendously Primus stoves operated at high altitude. But Dudley managed to figure it out and, while he spent weeks alone in the unforgiving environs, he never complained.

Below him, Jack struggled to reach the tents at Camp IV. When he finally did he looked up and saw Dudley once again keeping vigil at the top of House's Chimney in case any loads needed hauling up. Waving and calling out, the two men greeted each other for the first time in twenty-one days. That night Jack "reclined" but didn't sleep a wink as the sudden 1,000-foot increase in altitude wreaked havoc with his already struggling system. He had also had to haul Joe up the mountain, as the transport officer's inexperience and increasing altitude sickness became an enormous burden and danger to the others, particularly through the rain of rockfall below Camp III. In addition, the more Jack thought about actually going for the summit, the more a sense of panic descended on him, crushing him. In the morning, he choked down some Cream of Wheat and started out behind Fritz and Joe, his fear growing with every step up the mountain. After some terrifying moments in the chimney with Joe, who would suddenly stare off into space unaware of everything and everyone around him, Jack finally convinced him that he was at his altitude record. Joe agreed and retreated to Camp IV and then descended with Tony.

Finally reaching the top of the chimney, Jack greeted Dudley, who enthusiastically took his hand and clapped him on the back. Dudley showed them into Camp V, where he handed Jack a waiting cup of hot bouillon. Asking Jack if he could bother him for a medical opinion, Dudley quickly took off his boot to show his frostbitten toes, one of them already developing a blister. Jack remembered Charlie Houston's warning about frostbite and told Dudley that he should descend to lower altitudes in order for it to heal properly.

Dudley shook his head as he put his boot back on. *I'm going up. It'll be fine.*

But isn't it very painful? Jack asked, having had his ear bent by George's complaints the week before.

Sure, Dudley said, *but everything hurts. So you just keep going, right?*

He may be crazy, Jack thought, *but he's determined. I'll give him that.*

Jack told him to keep the toes dry and clean and whenever possible give them some sunlight without letting the sun burn them. Dudley thanked him and rose to help pack up the camp. Jack shook his head as he struggled to his feet. Then Jack, Dudley, Fritz, Pasang, and Dawa Sherpa continued on to Camp VI, a dismal collection of three tents perched on the edge of a 45-degree slope.

One of the unofficial rules of high-altitude climbing is to "Climb high, sleep low." As a climber moves up the mountain and reaches his high point for the day, he spends an hour or so there before descending to a lower camp to sleep, thereby enabling the body to experience the thinner air and make its immediate adjustments while allowing it to restore itself by sleeping in the thicker air. If a climber is doing well with the ever-thinner air, the rule is less important so long as he ascends slowly, usually less than 1,000 feet a day, but if he is already struggling, the rule is crucial for his condition. Unfortunately for Jack, in 1939 this rule was still unknown.

After a hot meal, Dudley and Jack bedded down for the night, but Jack could barely lie flat due to the overwhelming feeling that he was suffocating under a great weight on his chest, like a blanket of rocks. Yet, despite his own inability to acclimatize, Jack felt it necessary to once again tell Dudley that he should not climb any higher on the mountain, that his lack of experience and skill made him dependent on someone else to bring him down and therefore he was a burden that became more perilous with every foot he ascended.

While Dudley knew that Jack's charges had some merit—hadn't he himself asked Fritz if he had the skills and experience for K2?—they also stung. Not only was he the only member of the team who was actually climbing and helping Fritz build camps, he had made Jack's trip possible by providing the $1,300 balance to the expedition coffers that Jack had not been able to contribute himself. Rather than thanking him, it seemed as if Jack had taken one look at Dudley and dismissed him as a climber and team member. Dudley had had enough of the younger man's arrogance and shot back that it was he, Dudley, who was feeling fine, strong in fact, while Jack was unable to climb much above Camp II at 19,000 feet without crippling illness—a charge obviously true, with Jack dizzy and struggling to breathe as they spoke. Still, Jack was unwilling to admit to Dudley or to himself that Dudley was simply stronger at altitude. Instead, Jack blamed his own weak performance on the fact that, unlike Dudley, he hadn't had the "luxury" of climbing and resting at each camp. Rather, he had had to organize and pack loads, tend to the sick, and keep the low camps serviceable while the other two climbed like pampered clients on a guided tour. He was exhausted.

Even though Jack's outburst felt like a child's petulant whine, in the morning Dudley once again went to Fritz. He didn't want to be a burden or a danger to anyone, and he asked Fritz one more time if Jack's charges were true. Was he a liability on the slopes above? Would he be stuck high on the mountain unless somebody was there to bring him down?

"Don't worry," Fritz assured him. "If you should get too slow or find it too difficult higher up, you will stay in reserve."

Ironically and tragically, Jack was probably right, and may have been observing in Dudley's clumsiness and stubbornness the early signs of acute mountain sickness, caused by lack of oxygen, dehydration, and exhaustion. Much like a person who has had too much drink and boasts, "Of course I can drive, just watch me!" Dudley was no doubt impaired by the lack of oxygen yet oblivious to just how severely affected he was. But with Fritz only looking up to the summit and Dudley unaware of his weakened condition, Jack's warning again went unheeded. The matter was closed. In the morning the men headed up toward Camp VII across some of the mountain's most treacherous sections of steep, blue ice.

After only a hundred feet, Jack was filled with a crushing panic: *If I don't get off this mountain now, soon I may not be able to.* He couldn't breathe. He was so dizzy he had to walk with his hands stretched out like a B-movie zombie to protect himself from a fall. He felt as if he would vomit at any minute, if in fact he had been able to eat anything. He called ahead to Fritz, telling him he needed to go back to Camp VI and recover. After a quick conference, it was decided that Jack would descend with four Sherpas for the night and see how he felt the next day. If he was still sick in the morning, he would send the Sherpas back up with supplies and continue down alone.

Fritz watched him go, shaking his head in disgust at Jack's refusal to push through the pain as he and Dudley had done and continued to do. You didn't get to the top of a mountain like K2 without a lot of suffering and, yes, pain. Even as he watched the broken, sick man descend, Fritz still believed that all Jack needed was a rest and he'd be able to rejoin him and Dudley for the summit assault.

As he climbed down, Jack stopped to pant and choke every few feet, clinging to the rope between him and Dawa Sherpa as if his life depended on it—as indeed it did. That night back at Camp VI, his heart pounded so wildly he thought it would explode in his chest and he breathed air in great, gasping gulps but never felt satisfied. It was as if he were running through thick sand while trying to breathe through a straw. He could never get enough air. Finally, fearing he would die in his sleep, he asked Dawa to lie close to him to monitor whether he was still breathing. At 5:30 in the morning, he awoke the four Sherpas who had descended with him and, instead of sending them back up the mountain with supplies, Jack ordered them to descend with him because he felt unsafe. Often crawling on all fours, Jack made Camp IV by late morning. There, he instructed two of the Sherpas, Phinsoo and Tsering, to climb back up to the summit team with supplies, and he continued down to Camp II, taking Dawa and Kikuli with him. Kikuli, their strongest and most experienced Sherpa, had suffered a serious recurrence of frostbite while establishing the high camps with Fritz. Unwilling to lose his toes, maybe even his feet, and therefore his career, Kikuli had told Fritz he was finished high on the mountain, but would remain in the low camps to help organize loads for the summit assault team. Again, Fritz stubbornly refused to accept he had lost another climber and assumed all Kikuli needed was a rest at lower altitude and that he would soon re-ascend to attempt the summit with him.

When Jack arrived in Camp II, he found it an utter shambles. Tony was exhausted from having brought down Joe and the wounded Sonam, who lay dazed and bleeding in a corner. Around them was squalor; filthy dishes, remnants of food, and scattered gear littered the tent. It looked like a scene from a battle, and these guys were definitely not looking like the victors. But as Jack tried to tidy up and organize the next day's loads, he was stricken with a coughing spell and could do nothing but get in his sleeping bag and nap.

Seven thousand feet above them, the climbing team was officially down to Wiessner and Wolfe with Sherpas Pasang Lama,

Tendrup, and Kitar carrying heavy loads of gear for the upper camps. Cutting steps into the icy slopes, the ragged quintet finally established Camp VIII at 25,300 feet on a narrow ice shelf they carved out of the slope that afternoon, July 14.

Both Fritz and Dudley had frostbitten feet and, like those below them, they were well worn by their nearly six weeks on the mountain. Because the 1938 team had left many of its ropes on the route, Fritz had something of a map as he led the way up the mountain, but the task of breaking trail and anchoring new safety ropes where the old ones looked too weather-beaten to be safe was still enormous. With Dudley doggedly following in his cut steps or on the thin rope, the two crawled upward toward the roof of the world.

Chapter 7

A Family Waits

The ordinary man looking at a mountain is like an illiterate person confronted with a Greek manuscript.

—ALEISTER CROWLEY

Alice and Dudley Wolfe (on the right) on their honeymoon cruise, November 1934. *(Courtesy of the Dudley F. Rochester and Dudley F. Wolfe Family)*

Twelve thousand miles and a world away, Alice Damrosch Wolfe sat on the porch of her family's estate in Bar Harbor, Maine, reading a letter from Dudley. It had been filled with sand and she absently brushed at the tiny crystals in her lap as she read the letter. She looked out to the table-flat Atlantic Ocean, the last of the day's light playing across the surface of the water. Imagine. Halfway around the world, Dudley was dipping his toes in the Indus River. Well, he had been, anyway. She checked the date of the letter: May 11. He had dipped his toes seven weeks ago. Seven weeks. She wondered where he was now, trying but not succeeding to imagine his travels from the sandy banks of the Indus through the wild river gorges and terraced villages to the towering mountains of northern India. According to the rough schedule he had given her, he should be well on his way toward the summit by now.

Although she had promised herself not to burden him with her concern, it had not abated. It hadn't helped that their friends in St. Anton who knew him well and had been with them at the hunting preserve had filled her head with new worries.

"But Alice," Johann Falsch, the owner of her apartment in St. Anton had warned, "Dudley has never had to take care of himself—he has always had guides. These expeditions don't allow for that sort of caretaking on the mountains."

By then, Dudley had departed on the trip and she was left to worry and wait for his letters. When they came, she devoured every word he had written. She only wished he'd write more. His details were wonderful, if a bit glossed over. She felt as if he were holding back some of the more grueling details, maybe to spare her any more worry. He had written about concerns he had with the expedition, but he didn't elaborate—he never did talk much about troubles. He was not one to criticize; she had always loved that about him. She was quick to find fault and tell the person flat out, but he wasn't. He was apt to simply walk away from an offending comment or situation rather than engage the offender. She had marveled at an exchange between Dudley and his brother Clifford over the family business. While Clifford had rather nastily attacked his younger brother's lifestyle and lack of profession in a series of letters over the past couple of years, Dudley had remained calm and measured, giving Clifford straightforward answers to his snipes. She wondered whether Clifford cared more about the money than he did about his brother, or his happiness.

Well, she thought, *I suppose Clifford considers happiness bourgeois and overrated. If it's not on a spreadsheet, perhaps it doesn't enter in his realm.*

She looked out again at the ocean: Dudley's ocean. She half expected to see the *Highland Light* come around the corner of Frenchman Bay with Dudley waving from the helm as he had so many times before. It was somehow unfathomable that Dudley was in such a foreign, wild place. And even though he said he was thriving, she felt a growing apprehension. She had opposed the trip from the outset, but Dudley had been insistent, assuring her that he was up to the expedition's demands. She couldn't help but feel the trip was more about Dudley proving something than just another of his wild exploits and, as a woman with her own record of daring pursuits and near misses, she knew the danger of adding an agenda to an adventure. She put his letter down and looked out at the full moon rising from the water, finding a measure of comfort that Dudley was under the same sky. She couldn't wait until he came home with all of his stories; he promised he was keeping a detailed diary and that he would read her whole sections describing the rich tapestry of where he had been and what he had experienced.

The past year had been hell on her. He had tried to explain why he wanted to end their marriage, that as much as he loved her, he wasn't in love with her and that he'd be happier if they divorced. Her first marriage to Pleasants had been so devoid of passion that she had barely noticed its passing, but this was different. She and Dudley had had a life together and she cherished him, his opinions, and his perspectives on the world, particularly now that it appeared the world was headed for another war. Mostly she had adored just having him there, his quiet and gentle presence in the other room or on the preserve or in their apartment in New York. Before she met Dudley, she had been independent so long she hadn't known what it was like to have the security of a companion. Then, as she faced losing him, she nearly collapsed. She missed him more than she thought possible. Thankfully, the Falsches had taken care of her and helped her through the worst of it. But it hadn't been easy and she still longed for him every day.

Before she had left Austria for Maine a few weeks before, she had stopped and bought Dudley a box of his favorite handkerchiefs in Salzburg. Even though she had given him a brand new box before he left, she couldn't think of anything else she could send that might actually make it to the mountain and not be unduly heavy. Besides, she reasoned, given how filthy the ones he had must be getting, he would need new ones anyway.

Picking up her pen, she tried to sound light and playful.

"My dear Dudley Francis," she began as she often did, poking gentle fun at his stuffy Brahmin name, and wrote a chatty letter about nothing in particular, hoping to convey all of her affection and none of her worry. After all, she wasn't even married to the man any more.

She closed the letter, "Write me often. Always, Your loving Alice."

Down the coast a few miles in Glen Cove, Maine, Clifford paced back and forth across the long porch which overlooked the ocean. As June turned to July, Dudley's letters had come less and less frequently, and they were more and more troubled. At the start of his trip, the letters were newsy and cheerful, and Clifford had responded to each immediately, filling Dudley in on the stagnant markets and his ardent desire to see Roosevelt ousted from the presidency before he took the country down his socialistic drainpipe with him. But somehow telling Dudley about their sister Gwen's boys in summer camp near Wiscasset and the caretaker's repaving the drive seemed silly in comparison to leprosy-ridden villages, river crossings on goatskin boats, and avalanches sweeping thousands of feet down the mountain and across a two-mile-wide glacier. Even though he had resented Dudley's sudden and prolonged absence, Clifford had had to admit, *What a hell of an adventure he's on.*

Then in early July, Clifford had received news that one of Dudley's teammates was close to death. Death! They weren't even on the mountain yet! Clifford had tried to contact the US consulate in Calcutta, but he'd gotten nowhere. He supposed no news was good news, but how could a boy die at base camp? Didn't they have a doctor on board? To make matters worse, just last week Clifford had received an odd call from Dudley's secretary, Henry Meyer, and he couldn't get it off his mind. Meyer had received a letter from Dudley warning him not to let anyone have access to the film he had shot on the expedition, "not the leader of the expedition or any member of it." Meyer had quoted the letter over the phone. It was rare for Dudley to speak so vehemently, and Clifford did not at all like imagining what had provoked it.

His film? Why on earth, Clifford wondered, *is he worried about his film? First one of his teammates nearly dies of pneumonia and now he's worried about being robbed or swindled by his own teammates?*

Clifford stopped to look east across the moon-drenched Atlantic. Dudley's letters had become increasingly—well, almost paranoid, as if he didn't trust the men with whom he was climbing a mountain many considered unconquerable. For the thousandth time Clifford wished he had objected more strenuously to his brother's insanely dangerous adventure. He also wished he had insisted on meeting this Fritz Wiessner before the expedition. Clifford didn't even know the man to whom he had entrusted his brother's life. And now, with things apparently disintegrating, Clifford was powerless to help. He did not like the feeling.

Clifford remembered that Dudley had stayed on in Europe after the war in order to help gain his brother's freedom from the German prisoner-of-war camp that held him. Dudley had spent months writing letters to the American field offices, imploring any officials he could think of for help, and cabling the family back in Omaha and Maine every day with updates. Clifford wondered now if he had ever truly thanked his brother for his efforts, and worried that he hadn't.

He walked to the edge of the porch and looked out over Penobscot Bay and the Atlantic Ocean beyond it, thinking, *What the devil is going on over there?*

STILL FARTHER away, Gwen Wolfe Sharpe sat in Minden, Nevada, looking out over her new husband's ranch in the hot Great Basin desert.

She and Dudley had always exchanged a lot of letters and postcards, and she cherished a stack of them she'd received from the front lines in the war and now from his adventure to the Himalayas. But recently there had been an odd and unsettling silence. Cliff had explained how difficult it was to send and receive mail, and yet this absolute lack of communication was very troubling. They had always had a connection, even through the war; this void was painful.

Thankfully her boys, Dudley and Paul, were in summer camp in Maine, so she didn't have to constantly answer their questions about whether another postcard had arrived from Uncle Dudley with a colorful foreign stamp for them to fight over. Today's mail had again brought nothing. Maybe tomorrow she'd go into Carson City and check at the big post office and see if they had anything.

Looking out beyond the dry sagebrush, she saw the first glint of the moon rising over the distant Sierra Nevada. She thought of her brother, half a world away, on a peak two or three times as big as the ones on her horizon, and she could only close her eyes and say a prayer for his safety.

Come home to us, dear Dud, come home.

Chapter 8

The Highest Men on Earth

The tops of mountains are among the unfinished parts of the globe, whither it is a slight insult to the gods to climb and pry into their secrets, and try their effect on our humanity. Only daring and insolent men, perchance, go there.

—Henry David Thoreau

View below Camp IV. *(Courtesy of the George C. Sheldon Family)*

After Tendrup and Kitar dumped their loads of food, fuel, and reserve sleeping bags at Camp VIII at 25,300 feet on July 14, Fritz sent the Sherpas back down to Camp VI for more supplies. As they disappeared down the lower slope, Fritz and Dudley watched a storm approach from the northwest and retreated to their tent for cover. Despite the weather, they could feel success within their reach. While trying to keep hydrated and nourished for the summit attack to come, the men sat back, satisfied at what they had accomplished and excited about treading on ground no man had ever touched. They were the highest men in the world and, looking up toward the summit cone of K2, they raised their tin drinking cups of tea to their achievement.

But even as they celebrated, Fritz realized he too was now worried about Dudley's ability to go higher. He and Dudley had been on the mountain six weeks, longer and higher than any of the other team members. For the first time in the expedition's three and half months of progress toward the summit, which was still 2,000 feet above them, Fritz finally acknowledged that his team of six had dwindled to only the two of them, of whom one, Dudley, was critically inexperienced, had spent too much time idle in the high camps, was suffering frostbitten feet, and was increasingly weak from lack of proper food and fluids. While Fritz himself still felt strong, he knew he might have to leave Dudley in camp if he became too slow for Fritz's progress toward the summit. Even though he considered it an unpleasant alternative, he might have to continue alone with a Sherpa, most likely Pasang Lama, although he wished it could be Kikuli, Charlie Houston's trusted sirdar, who had performed so well the year before. Kikuli was more refined than Pasang, who was too "native" for Fritz. But the situation couldn't be helped. Kikuli was nowhere in sight. *Where was Kikuli, by the way*, Fritz thought in irritation? Where were any of them?

The one option Fritz never considered was descending; the rest of his team was gravely weak, but he was determined to continue, with or without them. *If I'm going to climb this mountain, I'm going to have to do it my way.*

Two DAYS LATER, the storm cleared and the three resumed their climb. Almost immediately out of camp, they encountered a trough-like crevasse filled with snow. When crevasses, or large cracks, form in the ice of a steep slope, avalanches and snow partially fill the gap. This creates a terrifying unknown for climbers; not knowing how deep the crevasse is, any step could take them one or 100 feet into the dark void. Going first, Fritz hoped to feel the crevasse floor under his feet, but instead sank into the snow up to his neck. He fought the urge to panic but knew that every minute he spent in the crevasse he was exposing himself to unspeakable dangers. He pushed and pulled through the snow, looking a lot like a swimmer walking through a pool of crushed ice. Finally he reached the other side and pulled himself up the trench's overhanging lip of ice. Gasping from the effort, he got himself into a seated belay position with the rope around his waist for purchase, and guided Pasang through and up after him. Exhausted and out of breath in the thin air, the two men looked back at Dudley. It was his turn.

Dudley had watched the other two struggle. Fritz took two hours to cross the treacherous hundred-foot section and Pasang, on the rope and with Fritz's help, took another hour. He could see that it had taken everything they had to make it through the snow and climb over the protruding lip of ice at the far side. Even if he were able to get across the crevasse, could he get over its thick edge? It was a difficult move for the lithest rock climber, to say nothing of one at 26,000 feet. But he had to try.

Dudley started across and immediately sank even deeper into the snow than Fritz or Pasang had. Trying to imitate their moves, he freed his arms and used them to swim through the upper layers, only to feel his legs disappear into the trough below. While his bulky power had always been his strongest suit, suddenly he felt every muscle like a barbell strapped to his legs, pulling him down rather than helping him power through. The heavy snow was like quicksand and he struggled against a feeling of terror as it seemed to drag him down.

From above, Fritz urged him on, but it was no help. The passage was only 100 feet but it might as well have been a thousand. Even if he made it across this hole of snow, there was no way he would be able to manage the overhang, particularly given that there were no footholds for him to push up against. Like most skiers, his strength was primarily in his legs, not his arms, and this move demanded a rock climber's upper-body agility and strength, not a workhorse's leg power.

He looked below him at the 10,000 feet he'd climbed to get here. *Hell, it was more like 26,000 feet since he'd started at the ocean. And here was the end of it all; a small, almost trivial ditch of snow.* Maybe with help from more Sherpas he would be able to do it, but not with an already exhausted Pasang and Fritz.

"It is hopeless, Fritz, I just cannot make it. I'll go back to camp," Dudley said.

Fritz did not argue.

Dudley told Fritz he would try again when Tendrup and Kitar came up to restock Camp VIII. Then he turned and retraced his steps through hip-deep snow back to the tents. Carefully putting his rucksack outside the tent, he sat down next to it, made himself comfortable and watched the two men climb.

It wasn't all bad. It was a beautiful day and although the crevasse had bested him, he'd made it higher than any other man on the team except for the two above him, and nearly as high as Charlie Houston and Paul Petzoldt had made it the year before. Not a terrible showing, all things considered. He desperately wanted a cup of tea, but the Primus was tricky to light in the best of circumstances, and 26,000 feet was hardly optimum. Besides, until more supplies came from below he had only a limited supply of matches, so tea would have to wait until after dinner. He settled back against his pack and watched Fritz and Pasang inch up the slope above him.

BELOW THEM, the rest of the team had become even more unraveled. Much like Fritz's failed Nanga Parbat expedition in 1932, the summit team was cut off from the support team below it without radio contact or even the vaunted smoke signals, and the men lower on the mountain had no idea what was happening with the summit party above. As curiosity became worry and then annoyance, and with their planned departure date looming, instead of climbing up to find out if everything was all right, the men at base camp began organizing the team's march away from the mountain. As Fritz had instructed and they had agreed, with the summit team still on the mountain, the team would have to split and leave in two groups, with Jack staying to wait for the summit team to descend, while Tony would go out with the first group of porters.

With the men at base camp now energized by packing for their departure, Chap Cranmer and George Sheldon decided there was no reason for them to hang around. Chap had finally recovered enough to hike above base camp, but his one trip to Camp I in early July took him nearly twice as long as the rest of the men and left him utterly exhausted. Now he was just biding his time. George had descended from the mountain for what turned out to be the last time on July 8. Ten days later, enough was enough. He and Chap had never expected to be marooned at base camp without knowledge of what the rest of the team was doing high on the mountain. Their dream adventure had turned into a nightmare of sickness, frostbite, and boredom. With the excuse of a geological exploration of the lower glacier, they told Tony Cromwell they were leaving base camp and, with no one challenging them for abandoning the rest of the team, they went on with their plan. Exclaiming that it was "a wonderful feeling to be on the way back" home, they headed away from the mountain on July 18.

After he watched them leave, Tony decided he too had had enough. He had neither forgiven nor forgotten Fritz's public dressing-down the week before. They had started out as close friends and comrades, but somewhere along the way Tony came to see Fritz as an ugly tyrant, or worse, an ugly German. Ordering the men around like his servants, parading through camp like a commandant, Fritz, in Tony's opinion, was a humorless, overbearing bully, hell-bent on his own achievement of the summit. The rest of them were merely pawns to that end. Picking up his pencil and pad, Tony wrote a note to Jack in Camp II announcing that it was time to start packing up the lower camps for the team's departure from the mountain on the 24th and to "salvage all the tents and sleeping bags you can."

Thus began the clearing of the high camps, an action that would be the subject of controversy for decades to come. With Tony's instructions in hand, Jack began organizing the camps' clearing. When he and Kikuli had retreated from the mountain a week before, he had treated Kikuli's re-frostbitten feet daily, massaging them with histamine to stimulate blood circulation. Layers of dead skin flaked off and, more worrisome to Jack, the skin around Kikuli's toes was limp and lifeless, like the skin of a Concord grape. Kikuli was definitely out of commission for work high on the mountain. He might even lose his toes. Nonetheless, needing him to help carry loads, Jack sent Kikuli and Dawa up to Camp IV for its tents, food, and sleeping bags (Camp III had been eliminated and the supplies at Camp V had already been moved up the mountain).

At Camp IV, Kikuli found Kitar and Tendrup, whom Fritz had instructed four days earlier to descend only to Camp VI for supplies and then immediately re-ascend to Camp VIII. But, without sahib supervision and afraid of the steep slopes above Camp VI, they had descended all the way to Camp IV—not only was it 2,000 feet lower on the mountain than Camp VI, it was a larger and relatively more comfortable camp. Kikuli was furious at their insubordination and immediately commanded them up to Camp VIII with more matches, fuel, and food for the summit team's bid for the top. Reluctantly, Tendrup and Kitar headed up, heavily laden. Kikuli and Dawa then headed back down the mountain with Camp IV's extra sleeping bags, air mattresses, and food.

As he packed up Camp II, Jack decided that he too would leave his lonely outpost and head down with Kikuli and Dawa. He had continued to suffer from insomnia and exhaustion, he hadn't heard from the summit team since he'd left them at Camp VI on July 13 six days earlier, and now he was finished. No amount of eleventh-hour pep talks from Fritz could re-energize him now. He was going home.

When Jack, Kikuli, and Dawa descended to base camp on July 19 they had with them 170 pounds of tinned beef and ham, two Yak tents, and nearly a dozen Sherpa and sahib sleeping bags.

As Jack walked toward base camp, he thought the barren, squalid outpost looked like the Garden of Eden after his six weeks at or above Camp II. Stripping off his clothes to take his first bath in fifty days, he stood naked on the glacier waiting for his bathwater to heat and realized it was his twenty-seventh birthday. "Happy Birthday to me," he thought, relieved to finally be off the mountain but also feeling slightly sorry for himself that he was so far from any semblance of celebration. He looked down at his skeletal frame, picking at his ribs with his fingers like a raven at roadkill, figuring he'd lost about thirty pounds. He could only imagine what Fritz and Dudley looked like. The once stocky Dud, whom Jack had derided and whose physique he had ridiculed as not being that of a mountaineer, was still up there, thousands of feet above where Jack had wasted away to a weight he hadn't seen since he wore short pants in the Florida Everglades.

As Jack sat in his basin of warm water at base camp and Dudley rested inside his tent at Camp VIII, the Sherpas whom Kikuli had sent up with supplies reached Camp VII. Three of them refused to go any further. The slope ahead was treacherous, they were alone, had heavy loads and no crampons, and they were unwilling to take the risk. They had been virtually alone on the mountain for weeks, they hadn't seen any of the sahibs taking loads above Camp VI, and suddenly they'd had enough. Tendrup, the team's most reliable climber next to Kikuli, was left to do the carry to Camp VIII himself. He started up, but got only a few yards out of camp before a steep wall of blue ice stopped him. Although there were only 600 vertical feet separating Camps VII and VIII, without crampons and a safety rope and with no sahib in sight to instruct him in step-cutting, he didn't know what to do. Finally, he decided not to risk it. Putting his load down, he called up the slope to see if anyone from Camp VIII would appear over the edge to help him or to come down for his load. No one did. He called again, *Bara Sahib! Wolfe Sahib! Pasang!* Silence. There was a slight breeze and his words seemed to evaporate in the thin air, like a handful of flour in the wind. *Wolfe Sahib! Bara Sahib! Pasang!* Again, nothing. Perhaps they were dead? Perhaps they'd fallen or been swept by an avalanche off this very ice slope which now stopped him? He tried calling out a third time and then stood on the barren slope waiting in the otherwise quiet wind. Nothing.

With little else to go on but the silence, the avalanche slope, and his own fears of the mountain spirits, Tendrup decided that the three above them must have perished. Returning to Camp VII, he told Kitar and Phinsoo of his fears that the sahibs above were dead. They talked at length, trading their theories and fears, and kept coming back to one undeniable truth: they hadn't seen nor heard from any one of the three in nearly a week. Surely something must have happened. What could they do? They were too afraid to stay here, particularly if the mountain spirits had already been angered by the sahibs—they could be next. There was nothing left to do but descend, and because the sahibs had told them repeatedly how valuable the sleeping bags were, they knew they had better take them and the larger food tins with them as Kikuli, Dawa, and Doctor Sahib had done further down.

They turned and started off the mountain, clearing anything of value out of Camp VII and then Camp VI further beneath it.

Below Dudley at Camp VIII, the mountain was now bare and soon to be empty.

AT THAT MOMENT, Fritz stared up a ramp of unstable ice which would later come to be known as the Bottleneck, a steep avalanche gully of loose rock and frozen scree. Beyond it was a 200-foot vertical wall of ice over which a gigantic overhanging bulge of ice, or serac, loomed. To Fritz, the bulging ice looked too fragile and avalanche-prone to traverse under.* He hated the perilous exposure they would endure climbing beneath it, and decided that, rather than flirt with the chance of a chunk of ice breaking off the serac and flooding down through the gully, he would traverse around the most dangerous section and climb on a surface where he felt more in control: rock. After explaining the move to Pasang, Fritz and the Sherpa carefully removed their crampons so that they'd have better traction on the rock and tied them to Pasang's pack. Then, taking off his gloves (at close to 27,000 feet, an amazing demonstration of fortitude) in order to get a better feel of the rock beneath his fingers, Fritz led Pasang up the rock face in what was undoubtedly the highest technical rock climb in history, at an altitude never before reached on K2. It took hours, but the men did it, exhausted and elated to have that section behind them.

Fritz looked toward the summit with growing excitement. It was only a few hundred vertical feet above them. *It is mine.* The summit of K2. After generations of explorers who had only been able to guess what the mountain felt and looked like at this height, here he was. As he had told Charlie Houston before he left, he was about to make history and be made for life.

In his elation he hadn't heard troubling sounds behind him. Pasang was muttering to himself. Then the words became chanting prayers to Buddha. Suddenly the rope at Fritz's waist went taut. Carefully he turned and looked down to Pasang, who stood there slowly shaking his head no. While Fritz later claimed that Pasang had refused to go on out of fear of mountain spirits, it was equally plausible that his fear was more pedestrian. After spending

---

* It was this serac that broke off in great chunks in 2008, killing eleven climbers who were swept off the route in a series of ice and rock avalanches.

most of the day standing stock still while belaying Fritz at 27,000 feet, Pasang's feet were probably in danger of severe frostbite. His cheap-issue Sherpa boots were not designed for subzero temperatures and Pasang might not have been willing to risk his future as a mountain guide for Fritz's glory on the summit. Besides, he believed—with very good reason—that they would not survive a night exposed to the elements on the summit ridge of K2. As the mountain's subsequent history eventually confirmed, it is the deadliest of the 8,000-meter mountains on descent, proving that Pasang's fears were well founded.

Fritz looked at the Sherpa in disbelief, and with rising anger. *We are almost there!* he insisted. He could almost see the summit from where they stood. It was 6 p.m. His plan was to climb through the night, the half moon providing enough refracted light off the slopes to adequately see, reach the summit before midnight then head back down, returning to their tent by daybreak. Without proper food and hydration, warmth, and rest, a nighttime summit bid at those altitudes is wildly risky, but to Fritz, whose judgment was probably compromised after several days above 26,000 feet, it made perfect sense. *It's more dangerous to climb down at night than it is up!* he urged Pasang. *We'll be safer climbing the easier snow fields to the summit rather than descending that rock wall at night!*

No, Pasang said firmly. *No*. He began to untie the safety rope that connected him to Fritz so that he could start down alone, if necessary. He had had enough.

Fritz's only options were to continue on alone in the dark or to turn his back on his dream and follow Pasang down. Fritz looked up at the mountain. *It is right there.* The pull of the summit was physical, painful. But he knew he couldn't, at least he shouldn't, try it on his own. This was not a mountain to climb alone, in the dark, at 28,000 feet. He also felt a flicker of dread of what the climbing community would make of his abandoning his climbing partner. Years later he would tell his biographer, "People would see me as 'that lousy damned Nazi German who must be crucified' if I had left Pasang." Fritz decided he had no choice but to follow Pasang down.

Okay, Pasang, okay. Don't untie the rope. I'm coming.

As they rappelled each other back down the rock face, the rope became caught on their two pairs of crampons tied to the Sherpa's pack. In his desire to get off the cliff face before the sun disappeared behind Chogolisa to the west and the temperature dropped dramatically, Pasang yanked at the rope to free it. Fritz was above and saw what was about to happen but, before he could speak, Pasang gave the rope a final, savage tug and the two men watched as their crampons went spinning off into the void beneath them and disappeared down the south face of K2.

Fritz watched them go with a sick sinking in his stomach. Climbing rock walls without crampons was one thing, but climbing across the windswept ice fields which were above them, and then descending back down without them, was unthinkable. *But maybe,* Fritz quickly reasoned with his take-charge thinking, *I could cut steps through the worst of the exposure. I've cut hundreds, maybe thousands of steps below me, why couldn't I cut a few more dozen above me? Besides, we are through the worst of it. It's merely a snow slope from here.*

With that, he had a plan. He continued down behind Pasang, organizing his thoughts and planning for his summit assault in the morning. He had kept his eye on the overhanging serac all day and had seen nothing discharge down the ice gully. Because its smooth surface was far easier than the technical rock wall they had climbed this morning, he decided that that would be their route. Starting early and getting onto the final summit cone around sunrise, they would reach the summit itself before noon and could get back to their high camp that afternoon, possibly even all the way down to Camp VIII. The plan cheered him up. But when they finally regained their tent at Camp IX it was 2:30 in the morning; they hadn't eaten or drunk a drop for hours; melting snow and making food and tea to replenish and rehydrate would take most of the remaining night. Given that most summit assaults begin hours before sunrise in order to make it back to camp before nightfall the following day, Fritz decided they would take a rest day and proceed for the summit the morning after that.

On July 20, as Jack was luxuriating in his birthday bath far below them, Fritz and Pasang awoke around ten o'clock to a beautiful, cloudless, windless day. Fritz removed his clothes and lay naked in the door of the tent, soaking in the warmth and exotic luxury of sun on his bare skin. Pasang lay next to him. They had reason to celebrate and bask in the warmth. They had climbed to within 800 feet of the summit. They had nearly reached the top of K2 without support or oxygen; it would be forty years before anyone matched that feat.* And they had done all of this on what many already considered to be the world's hardest mountain. Even though the summit had eluded them so far, they were already victors and they had every reason to savor their success. And, they would try again tomorrow.

While it was undoubtedly a sumptuous sun bath, it also was a potentially expensive one in terms of Fritz's and Pasang's strength. The power of the sun's rays in the thinner atmosphere at 27,000 feet, to say nothing of the debilitating effects of altitude, can strip a body of energy. Fritz and Pasang, after eight weeks of exhausting work on the mountain, the last few days of which was at altitudes only reached previously with bottled oxygen, must have already

---

* While an Italian team became the first to summit K2 in 1954, they did so with supplemental oxygen. It wouldn't be until 1978 that two American climbers made the summit without it.

been on borrowed energy and time. In hindsight, their sun bath may have been their undoing.

BELOW, AT CAMP VIII, Dudley licked at a tiny pool of water in a flap of the tent. He had run out of matches the day before and, although he had tried to melt enough snow to supply him for another day or two, he'd melted only a few cups before the last match was gone. Luckily, the weather had held so he had been able to melt snow in the sun, but at 26,000 feet the snow didn't have enough moisture in it to provide more than a couple of tablespoons at a time. Still, it was liquid and he lapped at it greedily, trying to hold it in his mouth and wet his lips with it before swallowing.

He'd been in this camp seven days, five of them waiting for Fritz to return or for help to come from below so he could try the overhanging crevasse again. He had fought hard for this mountain and gotten further than almost anyone else. To have his daring adventure come down to such an ignominious end insulted everything he'd ever done in his life. In the face of the younger men's ridicule, he had not given up. He knew he wasn't the best climber, or the most agile, or the most gifted. But he'd made it this far.

He had thought about making another go at the crevasse alone; the snow had most likely settled and crusted over, and with his crampons he might be able to just "walk" up the wall. But as much as he wanted to get moving and make a stab at the summit, somehow he just couldn't do it. Not alone. Besides, all of the inaction had caused the frostbite on his feet to get worse and he had had to spend most of his days rubbing circulation back into his painful toes. Looking toward the slope above him for the thousandth time, he searched for signs of Fritz and Pasang, wondering where in hell they'd gone and what he would do if they never returned.

As another night fell, Dudley lay in his sleeping bag with the half moon overhead. His feet throbbed; hunger and thirst gnawed at his stomach. Finally he fell asleep.

THE NEXT MORNING, Fritz and Pasang arose before dawn. After a quick breakfast, they suited up and started out toward the gully below the serac, but soon realized the warm sun the day before had melted the surface snow, which had then frozen overnight into a thick sheet of ice. Fritz looked at the 1,500 feet of mountain above him, calculating that he would need to cut nearly four hundred steps. It simply wasn't possible. He didn't have the strength or the time for such an effort. They would have to descend to Camp VIII and "expropriate"* Dudley's crampons—the only pair left high on the mountain—or get a pair from the reinforcements coming from below. Reluctantly and with rising irritation that once again Jack and the Sherpas were nowhere in sight, the following morning Fritz descended with Pasang to Camp VIII. It was July 22.

---

* From Fritz Wiessner's notes for his biography.

Chapter 9

The Descent

> *To those men who are born for the mountains, the struggle can*
> *never end, until their lives end. To them it holds the very quin-*
> *tessence of living—the fiery core, after the lesser parts have been*
> *burned away.*
>
> —ELIZABETH KNOWLTON, *The Naked Mountain*

Paul Petzoldt's 1938 shot of the infamous ice slope above Camp VI.
(Photo by Paul Petzoldt, courtesy of the Houston-NOLS Archives)

Fritz began what he thought would be a short descent to Camp VIII for food and crampons "from the expected support party"* to traverse the ice gully and slopes above Camp IX. Knowing that reserve sleeping bags had been stocked at Camp VIII, he left his own at Camp IX to reduce his load. He had to conserve his energy for another summit attack, and every ounce counted.

As they began their descent on the relatively easy slope, Pasang lost his footing and started sliding toward the cliff edge of the south face. Fritz moved quickly and dug his ice axe into the slope before the rope between them pulled him right off the mountain after Pasang. Pasang was clearly finished. Dizzy and disoriented from the five days above 26,000 feet, the Sherpa was so weak that his condition was becoming a critical hazard.

As every Himalayan climber soon learns, going down is deadlier than going up because gravity is working perversely against you. When you slip on the way up, you merely fall into the slope at your face. When you slip on descent you fall into the abyss at your feet. Still, Fritz had no other options for a climbing partner with whom to attack the summit, unless one had arrived at Camp VIII. If not, Pasang would have to rest at Camp VIII and be ready for another summit bid.

Instead of provisions and fresh Sherpas awaiting them at VIII, they saw a desolate tent, somewhat collapsed after nearly a week

---

* Fritz wrote in his diary that he expected to find crampons in Camp VIII. However, when Charlie Houston was asked whether the high camps typically would be provisioned with extra crampons, he responded, "Unlikely. We didn't have extra crampons in those days. Every man had his one pair and that was it." Therefore, it seems that Fritz was counting on taking another climber's crampons for his summit bid, leaving the man to descend the mountain without them.

of wind battering it, its front enclosure loose and blowing in the wind. It looked empty but Fritz called ahead and was surprised to see the tent move and a figure slowly crawl out.

It was Dudley. He had spent another five days alone on the mountain, this time at 25,300 feet. He was exhausted, dehydrated, malnourished, and had badly swollen and frostbitten feet. He struggled to get out of the tent and then to his feet to greet them. He had run out of matches two days before and was reduced to melting handfuls of snow in small folds of the tent. He had had no cooked food and the food he did have was dried and heavily salted, which further stripped him of liquids: canned ham and pemmican, Ry Krisp crackers, cheese, dried peaches, dried apricots, and raisins. His stores of dried vegetables, cereals, cocoa, macaroni, tea, bouillon, soup cubes, and rice had gone untouched. Unwilling and unable to descend the treacherous slopes below him alone, he had sat vigil waiting for men and supplies which never came. While weak, he was still functioning and mentally alert enough to be alarmed and angry that no one had come from below. Whether or not he still thought the summit was in his grasp will never be known, but after his two months on the mountain, it's hard to imagine that his thoughts were on anything but descent, safety, and home, and not on climbing slopes and navigating crevasses which had already defeated him or of more nights spent trying to sleep in the suffocating air.

Fritz was irate. He felt as if he had been close enough to the summit to see the view from the top. He had solved the last riddle of this confounding mountain that had eluded men for generations, and it was now his for the taking. Yet instead of climbing toward it, he had to walk further away. Descending to Camp VIII had been frustrating enough; now they would have to go even further, to Camp VII, hoping that it still had men and supplies in it, although he was beginning to doubt it did.* Something had gone seriously wrong on the mountain below him. He didn't know what had happened to Jack, Kikuli, and the others, but if they hadn't resupplied Camp VIII as instructed, there was every possibility Camp VII was also empty. The insubordination of his team was more than he could comprehend.

With a handful of matches given to him by Pasang, Dudley was finally able to prepare a hot meal and quickly handed out soup and crackers to the two men. Then he packed up his sleeping bag, journal, and camera, and prepared for the painful descent on his blistered feet.

Here, Dudley's decision to descend to Camp VII deserves examination. Fritz later testified that Dudley was "in great shape," so much so that he "insisted" on joining Fritz on a final summit bid, and that he descended to Camp VII only to help bring up supplies for that bid. The distance between the camps was only 600 vertical feet—a distance covered in hours, not days. If he were bent on going for the summit, surely it would have been easier for Dudley to wait at Camp VIII while Fritz and Pasang hopped down to Camp VII, grabbed some food and fuel for a summit bid, and reascended. But Dudley didn't wait at Camp VIII, and, because he took his sleeping bag, air mattress, journal, and camera with him, it seems likely that his intent was to continue all the way to base camp.

Another curiosity is Fritz's decision not to grab one of the extra sleeping bags which had been stocked at Camp VIII. A climber's bag is one of his few securities on a mountain; for Fritz, who had left his at Camp IX, to have one available at Camp VIII and not

---

* Fritz Wiessner, diary entry, July 22, 1939.

utilize it was perhaps an indication of his reduced mental capacity after so many days near 27,000 feet, particularly since he was already worried that Camp VII might be empty.

Regardless of hindsight logic, three men with only two sleeping bags decided to head down the mountain on the afternoon of July 22. Tying the three of them together on a rope, Wiessner started to inch them down the slope. While it is customary for the strongest climber to take up the rear on descent in order to arrest any falls on the rope below him, Fritz didn't trust Pasang to find the route down the tricky, steep slope; plus, there was nobody better at discerning a mountain's mysteries than Fritz. Even though Pasang was severely depleted by that time, Fritz went first, with Dudley in the middle and Pasang in the rear, the most powerful position in the three-man team. Dudley was presumably wearing the only pair of crampons between the three men, and with the tricouni nails in both Fritz's and Pasang's boots worn down after weeks on the mountain, Fritz was forced to cut steps for purchase on the slick incline. Bending forward, he cut into the ice with quick, sharp bites of the axe as he moved laboriously down the slope.

Above him, Dudley was moving even more slowly. Between his seven weeks on the mountain, the last week in a tent at nearly 26,000 feet, and his depleted physical strength, he wasn't taking any chances. As he inched along, he looked down a slope so steep he couldn't see where it ended beneath him. It was like climbing down the side of a roller coaster. If he could have inched down on his rear end with his crampons digging into the ice for purchase, he would have.

Below him, Fritz was annoyed. He wanted to get to Camp VII and crawl into a sleeping bag and rest. After he cut the third step and leaned toward where he would cut the fourth, something happened which caused Fritz to lose his footing and soon all three men were sliding down the slope out of control.

Re-creating what actually happened in the accident is impossible, but it's not hard to imagine how frustrated Fritz was or how desperate he must have been to lay his head down and sleep. He had been higher on a Himalayan peak and for longer than any man in history, most of the time breaking trail and anchoring the safety rope to the rock and ice walls on the route. Perhaps the rope around his body tightened between him and Dudley and he tugged it out of impatience. Or, perhaps Dudley became tangled with the rope, stepping on it and causing it to pull at Fritz's waist. Or, perhaps Fritz simply fell forward as he leaned over to cut the next step, and Dudley and Pasang in their diminished states were unable to properly belay him.

No matter how it happened, something pulled Dudley off the mountain so strongly that he somersaulted over Fritz and began careening down the precipitous slope, pulling Pasang and then Fritz after him. Soon all three were tumbling down the icy grade, the rope playing out and then catching between them as their bodies fell. Fritz kicked his boots into the slope trying to gain purchase in the ice as the men slid with ever-increasing speed, bouncing against the rocks as they plummeted. After several wild swings of his heavy ice axe, which glanced off the frozen slope as if it were a baseball bat, Fritz finally felt the rope catch and braced himself as the other two men's weight became taut on the rope at his waist. They all stopped, less than 200 feet from a sheer drop-off to the Godwin–Austen Glacier 9,000 feet below. While Fritz later said he was finally able to sink his axe far enough into the ice to hold the three men, Pasang reported that the rope had caught on a rock. Either way, their fall had been arrested and they were alive, if bruised and badly shaken by their close call. Looking down, Fritz could see that Pasang had suffered some sort of injury to his back or possibly his kidneys, while Dudley's rucksack (with his sleeping bag, air mattress, and one of his cameras) tumbled down the slope and disappeared into oblivion.

After picking up the pieces and dusting themselves off, the three men limped carefully down to Camp VII, only a few hundred feet below them. But instead of men and supplies, they found the camp not only empty but stripped; its tents had been left open to the wind and were half-filled with snow, food and matches were scattered on the slope, and, most critically, no one was in sight whose crampons Fritz could use for his summit bid.

The three men stood staring at the ruined camp, dumbstruck.

What in hell happened here? Fritz wondered. While it was one thing for Jack and Kikuli not to have reached Camp VIII, for them to have evacuated Camp VII was an outrage. He had left exact orders detailing who was to bring what supplies and when, and he was infuriated that his demands had been ignored. He had reprimanded Tony and Jack several times before and now to be so utterly disregarded was unthinkable. Had he and Dudley been sabotaged by the Sherpas, even though Kitar and Tendrup had been so "cheerful" the last time he had seen them at Camp VIII? Fritz stomped about the camp, his temper, anguish, and exhaustion boiling over in equal measure. His own team had "sacrificed this great goal," *his* great goal. Not only had they been abandoned, but they had been left without spare sleeping bags and air mattresses high on K2. Standing on the edge of the mountain in the fading light, after his white rage finally passed, Fritz had one overriding thought: *What the hell am I going to do now?*

As Pasang gathered some of the scattered food and prepared a small meal, Fritz and Dudley re-erected the most usable tent.

When it was finally standing, the three crawled into it for the night.

Fritz wasn't exactly clear on what had happened on the slope above, or why they all fell, but he knew that they had almost disappeared down a 9,000-foot face. Did he have the strength for another close call? Could he stop all three of them again if there were a next time? Could he take that chance? The nails on his boots were almost butter-smooth by now—he hadn't been able to sharpen them in over a week. Also, his six days above 26,000 feet had cost him more in terms of his physical strength than he'd thought. He was exhausted. The idea of descending, with the summit so close, infuriated him. However, without crampons and a climbing partner, it was impossible to even consider another try. He needed to replace Pasang, but there were no Sherpas in sight. There was only Dudley and his one pair of crampons.

For nearly ten hours the three sat upright huddled beneath Pasang's thin sleeping bag while the frigid cold bore into their bones through the tent floor. With sleep impossible, Fritz and Dudley talked through the night, Fritz bitterly accusing the men below of having stolen his summit out of jealousy and revenge, and declaring that Dudley, with his money to buy a team of lawyers, could have them all sued for stripping the camps, even put in jail for criminal negligence. It was the longest night of Fritz Wiessner's life and one from which he felt he never truly recovered his strength. Years later, he would tell his son that that one night at Camp VII cost him more physically than anything else ever would in his life.

As they waited for the first light of morning, Wiessner thought of the descent ahead and knew that the worst of the steep and icy slopes was still below them: a treacherous 65-degree pitch with ice so smooth they called it blue. They'd have to traverse across it in order to avoid facing directly downhill, but that would only lengthen their descent. Even if Fritz were to wear Dudley's crampons, there were few rocks to arrest a three-man tumble down the slope and none of them had the strength or skills to hold the weight and momentum of all three careening out of control down the mountain.

Whether Fritz accepted it or not as they sat upright that long night, perched on the edge of K2, his ability to get Dudley Wolfe down the mountain was gone. Their fall the day before had been devastating for Dudley; after two months on the mountain he was a frail shadow of the man who had boarded the *Biancamano* four months before. His somersault down the slope, losing his rucksack, and nearly falling off the east face cliffs, had taken the last of his already spent reserves. He was done.

The debate about mountain ethics, and what one climber's responsibilities are to another, is as old as the ropes and pitons of the earliest adventurers. Many, including Charlie Houston, believed that the glory of climbing is found not on the summit but in the shared experience of getting there, and back, alive. Judging by their behavior, just as many other climbers believe that it's "every man for himself," and that no one can or should rely on anyone else to take care of them in a place called the death zone. The question is not without its sea-level equivalents. Like the captain of a sinking ship, is it the leader's responsibility to make sure every man is off the boat (or the mountain) before he saves himself? And does it matter, morally, if the leader is so incapacitated by exhaustion and mental haziness that the mountain may end up claiming not just one, but three lives if he doesn't save himself?

While we will never know what the two men said to each other as the first slate gray of dawn appeared in the sky, what we do know is that a decision was made for Dudley not to continue descending with Fritz and Pasang. There are two possible reasons. Either Dudley thought he was strong enough for a summit bid and wanted to rest in preparation for it, as Fritz later testified, or Dudley acknowledged that after two months on the mountain he was too weak, too inexperienced, and too hobbled by frostbite to get down safely, and that Fritz alone couldn't provide that help.

Because there was adequate food for a summit assault between what remained of Dudley's Camp VIII stash and what they found at Camp VII, food was not the reason for Fritz and Pasang to descend. And because there were extra sleeping bags at Camp VIII, sleeping bags were not the issue. The only viable reasons for Fritz to continue descending were his and Pasang's mental and physical deterioration, their lack of crampons to climb above the Bottleneck, and the need for help in getting Dudley down safely. But that's not what Wiessner later said.

In all of Wiessner's accounts after the expedition, verbal and written, he said he descended to Camp VI in order to resupply another summit bid, and he left Dudley at Camp VII to rest (without explaining why, if rest were the issue, he hadn't left him at Camp VIII). He also never specified what supplies he needed, and no one ever asked.

While it seems heavy-handed to label Dudley's decision to stay at Camp VII "sacrificial," his staying with only Pasang's cheap sleeping bag, which was just two-thirds as tall as he was, and only two or three days' worth of matches poses the question: Did he remain on the mountain because he realized he was a liability to the others and didn't want to risk their lives as well as his own?

THE FRIGID, miserable night left the three men disoriented and exhausted. In the morning, Fritz and Pasang readied themselves for their descent but in their weakness and delirium it took them nearly six hours to pack up and put on their boots. When they were ready, Fritz counted out the remaining matches and handed Dudley fifteen of them, taking the last full box for his and Pasang's descent. Dudley put his fifteen into his stainless steel match case, careful to tighten the screw top firmly back into place. As they left camp, Fritz turned and saw that several matches remained scattered in the snow.

"Dudley!" he called.

Dudley stuck his head out of the tent.

"You'd better collect those matches and dry them out. You may need them."

Dudley waved and nodded that he understood.

With a promise that he'd be right back, Fritz turned and headed down the mountain.

AT THAT MOMENT, Tendrup, Kitar, Phinsoo, and Tsering were resting at Camp I at 18,600 feet, after an exhausting descent the day before all the way from Camp VII, laden with gear and feeling guilty over their decision to vacate the high camps without orders from the leader. Almost reluctant to return to base camp, which had become a fractious place, they finally left the tent by midday and made it into base camp that evening.

As they neared camp, sentries who had been waiting for any signal from the summit team saw the Sherpas coming and a cry went up that four members were moving down the glacier toward the tents. The entire team rushed out to meet the men as they approached. There Tendrup told Jack, Tony, and Joe that he and the other three Sherpas had not seen or heard from Bara Sahib or Wolfe Sahib since July 14, the day after Jack had left them above

Camp VI. In fact, Tendrup told them, he believed that the summit team was dead, telling how he had gotten to within 500 feet of the Camp VIII tents and had called for help to cross the slope, but no one had responded. He also showed Jack and Tony that the four of them had brought down all the sleeping bags and valuable foodstuffs from Camps VI and VII, just as Jack, Kikuli, and Dawa had done from Camps II and IV.

If Jack and Tony were concerned that the team's laborious work in stocking the high camps had just been entirely erased, they never mentioned it. Instead, they listened to the Sherpas and were perplexed. The weather, save for a storm on July 15 and 16, had been relatively good, and they figured that from Camp VIII at 26,000 feet, all Fritz and Dudley would have needed was three days to reach the summit and return to a lower camp, maybe even all the way to base. Here it was the 23rd and no one had seen or heard from the summit team in nine days.

Where are they? they wondered, looking up at the mountain. *Could they in fact be dead?*

Jack and Tony went to Dudley's base camp tent, got his powerful nautical field glasses from the leather case embossed with *Highland Light*, and scoured the mountain for any signs of life, or death. They saw none—just oceans of snow, rock, and ice. As they searched, Chandra, the schoolteacher and translator from Srinagar, approached and told them he was concerned that all of the bags had been removed and thought that at least a few should be returned to the high camps for the retreating summit team.

They looked at the man in annoyance. He had been nothing but a complaining hindrance to the team and a frightful gossip all summer. Joe Trench thought him a laughingstock who was desperate to befriend Fritz for future work and who would agree "black was white if Wiessner said so."

Jack and Tony needed time to figure out what to do. The last Sherpa to get within shouting distance of Camp VIII had concluded that the summit team was dead. The porters had arrived, as scheduled, to take the team out of base camp. And now this bothersome man was telling them to rush back up the mountain and restock the camps which had been stripped in preparation for the team's departure, a departure they hoped was imminent.

Hoping to quell Chandra's instinct for wagging his tongue, they told him they were going to survey the glacier in the morning for any signs of the summit team and instructed him not to share his concern about the clearing of the camps with any of the other Sherpas. The last thing they needed was a rumor starting a revolt.

With that, Jack and Tony returned to their private conference about what to do next, leaving Chandra standing on the glacier angry and embarrassed at having been spoken to like a child. The schoolteacher had had a long summer suffering the arrogance of the Americans and the bigotry of Trench, the man hired as the porters' supposed liaison who couldn't be bothered to learn their language. Bruised and resentful, Chandra returned to the Sherpas' tents where he, true to form, kept the men busy chatting with speculation, accusation, and second-guessing Tony and Jack's management of their splintered team. Even if Jack and Tony had been able to silence Chandra, it would have done little to calm the babble at base camp, where, when disaster strikes, those not on the mountain are mostly left to speculate about those who are. The trouble above is simply too far out of anyone's reach to do anything constructive. All that's left is talk.

That night, with little else they could do, Jack and Tony, the men in charge, went to bed. In the morning Tony headed up the glacier with Kikuli and Dawa to examine the ropes and upper campsites from the base of the climbing route. As Tony went to look for concrete evidence that their teammates were dead, Jack stayed in base camp to manage the thirty porters who had arrived to take the men home.

Whether through malfeasance or simply because they didn't think to do so, neither of them ever mentioned returning any gear to the high camps for the descending summit team.

The Last Man on the Mountain

These mountains do not forgive mistakes.

—ANATOLI BOUKREEV

The highest-known photo from the expedition, taken most likely at Camp VIII. *(Courtesy of the Fritz H. Wiessner Collection)*

When Fritz and Pasang reached Camp VI at 23,400 feet on the afternoon of July 23, they found it too was deserted. Fritz was at a critical juncture. He could either re-ascend the 1,400 feet back to Camp VII and bring Dudley down, or he could continue down the mountain hoping beyond reason that someone was still in either Camp IV or II who was able to rescue a failing man (he knew Camps V and III had been dismantled and served only as supply depots). Without the strength to climb back to Camp VIII, where the only extra sleeping bags were, going back up would have meant another miserable night on the mountain with three men again sharing one bag. Evidently, for Fritz, that was an unthinkable alternative. By now, he was near or at the end of his tether; he had to get down. Up was no longer possible. Instead of going back for his last man, Fritz continued down, taking Pasang with him.

As they descended, they found more of the same: the remnants of Camp V at 22,000 feet, an evacuated Camp IV at 21,500 feet, and the old equipment depot which they called Camp III. With all evidence to the contrary, Fritz still held out hope that Jack and a few Sherpas remained at Camp II, the mountain's main staging area at 19,300 feet. But as Fritz and Pasang drew near the tents, Fritz's last flicker of optimism was extinguished. Camp II was clearly empty. Its tent doors were open and blowing in the breeze with no sign of life or sound of a hissing stove cooking dinner.

With night falling and unable to put one foot in front of the other, further descent that day would have been suicidal. With their arms and legs feeling like lead, Fritz and Pasang took down one of the remaining tents and wrapped themselves in it. They huddled together for yet another frigid, wretched night in the cold.

It's hard to imagine what physical and mental state Fritz and

Pasang were in after their weeks on the mountain, the last five days above 26,000 feet clawing for the summit. Climbers who have spent similar amounts of time at that altitude, straining every fiber of muscle and brain matter to reach the top, have experienced a range of miseries when they finally turned to head back down the mountain: cerebral edema, hallucinations, fatigue so severe that the only desire is to lie down and sleep even though every last ounce of their survival instincts is screaming, "NO!! If you sleep, you DIE!" It's a tribute to the men not only how close to the summit of K2 they climbed, without any support, but what they accomplished on descent. During those two desperate days of retreat from the uppermost summit slopes, they survived severe dehydration and malnutrition and were exposed to the raw and frigid elements, exhausted beyond measure.

While Pasang was simply grateful to be alive, Fritz felt they had been utterly deserted and he was tortured by thoughts of their abandonment. *They left us on the mountain for dead. Forgotten. Perhaps even sabotaged.* His grand plan for K2 and his future seemed destroyed. Not only had he not made the summit, he still had a man high on the mountain. And not just any man, but Dudley Wolfe, one of the richest men in America, a man who could have meant a lot to his financial and climbing future, a man whom he could have talked into returning the next year, and then to any number of expeditions in the Himalayas. But Fritz had left him on the mountain. He'd send help to bring Dudley down as soon as he got himself to the base; but still, it wouldn't look good to the outside world and for his future as an expedition leader.

As he and Pasang stumbled down, each in a semi-coherent trance, Fritz began to silently chant to himself, *Come on, keep it going.* Fight it. It became almost a mantra as he focused intently on the ground at his feet. *Keep going. Fight it.* A misstep now would surely mean death. Neither he nor Pasang had the strength to hold the other in a fall. Thankfully, with every foot he descended, the thicker air became food and energy for his ravaged body and brain. While he grew weaker and more desperate for sleep, he nonetheless knew now that he would make it down and survive.

On July 24, Fritz and Pasang finally reached the glacier, mere shadows of the men who had left weeks before. Wiessner was so emaciated he could encircle his ankle with his thumb and fore-finger. Pasang, doubled over in pain and passing bloody urine, had bruised a kidney in the fall below Camp VIII, and every step felt like a knife in his back. Each man clung to the other as they lurched across the glacier, often falling to the rocks.

Further up the glacier, Tony Cromwell was returning from the base of the Abruzzi Ridge, where he had hoped to get a glimpse of the three men on the mountain, or a sign of what might have happened to them—avalanche or fall. Finding neither, he had started back when he saw two men far off the usual route to base camp. Each was stumbling, falling to the rocks and struggling to get back up.

It was Fritz and Pasang. Tony approached the men and exclaimed how glad he was to see them. Everyone at base camp was worried there had been an accident.

Looking up from the rocks, Fritz struggled to stand. Then, still holding onto Pasang, he pointed a shaky finger in his deputy's face and demanded, "Why was the mountain stripped? What is the meaning of this!? You know, Dudley could have you put in jail for this insubordination! This sabotage!"

But his voice was gone. The words came out a crackled rasp. Still he raged on, as perhaps his guilt over having left Dudley yielded to the much easier emotion of blame.

Tony was stunned and infuriated. How dare Fritz accuse him of anything? Wiessner was their supposed leader and he had been on his own crusade for the summit, ignoring the team and its increasing problems, for his own vainglory! Now he was accusing *him* of incompetence and neglect? Besides, where the hell was Dudley?

Fritz waved his hand toward the mountain. *He is at Camp VII. Someone needs to go.*

Whom did you have in mind? Cromwell demanded. He told Fritz that everyone on the team was either exhausted, suffering frostbite, or had already left for home. *There's no one left!* he shouted. *Besides, Sherpas are not high-altitude guides, they are high-altitude porters! They are not trained or equipped to make such a rescue.*

We'll send the Sherpas up, Fritz persisted, as if not hearing. *And then, when I've recovered, I'll try again for the summit. I was nearly there . . . I could see the summit. It was right there. I nearly did it!*

As Fritz described his summit attempt and how close he had been to the top, Tony, disgusted and enraged, turned on his heel and headed back to base camp. Fritz stumbled along behind with Pasang.

WHEN THE REMAINING team at base camp saw the men approaching, they came running from every direction to greet them. Many had thought they were dead and were enormously relieved to see their friend, Pasang, and their leader, Bara Sahib, safe and back at base camp, although he was just a frail whisper of a man. But he didn't act frail. Fritz immediately confronted the smiling Sherpas. *Why didn't you come up to Camps VIII and IX with supplies as I ordered?* he demanded, leaning into their bewildered faces. *Why did you strip the camps?* he screamed at them in a screechy rasp.

Tendrup, the man considered by some on the team to be their best Sherpa aside from Kikuli, tried to explain what had happened.

They had been afraid of traversing the slope above Camp VII without steps, and he had called but no one had appeared from the tents in Camp VIII. They had not heard a sound or seen any signs of life from the mountain above them for more than a week and thought them all dead. They were cold, exhausted, frightened, and running out of food and fuel. With no sahib to give them direction in Camp VII, they did the one thing they thought most important for the team: they saved the last of the valuable equipment and fled for their lives.

Finding a target for his rage, Fritz attacked Tendrup. Tendrup had robbed him of the summit and caused Dudley to now sit thousands of feet above them waiting for rescue. *It is all Tendrup's fault!* As far as Fritz was concerned, the summit had been stolen from him through others' actions, not his own. He had been within a few hours of the top but their laziness, insubordination, and sheer evil intent had ruined the mission. Not only would he never forgive them, he would have their hides and Dudley would sue them all.

Dudley! He is going to have you all put in jail! Fritz raged.

As Fritz paused for breath, Tony pounced. *Us, put in jail? You're the one that owes him $1,300 and left him on the mountain! If anyone is getting sued and going to jail, it's you!*

As Fritz reeled from the accusation, others took their opening and started questioning him. *Why did you leave Dudley alone? How could you leave him with only a Sherpa's thin bag and a handful of matches? Why didn't you turn back at Camp VI, when you saw that it was empty, and go get Dudley?*

Fritz explained, through a throat so dry and swollen that every word was painful, that Dudley was okay but that he was weak, his feet were blistered, and he needed help to get down. Finally, unable to answer the last of the questions and feeling increasingly cornered, Fritz countered that Dudley had stayed at Camp VII because he "insisted" on going for the summit—that he was in fine shape, totally fit and strong, and all he needed was a rest. That provoked a question for which he had no answer: *If Dudley wanted to go for another summit bid, then why did he descend from Camp VIII?*

Fritz had no answer. It didn't make sense for Dudley to leave Camp VIII if he in fact wanted to go for a summit bid. He'd had enough food and fuel at Camp VIII for a few days, particularly since he had run out of matches and been unable to cook food for two days until Fritz and Pasang arrived with a new supply of matches.

Fritz was trapped, and like all trapped animals he lashed out. "After all, a Himalayan mountain is like war! You must expect a few casualties!"*

The men stood staring at him, their mouths agape. Had he really just said Dudley was expendable? Death was to be *expected* on high-altitude expeditions? No one said a word as the statement hung in the still, cold air.

ALTHOUGH THE TEAM still had a rescue to launch, Fritz ordered Tony and Tendrup out of base camp, commanding them to leave in the morning with Joe Trench and the first group of porters and wait for him in Srinagar. Jack, who stood nearby, thought the banishment out of place; every man was needed to launch the rescue of Dudley, particularly their strongest Sherpa, now that Kikuli was hobbled by frostbite. But again he said nothing and Tony and Joe packed their bags.

The confrontation seemed to drain Fritz of his last energy.

---

* Letter from Lt. George "Joe" Trench to Clifford Smith, May 16, 1940.

Soon after, he crawled into his tent and fell into a coma-like sleep. Later he wrote:*

> The mountain is far away. The weather is the best we've had so far. Will it be possible for me to go up after a rest with some Sherpas and with Jack, if he is in shape, pick up Dudley and then call on the summit? 7 days of good weather will be necessary. Maybe the Gods will be with me and let me have what is due to me.

The next day, Tony headed down the glacier and back to civilization in a rage, already formulating his version of the ill-fated expedition. With him went Joe, Tendrup, and twenty-two of the porters laden with most of the team's gear. As they walked, Joe and Tony compared their notes, their thoughts, and their memory of what had just happened. Tendrup, thoroughly dismayed and confused by Fritz's angry accusations and banishment, followed close behind.

With Fritz physically and mentally exhausted and Tony gone, Jack was left to organize the rescue. At 9 a.m. on the 25th, he set out with Dawa, Kitar, and Phinsoo to get Dudley. They reached Camp II by 3 p.m. and reset the tent that Fritz and Pasang had huddled beneath the night before. The morning of the 26th they left Camp II as soon as the sun hit the tents. But above camp they found that much of the length of the fixed safety ropes was unusable because the hot midsummer sun had melted out many of the anchor pitons. Another increasing hazard in the warm sun was rockfall, ranging in size from marbles to steamer trunks, which melted out of the snow and showered down around them with

---

* It is unclear exactly when Wiessner entered the events into his diary. Trench mentioned he didn't keep a daily journal and Chap Cranmer commented in his diary that "Fritz didn't keep a journal so he wasn't clear on what happened what days."

increasing frequency and velocity. One, sounding like a sewing machine at full throttle, missed Jack's head by inches and whizzed by him so fast he felt its whoosh rather than saw its size.

As they moved from Camp II to Camp IV the next day, Jack once again began to feel sick and dizzy. Given his previous collapse above Camp VI, Jack knew that his chances of getting much higher than where he was now on the mountain were slim. Beside him, Dawa complained of a pain in his back and chest, and Kitar simply refused to go any higher without Jack or Dawa. Once again Jack turned to the Sherpas, ordering Kitar and Phinsoo to go for Dudley, while he turned and descended with Dawa. On their way down the mountain, Dawa recovered sufficiently at Camp I to gather old cigarette butts from around the camp and make Jack a "horrible" cigarette out of their remains and a sheet of brown paper.

While each of their sahib bosses had quit the climb and now the rescue, Kitar and Phinsoo bravely continued up alone to Camp IV. There they stopped and waited for assistance to come from below.

When Jack made it to base that evening, he immediately went to Fritz's tent to discuss their next plan. Fritz had hoped to recover within a few days and was even still considering another summit bid. But he had remained weak and totally unable to head back up the mountain. That left Kikuli. After two months on the mountain, most of it managing loads to and from Camp IV, and now with frostbite threatening his feet, Kikuli stepped forward and said he and Tsering would leave at first light. Having seen the ravages of frostbite all too clearly, Kikuli undoubtedly knew this rescue could cost him his toes, even his feet, but still he went, not only for Dudley but for his two friends Kitar and Phinsoo, who would otherwise be abandoned as well.

Fritz gave Kikuli instructions to burn gasoline-soaked paper for a fire signal in case of trouble, and then sent him up the mountain.

In what is considered by many mountaineers to be the most Herculean effort in Himalayan climbing, Kikuli and Tsering reached Camp VI in a one-day ascent of 7,000 feet on what is arguably one of the most difficult, dangerous routes in the world, using ropes which were pulling their anchors and under constant threat of rockfall. On the way, they found Kitar and Phinsoo waiting in Camp IV; once again, the Sherpas had been afraid and unwilling to traverse the ice slopes above without proper equipment or leadership. With Kitar and Phinsoo now in tow, the four men reached Camp VI by nightfall.

In the morning, Kikuli, Kitar, and Phinsoo left the tent, leaving Tsering behind. The rapid ascent had left him with acute mountain sickness, and Kikuli instructed him to rest and have tea and food waiting; they would return that evening with Wolfe Sahib.

Shortly after 10 a.m., the Sherpas reached Dudley at Camp VII, seven days after Fritz had promised to "be right back." They were stunned at the desperate condition of their refined and gentle sahib, and embarrassed to see that he had relieved himself on his remaining food and in his sleeping bag, apparently unable to crawl out of the tent or even into a corner.

As if awakening from the dead, Dudley slowly focused on the faces staring at him. Reflexively he reached up to smooth his long and matted hair. It had turned totally white and hung in his ashen, gaunt face. He had always taken such pride in his appearance and here he was, reduced to this.

"Wolfe Sahib," Kikuli said, "it is Kikuli." He tried to hand Dudley his mail and a note from Fritz.

Dudley feebly took the letters and note but they fell out of his hand. He lay there, his brain trying to comprehend what was happening.

"I ran out of matches," Dudley said, the words coming as a

whisper. They were the first words he'd spoken to another human being in a week.

"Yes, Sahib, no problem. We have matches. Mister Dudley, I help you up," Kikuli urged, taking Dudley under the arms. He noticed Dudley had sores on his left hand, probably frostbite or even a bad burn from the stove. Kikuli tried to be gentle; he knew sores easily get infected because they can't heal at high altitude. He had seen it before on Nanga Parbat and Kangchenjunga. Only after the men descended the mountain and started down the glacier did their wounds stop oozing pus and crust over.

Dudley shook his head feebly but struggled to obey. Half crawling, half being pulled out of the tent, Dudley was hauled to his feet. It had been days since he'd stood, and his blistered feet sent shocks of pain through his legs. He was dizzy from starvation and dehydration. Kikuli quickly tied a rope around his waist and secured it to his own but before he could start down the slope, Dudley fell to the snow in a soft pile. Kikuli barked orders at Kitar and Phinsoo to clean up the worst of the mess in the tent and to start the stove and make Sahib some tea.

Kikuli kneeled by Dudley, urging him to try again.

Perhaps embarrassed that the Sherpas were seeing him in such revolting shape, his pants soiled and his hair, hands, and teeth dirtier than they'd ever been in his life, even on the front lines carrying dead bodies to the camion, Dudley shook his head no. "I need to collect myself. Come back tomorrow. I'll be ready to go down then."

While a proper diagnosis of Dudley's horrific physical and mental state will never be made, he most likely was suffering from cerebral edema, a swelling of the brain which causes confusion, dizziness, and irrational, defiant behavior. While medical experts don't have all the answers as to why it happens, they surmise that it is a combination of the atmospheric pressure, a sodium imbalance in the blood, capillary damage from uneven distribution of blood through the brain, and the body's tendency to store fluid when confronted with the crisis of dehydration. The only cure is immediate descent. Today's climbers know that if a person stricken with cerebral edema is not brought to a lower altitude within hours, he or she will most likely die soon.

While he was not able to medically identify Dudley's condition, Kikuli saw that the gracious sahib was not right and tried again to get him up and to urge him to come with them, *now*. But Dudley again refused. "No. I'll be ready tomorrow. Not now."

Kikuli sat back on his heels. It simply wasn't in his social reference to tell Wolfe Sahib, any sahib, what to do. Servants didn't command the master, even if the sahib was sick and weak and clearly out of his head. Kikuli had no choice; he and the other two Sherpas had left their sleeping bags at Camp VI and they couldn't stay at Camp VII overnight without them. They would have to leave Dudley and come back tomorrow. Handing the wretched man a cup of hot tea and a chapati—a pancake-like flatbread which was a staple for the Sherpas and porters because it was easy to prepare and carry—the three men left, promising to return in the morning to bring Dudley down.

The Sherpas descended to Camp VI where Tsering waited with hot tea. Alarmed that they were alone and without Wolfe Sahib, Tsering sat crouched by the stove making soup while the other three told him the sad story of the sahib and his deplorable condition.

The next day the four men were forced to wait out a twenty-four-hour storm. As the storm battered the tent they sat huddled, discussing how to handle their stubborn, weak sahib at Camp VII. He was obviously sick in the head and too feeble to descend, but they couldn't simply go down without him; there would be too many questions and accusations. They knew all too well how the Sherpas were the first to get blamed during a crisis and the last to get thanked after a victory on big mountains. No, they would go back up when the storm broke and if they weren't able to get Wolfe Sahib moving or if he still refused to come down, Kikuli would get him to sign a note explaining that he wouldn't or couldn't descend. Hopefully that would satisfy the sahibs at base camp.

Finally on July 31, Kikuli, Kitar, and Phinsoo again left Tsering alone in the tent while they roped together and started out across the steep, avalanche-prone slope which had so worried Wiessner a week before.

The only trace of the Sherpas was found fifty-six years later. In 1995, American climber Scott Johnston was walking up the glacier above K2 base camp when he spotted something incongruous sticking out of the ice and rocks. As he neared, he saw that it was what remained of a human torso: bits and pieces of a spine and a pelvis, covered by shards of a blue and white cotton shirt, tattered cotton pants, and desiccated flecks of skin. A threadbare hemp rope was tied at the waist. As with nearly all climbers who fall or are avalanched off K2, the violence of the fall and then the movement through the churning glacier had removed the head from the body. Hoping to identify the remains, Johnston bent and pulled a small black leather wallet out of the pants pocket. It was full of Emperor George V Indian rupee coins, pennies to a Westerner, but hard-earned wages to a Sherpa in 1939.

Chapter 11

Dudley's Vigil

*Although we climbers usually don't admit it, we are always
more or less conscious that the strange and irresistible call of
the mountains is also a call towards the end of life. And for
that very reason we love them all the more, and find their call
more sublime. Our secret heart's desire is that our end should
be in them.*

—ELBRIDGE RAND HERRON

Match case found near Dudley's remains in 2002.
(*Jeff Rhoads*)

The study of high altitude and its effect on man is as old as the mountain sickness first suffered by explorers as they climbed out of the valleys and villages and moved upward toward the summits above. While men started experimenting with the density of air as early as the 1600s, the science of high altitude didn't properly develop until they braved the demons and dragons rumored to live in high mountains and climbed above 10,000 feet for the first time a century later, experiencing headaches, nausea, panting, fatigue, and insomnia. Early scientists believed that 10,000 feet was as high as man could safely go. But as adventurers and naturalists began exploring the mountains of Europe and eventually climbed 15,781-foot Mont Blanc in 1786, they realized humans could survive far above 10,000 feet and possibly go to even greater altitudes. Just how much greater remained a matter of debate for generations to come. By the turn of the twentieth century, balloonists had flown to 28,000 feet, several getting killed in the process because they ascended so quickly that they literally suffocated, but no one believed man could climb on his own feet to those same heights, let alone do it without supplemental oxygen. Simply put, if anyone who lives at sea level is quickly taken to 18,000 feet, he or she will be desperately ill within ten minutes and some will soon grow comatose and die. That same person, taken swiftly from sea level to 25,000 feet, has two minutes of consciousness before lapsing into a coma and dying within the hour.

With modern science, we know that from the moment a climber ascends above 18,000 feet his body is no longer building muscle. Above 22,000 feet, the lack of atmospheric pressure to force oxygenated blood through the circulatory, respiratory, gastrointestinal, and cerebral systems puts the body into mere survival mode. Wounds don't heal, slower circulation threatens hands and feet with frostbite, chronic coughing can break ribs and often produces frothy or pink sputum, lips and fingernails can turn an unsettling blue or gray, thinking is muddled, coordination and balance are compromised, and although the climber feels lethargic and drowsy, restful sleep is nearly impossible. Above 25,000 feet it gets even worse. At that altitude, the body is in a race against death, slowly suffocating from a dangerous lack of oxygen and languid blood flow. Meanwhile, the heart and lungs are pumping furiously, trying to force enough oxygen through the blood to keep the body alive. Unfortunately, this "panting" throws off a lot of carbon dioxide, making the blood very alkaline. The kidneys compensate for the alkalinity by excreting bicarbonate, thus increasing urine production, which robs the body of even more liquids. Soon, the blood thickens to something resembling the consistency of house paint.

All of the body's reactions to high altitude are designed to be short-term emergency measures, but if the climber remains in the highest altitudes without proper nutrients and hydration, the brain shunts blood away from the nonessential systems—skin, legs, arms, intestines, and other "less vital" organs—to keep alive the crucial ones: heart, brain, and lungs. Thus, digestion slows, frostbite looms as tissue dies from lack of oxygen, and kidney function sputters to a near standstill.

Mentally, the climber isn't faring much better. While his heart and lungs are on overdrive, trying to find enough oxygen in the thin air to keep his body alive, his brain is being robbed of the capacity for rational thought. Feeling much like a person with a hellish hangover—headache, nausea, dizziness, and debilitating ennui—the climber in the lethal air above 25,000 feet is stripped of all motivation. Climbers have actually recommended training

for high altitude while suffering a hangover so as to fully antici-
pate the misery that is in their future in the Himalayas. Rest is
the climber's only desire, but it's an illusion; at those altitudes the
body is incapable of rest because it is working so hard to stay alive.

The death zone, as it is known, has earned its name.

Today's climbers know all too well the lethal dangers of remaining above 25,000 feet longer than absolutely necessary, and that
they have to tag the summit and run like hell for their lives. In
1939, Dudley did not know that every minute he spent in the high,
thin air, even at base camp, he was slowly depriving his body of
strength, muscle, and immunity. He just kept climbing. Looking
back with the knowledge gained by seventy years of research and
experience, it is remarkable how far he got, how long he stayed,
and how relatively well he felt.

WHEN DUDLEY was left at Camp VII at 24,700 feet, he had already
spent all but the first week of the expedition above base camp, and
two weeks of that he had spent at 25,300 feet. He couldn't have
known it, but he made history by surviving in that lethally thin air
and ruthless environment longer than any man or woman before
or since.

It was an achievement for which he would pay dearly. Because
no man had been at such heights for such a prolonged period of
time, Dudley was charting new territory, not only on the mountain
but in his body.

After nearly two months on the mountain with inadequate oxygen, food, and water, Dudley's mind, like his body, was shutting
down, and his ability to distinguish reality from fantasy was rapidly fading. Medical experts agree that at best he could have been
only semi-coherent. As he lay in his tent slowly dying, ravaged by

starvation, dehydration, and exposure, the last of his bodily fluids leaked uncontrolled from his bowels. For a fastidious man who never was far from a hot bath and a clean, laundered shirt, his final days lying in his own filth must have been devastating.

Day ran into night and back to day as he waited, his only company the waxing moon above in the ink-black sky. Fritz and Pasang had only been able to leave him what little food they scraped up from the snow at Camp VII and a handful of matches. He had tried to keep the stove lit and the snow melting, but the stove was tough to light and he soon ran out of matches entirely. Again. At some point in his vigil, he badly burned his left hand, further incapacitating him. After that, all he could do was lie in the tent and wait, watching the day turn to night.

Few people have survived protracted exposure to the deadly combination of high altitude, starvation, dehydration, frostbite, and loneliness. The small handful who have did so with damaged hearts, livers, missing limbs, and often palsy, epileptic seizures, memory loss, and an abiding paranoia, most likely caused by the severe hallucinations and fantasies suffered during their hypoxic isolation. They also report having had visions so vivid they spoke, often argued, with their "companions" on the mountain during their long vigil. Regardless of the particulars of their experience, each said their mind often took over, taking them places and bringing them visitors as they slowly lost touch with reality.

Luckily for those who perish on the world's highest mountains, frostbite doesn't hurt as long as the tissue stays frozen. Further, the body is unaware of its fatal slowing, and as the brain shuts down, it allows only for random moments of dreadful clarity. Death by exposure, as death goes, is not as horrific as some, particularly if the climber gives in, lies down, and closes his eyes. But if that climber fights, if he is aware that sleep is death and that hope might mean survival, as the poet Dylan Thomas said, he "rages against the dying of the light" as he waits for something to happen to enable his living. Maybe rescue will come. Maybe the sun will enable movement. Maybe.

WHAT DUDLEY saw and the phantom conversations he had in his last days and hours disappeared with him, but, given other climbers' near-death experiences at the roof of the world, it is not hard to imagine where his brain went as hope of a rescue faded.

Perhaps he replayed his grandfather B. F. Smith's tales of Indians and gold mining and of sleeping atop his wagonloads at night, listening to the wolves and watching the stars. Just as B. F. described the stars above the prairies of Nebraska, those above Dudley were their own extravaganza of light and color, three and four layers deep, like a dark opera house with millions of diamonds suspended from the ceiling on invisible filaments.

Perhaps he thought of the time he had taken his young nephew, Clifford Junior, out on the open water for the first time and given him the helm. He had watched pure, unspeakable joy transform the boy's face as it once had his own when he connected the small movements of the tiller in his hands with the creaking melody of that great ship's turning to starboard or to port, as he willed. Up and down the Maine coast they had sailed that crystalline afternoon, alone together and at peace with the power and grace of the ocean, one among its flock of white-tipped vessels. He had hoped Gwen's young boys, Dudley and Paul Rochester, would fall in love with the ocean too, and he had even directed that part of his inheritance to them be put toward sailing school.

Surely he reconstructed his brief, tumultuous time with Alice, and its not entirely sad ending. He had loved her—her strength, her resolute beliefs, and her iron will. Maybe he chuckled, remembering how he had tried to impress her with his mastery of the slalom style of skiing, not realizing she had taught it to her Olympic protégées. She had generously and gently agreed to his ending the marriage, but it couldn't have been easy for her. She had always been the one to end her relationships. This time Dudley had beaten her to it.

Then there were the men below him at base camp. Although he was old enough to be the father of some of them, he had enjoyed their boisterous energy and how they had laughed at some of his raunchier limericks. He knew that when they first met him they had thought him a pampered old fool out to prove something to the world. But he'd seen their respect grow as he had shouldered loads and kept pace with the best of them, on the ski slopes of Gulmarg and then on K2. He hadn't always been able to carry as much as Jack or Fritz, but he had stayed the course when the others faltered. He had swallowed the pain, lowered his head, and kept going.

It had only been two months since he had first set eyes on the mountain where he now lay. Then, he had felt its power like a great weight in his belly. But after two months on the mountain, perhaps he began to feel its power as a thumping heartbeat far and deep beneath his own, and so long as he felt that rhythmic beat, he knew there was hope of survival.

He lay in his tent, the full moon creating an eerie light through the thick canvas. For a while he had listened to the avalanches thunder down the mountain, each time wondering if this was the one that would take the tent, and him, to the bottom. But after a time, even listening for the avalanches and worrying about their path took too much energy. Then he closed his eyes.

———

THE TIBETANS believe there are eight stages to death. In the first stage, all strength is lost as blood, air, and fire leave the body. The second dries up the nine orifices, causing a terrific thirst. The third brings a cleansing, cool out-breath as the body releases all control over defecation and urination. By the fourth stage, inhalation stops; there is only a constant exhalation. In the last four stages, the mind travels through white, red, and black light, and experiences a series of hallucinations reflective of the person's karma; a peaceful person will have calm, accepting visions while a violent, angry person will experience aggressive attacks. Finally, the breath stops and there is a deep fainting sensation, even a crushing weight, as the body falls deep into the earth. This stage, in which the person appears dead but consciousness and life force have not yet left the body, can take up to several days. Buddhists believe the body must not be tampered with until it has reached actual death. When death occurs, red and white fluids will release from the nostrils and the mind/spirit experiences a clear vacuity: the light of death.

Modern science describes the stages of death in very similar terms, particularly death caused by cerebral edema. Beginning with a headache, the climber soon experiences a loss of coordination (ataxia) and weakness, followed within hours by decreasing levels of consciousness including disorientation, loss of memory, hallucinations, psychotic behavior, and, finally, coma.

When the Sherpas left Dudley, he was somewhere between the third and fourth stages of Tibetan death and between the last two of medical death, those of incontinence, psychotic behavior, and coma. Whether or not he experienced spiritual peace, he was physically released from his struggle soon after he was left alone. His last physical awareness was probably that of being overheated, as the last of the circulating blood rushed to the surface simulating an intense, prickling heat. Many climbers who have died of exposure are found frozen solid but with their clothing stripped off—hat, gloves, parka, even their shirt cast aside in the snow.

The last hours of Dudley Wolfe's life remain unrecorded. What is known is that he was lying in his tent as the last of his constricted blood and air trickled to a stop. And if he had similar experiences to those who have technically died and come back to life to tell about it, his last thoughts and visions were of a warm, serene, welcoming place and he was at peace.

BELOW HIM, Jack and Fritz anxiously watched for any sign that Dudley and the four Sherpas were finally on their way down. But repeatedly, they saw the motion of only three men climbing and descending between Camps VI and VII. What did it mean?

"There are many possibilities . . . Maybe," Fritz faltered, his words fading off. He had no answers but he repeatedly tried to convince Jack that there was "absolutely no reason to be worried." Dudley and the Sherpas would be in base camp within days, he assured Jack. "Not to worry!"

But Jack did worry. Not only was the fate of one of their teammates increasingly dire, he also knew he would be the primary scapegoat for the team's failure, "as obviously someone must [be]." But he had merely been following Tony's orders to strip Camps II and IV. The descending Sherpas had been the ones to strip Camps VI and VII on their own, trying to save the team money. Still, Jack knew he had abandoned his post at Camp II. If he had still been there when the Sherpas descended with their huge loads, he could have easily ordered the supplies back up the mountain. Further adding to his sense of dread was that when the Sherpas finally reached base camp on the 23rd, he hadn't directed any of them to return the equipment to the mountain. He knew he would most likely be blamed for that as well.

While they waited, Jack and Fritz talked about the expedition, the mountain and, mostly, their failure to climb it. They napped, took pictures of flowers at the base of the Southeast Ridge, and ate too much—there was plenty of food in base camp. On July 31 they finally saw Kikuli, Kitar, and Phinsoo leave the tent at Camp VI and head back up the mountain for Dudley. They breathed a small sigh of relief. It shouldn't be long now before everyone was back in camp, they thought.

In Camp VI, Tsering also waited. Kikuli had told him to again have tea and food waiting for their return that afternoon. They would not take any sleeping bags or food with them to Camp VII because the plan was to get Wolfe Sahib and descend immediately. For two days, Tsering kept the tea warm and food ready, but no one returned. Afraid to cross the ice slope above camp alone, he called out for Kikuli, Kitar, and Phinsoo time and again, but no one answered. He searched the mountain for any sign of his friends. There was nothing. He waited, hoping and praying to Buddha. Finally, on August 2, after five days in the tent and sure that his friends could not have survived three days and nights without food or sleeping bags, he headed off the mountain for what he hoped would be the last time.

When he stumbled into base camp that afternoon and told his story, Jack and Fritz immediately ordered him to go back up; there was no one else. Tony and Tendrup had left, Jack had proven time and again he couldn't make it much above Camp II, Fritz was exhausted, Pasang Lama had frostbitten feet, and Dawa was a "whispering dwarf."

Tsering had, in all likelihood, just left three of his "brothers" on the mountain; their disappearance could only mean their deaths.

He was physically exhausted, emotionally drained, and now terrified of the mountain spirits who had swallowed up four members of the team. But Jack would hear none of his "balking" and commanded him and the hoarse Dawa to go up and check out the slope under Camp I for any signs of life, or death, while he and Fritz continued to watch from base camp. The dejected and exhausted Sherpas once again left base camp and headed for the mountain.

Jack and Fritz, still watching through Dudley's field glasses, had decided that if they didn't see any movement from Camp VII by noon, Fritz would have no choice but to head back up the mountain and bring Dudley down himself. Noon came and went. Exhausted, still with only a rasp for a voice, and now worried that he could lose some of his toes to frostbite, Fritz started up the mountain the afternoon of August 3. Almost immediately, it felt like his breath stopped in his throat. While he had hoped to make Camp IV by nightfall, he was unable to get any higher than Camp II. Calling up the mountain in the still night air, he and the Sherpas heard nothing in return.

ON THE MORNING of August 5, another full week since Dudley had been seen alive, the weather began to deteriorate and the first real storm in weeks moved across the mountain. As the first light snow began falling, Fritz declared he was too weak and that he "must not jeopardize my last reserves for the rescue." When the storm cleared days later, Tsering stood outside the tent and made one last call up the mountain.

Silence was the only response.

Finally on August 8, Fritz, Dawa, and Tsering descended the mountain for the last time.

How long Dudley lived at Camp VII will never be known,

but perhaps one of the last things he heard was the faint, far-off sound of Tsering calling up the mountain. Whether Dudley was still alive to hear it or not, the strange and beautiful tongue of the Hindustani language floating up the slope and through his silent tent was the last voice heard on K2 the summer of 1939.

Chapter 12

Coming Home

> *The real measure is the success or failure of the climber to triumph, not over a lifeless mountain, but over himself: the true value of the enterprise lies in the example to others of human motivation and human contact.*
>
> —SIR JOHN HUNT

Heading home through the Suez Canal. *(Courtesy of the Cranmer Collection)*

Their last day at base camp, while Fritz rested, Jack, Dawa, and Tsering made one last trip up the glacier and scoured the mountain with Dudley's field glasses for any sign of an avalanche or fall. Again, there was no sign of disaster, just the endless miles of snow and rock around them. Jack bowed his head and for one of the few times in his life quietly sang a song. It was from a collection of Schumann's *lieder* and it just seemed the right thing to do. He then turned and walked back to base camp. Behind him, the summit of K2 was bathed in the setting sun's golden light.

The following day, August 9, Jack and Fritz, the last members of the 1939 expedition to leave, finally walked away from K2. As they neared the confluence of the Baltoro and Godwin–Austen glaciers at Concordia, ten miles from the mountain, Jack turned and looked back for the last time at what had become a malevolent presence on the horizon. He later wrote, "Bade the old devil adieu—it was dutifully shrouded in clouds befitting the fate of those remaining in its clutches."

From the moment they left base camp, Jack and Fritz both began preparing their versions of what had happened and why they had left four of their men on the mountain. While they were cordial to one another on the long trek home, each later accused the other of expressing a guilty anguish. Jack said Fritz broke into his tent at base camp to read his journal and that once on the trek he kept asking Jack, "What are we going to say? How can we explain it?" Fritz said that when he repeatedly asked Jack why the camps had been stripped, Jack cried in anguish, "Stop it! Stop it! We have talked long enough." Fritz also suggested that Jack had removed the sleeping bags from the camps so that he could take one home and use it as a ploy with women.

Through all of the various accusations which were later lev-
eled, what is clear from the trek out was that Fritz was in appalling
condition, semi-coherent, and suffering fainting spells and fatigue
so extreme that he was forced to curl up on the rocks and take
naps along the way. Jack again stepped up as nursemaid, preparing him meals and often literally holding his hand lest he fall to
the ground.

Interestingly, in Jack's diary covering the twenty days from
Concordia to Srinagar, he never mentions the tragedy or the men
they left behind. Instead he gives great detail of every sumptuous meal he and Fritz ate, including a twelve-egg omelet (while
also noting that Fritz was worried that the Sherpas, whose rations
had been cut for the trek out, would complain to the Himalayan
Club), the joy of smelling grass and flowers again after nearly
three months on ice and rock, and the petty spats between him
and Fritz.

Fritz's diary ends on August 7, the day he called off the rescue
attempt and descended to base camp for the last time. His only
mention of the long trek out was years later, to interviewers and in
notes to the authors of his planned, but never completed, biography. In these instances, Fritz spoke mainly of Jack and his panic,
suggesting that Jack had cared for him "like a baby" because he
was afraid of what Fritz would tell the world of Jack's actions and
inactions on the mountain.

They reached Shigar, the first village with a telegraph station,
on August 18 and sent word to Tony Cromwell, who awaited them
in Srinagar, and the American Alpine Club in New York. Dudley
Wolfe and three Sherpas were dead.

As they approached Srinagar in late August, before time and
circumstance had revised their stories, Fritz and Jack wrote their
official expedition report for the American Alpine Club. In it

they carefully detailed the weather, the team's movement up the mountain, when and where the camps were established, the summit attempt, the descent, the discovery of the deserted Camp VII, and Fritz's retreat down through the stripped camps to base. Of the three-and-a-half-page report, nearly two of the single-spaced, typewritten pages detail Fritz's bid for the summit—the route, the rocks, the overhanging serac, and what he called "the greatest mistake I could have made" in turning around when Pasang refused to climb through the night; it didn't mention any of the problems or the final tragedy. Although Jack thought Fritz had "padded the story to his own fancy," all in all it was a very dry, very thin telling of the expedition's two months on the mountain. Jack and Fritz worked on several revisions before they considered the account finished.

Then Tony Cromwell appeared and all hell broke loose.

When Tony and Joe Trench had left base camp on July 25 and started their long walk out, Tony was still smarting from his last encounter with Fritz and anxious about his own decision to strip Camps II and IV. He knew that it would be Fritz's focus of attack in explaining why he had failed to make the summit, and although Tony had had nothing to do with the Sherpas' decision to clear Camps VI and VII, the fact was he had taken it upon himself to order the lower camps stripped. When he and Joe caught up with Chap and George outside Askole on July 30, they had already rewoven their story. In their version, Fritz was blinkered by summit fever, had refused to bring a hobbled Dudley Wolfe down, and had ordered the Sherpas to rescue him, a rescue for which they were woefully untrained. Most remarkably, in Tony's version of events, it was Jack (rather than himself) who had given the order to strip all the camps. Both George Sheldon and Chap Cranmer wrote in their journals that Tony had told them that "Jack, out of turn," had cleared the camps. George summed up the tragedy, mincing few words: "The blame, as has been said before, lies mostly with Fritz. The great K2 expedition is over and they have lost four men. Fine work."

Tony stayed in Srinagar a month after leaving base camp, anxious to see Fritz and find out what had happened. He learned the worst on August 19 when Fritz's telegram arrived from Shigar: four men were dead. Reeling from the news and anxious about how they would handle the crisis, Tony all but ran to meet Fritz and Jack as they approached Srinagar on the 27th. At first relieved to finally see them, Tony then read a draft of Fritz and Jack's expedition report and exploded, calling it a disgraceful cover-up. Further, he charged that Fritz was fully responsible for the deaths of Dudley Wolfe as well as the three Sherpas, because a rescue of that caliber, without sahibs to assist, was something for which the three Sherpas were clearly not trained.

Jack, always hoping to avoid a confrontation, tried to calm the two warring men, but Tony would not be mollified. He turned on his heel and stormed ahead into Srinagar. Once there, he sat down to write his version of the tragedy to Joel Fisher at the American Alpine Club in New York. Like Fritz and Jack's report, Tony's quickly detailed the weather and camps, but unlike what he told Chap and George, his written report offered no blame or speculation about the leadership or the stripped camps. Tony's report also stated that Fritz, Dudley, and Pasang's near-fatal fall occurred on July 17 during ascent, not on July 22 during descent, and that, after the fall, Dudley was too ill to leave the tents at Camp VIII during the week that Fritz and Pasang went for the summit.

Presumably gleaned from Pasang Lama, Tony's timeline of the accident and Dudley's subsequent illness offer a glimpse into an alternative scenario. Perhaps the fall had happened before Fritz went for the summit, not after he descended, and Dudley was left in Camp VIII because he was incapacitated. If true, Fritz's decision to leave Dudley sick, possibly injured, and alone while he went for the summit was certainly one he would have had a difficult time defending. It's interesting to note that in two major accounts in which Fritz detailed the expedition, he never mentioned the fall. The first was his own original report written with Jack in Srinagar;* the second was a 1969 interview for *Ascent.* Additionally, when Fritz later read Tony's report in New York, he made angry notes in the margin objecting to and correcting many of Tony's assertions, but he made no notes next to Tony's statement that the fall occurred on July 17, versus July 22, his own claimed date. The fact that there are two different timelines for the fall indicates, more than anything, that Fritz's memory of what and exactly when things occurred was severely compromised during his final days on the mountain.

Tony didn't stop with his formal report. He wrote a letter to Fisher with his more personal assessment of the failed expedition, and urged Joe Trench, who was still in Srinagar, to do the same. While Trench's letter was detailed and without any overt accusation, he did cite three failures by Wiessner which he felt contributed to the eventual tragedy. First, because Wiessner was "not very coherent" when he reached base camp on July 24 and as "he kept no diary,"† those in base camp were unclear as to where and when Dudley had been left and in what condition. Second, Wiessner's order to send up three Sherpas to "fetch Wolfe" was

---

* By the time Wiessner submitted his final draft to the American Alpine Club, he had inserted a brief mention of a "fall above Camp VII" but gave no details of how or when it occurred.

† Wiessner kept a log of the movement of the team and its gear on the mountain, but several of the expedition members noted that he didn't keep a diary while on the mountain. The diary he submitted for later perusal was a small flip-style notebook of the same type as his gear logs, with pages ripped out, lost or destroyed, and the dates penciled in. It's impossible to determine if the journal was written at the time of the expedition or later.

"hardly right" because the Sherpas were only high-altitude porters and not trained guides prepared for such a difficult mission. Finally, Trench wrote that if Wiessner had deferred his summit attempt until Camp VIII was fully stocked, "the lives of four first class fellows would not have been needlessly wasted."

Without explaining why, the American consul in Calcutta, Edward Groth, dismissed Trench's report out of hand, deeming it "superficial" to the point of having no credibility. Meanwhile, Tony Cromwell's letter was a scathing, if not libelous, attack in which he accused Fritz of murder. The letter was evidently so incendiary and vindictive that Groth and the British Resident in Kashmir, Lt. Col. D. M. S. Fraser, questioned Cromwell's motives more than the actions of the accused team leader.*

Finally, Lt. Gen. Sir Roger C. Wilson, the president of the Himalayan Club in Srinagar, wrote his own summary, stating that the expedition was "remarkable for the antagonism which developed between the members. Squabbles within parties are not unknown, indeed they are incidental to a prolonged stay at high altitudes, but nothing approaching this one in intensity has ever come to notice. It divided the expedition into hostile factions and even endured after the tragedy, for which, incidentally, it was mainly responsible." Wilson's report was sent to the secretary of state in Washington DC and was filed in the National Archives, but like so many other potentially damaging documents, it disappeared from the American Alpine Club archives.

Whichever account was closest to the truth, the argument was lost in the firestorm that followed; the war had begun, both between the expedition members and out in the world. On September 1,

---

* Like a lot of the original documentation from the expedition and ensuing inquiry, Cromwell's letter either disappeared or was destroyed; either way, it has not been seen publicly for over seventy years.

Germany's Blitzkrieg against Poland began and on September 3, after Hitler ignored an ultimatum to remove his forces, Britain and France declared war on Germany.

While the European powers readied for World War II, the remnants of the 1939 expedition found themselves adrift halfway around the world.

BACK IN NEW YORK, from the moment the American Alpine Club received word that four men on the team had perished, one of them Dudley Wolfe, club officials began circling the wagons; they knew they had a crisis of potentially devastating proportions on their hands. Not only had America suffered its second death in the Himalayas in only ten years,* but the fatality was a man from one of the country's oldest and wealthiest families, a family that would certainly demand answers. Further, the expedition had been led by a man whom many of the club's most august members had refused to join, reportedly because of his volatile temper and autocratic leadership style.

Having received Tony Cromwell's report in late August, and not knowing of the internecine battles brewing on the expedition, the club decided to distribute the account to its membership. Fritz was still in India but he was already under attack.

---

* The first death was E. Francis Farmer, a businessman from Manhattan with no mountain experience who nonetheless set out in 1929 to explore the foothills of Kangchenjunga, the world's third highest mountain and one of its deadliest. He was last spotted by his porters on or near the summit, but he never returned. If he had reached the top and made it back alive, his feat would have changed the course of Himalayan climbing and forever set the standard for ascending an 8,000-meter peak, as he did it alone and without oxygen or support of any kind. It would be another fifty years before a similar feat was recorded at that height in the Himalayas.

On September 4, Groth, the US consul, traveled to Srinagar to interview Fritz Wiessner and Jack Durrance. For seven hours he spoke to the men separately and together about what had happened on the expedition. While Tony and Joe were blaming Fritz and Jack, and Fritz and Jack had obliquely accused Tendrup for starting the rumor that the summit team was dead, once they were faced with Groth's questions about what went wrong, Dudley Wolfe was suddenly no longer the victim. He became their culprit.

In Groth's report, perhaps one of the least self-serving (if a bit xenophobic) of the many reports to follow, he firmly attributed the expedition's overall failure to a "clash of temperaments" due in large part to Fritz's "German bluntness . . . like every German, he is very forceful in giving commands and totally unaware that the abrupt, blunt manner in which the order may have been given might have wounded the feelings of his associates, who in this instance, being Americans, naturally had a different attitude and outlook in matters of this sort." He also examined the financial inequity as a source of conflict: "the general feeling of several of the expedition members was that, as they had borne their share of the expenses and had contributed liberally to the expenses of one or two members unable to pay the entire cost out of their own pockets, they were entitled to have just as much to say about the running of the expedition as the leader." As Jack was the only one who joined at a discounted rate, it would seem that this came from Fritz and was a direct criticism of Dudley Wolfe, a man he called his "brave comrade." Or perhaps it did come from Jack, and was an indication of his resentment and guilt at having been financially sponsored by a man he had then been unwilling or unable to rescue.

In telling Groth of Wolfe's fateful decision to remain at Camp

VII while Fritz and Pasang descended, Fritz insinuated that a sluggish ineptitude was the root of the problem. Groth wrote:

> It appears that Wolfe . . . was not as sure of himself as might have been expected. It also appears that he had a definite tendency to be lazy . . . As the time of the crisis approached, Wolfe, either as a result of the debilitating effect of the altitude, or through sheer laziness, expressed a desire to rest a few days at Camp VII.

The degree to which Jack and Fritz criticized Dudley's "sheer laziness" was interesting, given that while climbing the mountain it was his slow pace and clumsiness mostly on the steeper sections that troubled the men. In fact, in listing what each team member would carry from day to day, Fritz had assigned equal loads to Dudley and Jack.* Further, Jack had only witnessed Dudley's climbing and carrying of loads in the earliest days when the team was still low on the mountain, and then once between Camps V and VI when he himself collapsed. Other than that, Jack and Dudley spent no time together on the mountain.

By the time Groth wrote his report, Tony Cromwell had discredited himself, not only by writing and sending the inflammatory letter to the AAC, but in having left base camp with Wolfe still on the mountain. In fact, Groth seemed to be the only evaluator of the tragedy who publicly narrowed the focus to Cromwell, questioning why he ordered the lower camps stripped and then why he and Jack Durrance did nothing days later when the Sherpas descended with all of the high camps' gear. These actions, Groth felt, were the final and most devastating blows to the expedition.

After his day-long discussion with Groth, Fritz sat down and

---

* Fritz Wiessner's expedition log.

wrote Alice Wolfe a lengthy letter expressing his regret and sorrow. While it spoke of the "dreadful disaster" and how "depressed" he was about not being able to have had a "more active hand in the rescue attempts" of Dudley, his first and foremost regret was in not achieving the summit: "I have never been hit so hard in my life, first to lose the summit which seemed in my hands, and then the terrible realisation of Dudley's and the Sherpas death, and now a war."

Then he began the unhappy work of gathering Dudley's belongings and sending them to the American consulate in Karachi, from which they would be shipped to America. In addition to two locked suitcases full of items Dudley hadn't needed on the mountain (presumably including the tuxedo and gold cufflinks) which he had left in Srinagar, Fritz detailed what he had packed up from Dudley's tent at base camp. Curiously, the list he compiled on September 11, 1939, included a diary, but by the time Dudley's effects were catalogued by the US consul general several months later, the diary was not listed. Given Fritz's earlier curiosity about Jack's diary and his reported breaking into Jack's base camp tent to read it, perhaps Dudley's created just too much temptation for him. Or maybe it simply got lost in the long transit home. Also missing from the final shipment home to Maine were Dudley's movie camera and his final rolls of film from high on the mountain. They were never officially accounted for.

After some worry that transatlantic travel would be curtailed for months because of the war, commerce began to move again by mid-September and Tony Cromwell finally managed to book passage on the USS *Harrison* out of Bombay on September 24. Meanwhile, Fritz was still managing the expedition's last diplomatic affairs and getting Dudley's effects sent home to Boston. Unable to leave as scheduled on the *Harrison*, he flew on a noisy DC-3 to Alexandria the following week, caught up with the boat on October 6, and sailed home from there. One can only imagine the look on Tony's face when he saw Fritz, whom he thought he'd seen the last of in Srinagar, embark in Egypt. It is unknown if the two ever spoke on the boat, although it's possible. Shortly into the weeks-long passage, Fritz was thrown out of bed in rough seas and badly wrenched his back. He spent the rest of the trip in his cabin.

Jack also had been eager to part company with Fritz, but he was evidently not anxious to get home. He lingered for two more months in India and then Europe before finally boarding a ship out of Naples headed for New York on November 26. An interesting and unanswered question is: how did the penurious student pay for it?

IN ST. ANTON, Austria, Alice sat in her small living room and wept rare tears for the man she loved. In her hand she held Fritz's telegram: DUDLEY WITH THREE SHERPAS LOST VICINITY CAMP SEVEN ACCIDENT CAUSE UNKNOWN AS SEVERE CONDITIONS PREVENTED THEIR RECOVERY THIS SEASON STOP DEEPEST SORROW FELT BY ALL STOP.

As she struggled with her warring emotions, she had a small sense of comfort in knowing that at least Dudley would have been proud to die on the mountain. He had been so adamant about going, so sure that this expedition was his destiny, she had felt powerless to even try to talk him out of it. So perhaps it was his destiny and perhaps he was at peace.

He had been such a rare presence in her life, a man who kept her guessing. Yes, he had been reserved, withdrawn even, but always gentle and charming, generous and kind, to her and to everyone who crossed their threshold. Unlike his staid family in Maine, he had relished people with exotic last names and foreign accents, interesting people with stories to tell. He had loved finding his Jewish uncle and cousins in London and sharing their life, so different from his own, so full of music and laughter and lively debate around the dinner table. The Wolfs, as well as his own experiences on the ocean and on the front lines, had opened him to worlds beyond the gated stone walls of Warrenton Park in Maine, and perhaps, she thought, he's happier there, high on that mountain.

That afternoon she sorted through Dudley's letters and postcards, putting them into two piles, one containing more of their personal history than she cared to share, and the other with his more newsy, impersonal letters from the expedition. With tears streaming down her face, she walked to the small stove in the corner of her living room and burned the first stack. She tied the second stack into a bundle and tucked it into her suitcase. She would deliver it to Clifford, Dudley's brother, when she returned to America next month, if she could ever make it out of Austria.

Alice felt Dudley's loss as a great void she could never quite fill. While she soon remarried and lived well into her seventies, years after Dudley's death she wrote Fritz that she was haunted by his memory. "I still think about poor Dudley lying up there in the snow and probably will until I die."

IN LATE AUGUST, Gwen Wolfe Rochester Sharpe arrived at Clifford Lodge, the massive house her grandfather had built overlooking the ocean in Rockport, with her sons, Dudley and Paul, whom she had just picked up from their summer camp down the coast. Young Dudley had particularly loved spending the summer sailing on the *Kestrel*, one of his Uncle Dudley's sloops which he had loaned to the camp for the summer.

As the car rounded the last bend in the long drive in from the main road, young Paul looked at the enormous house appearing over the hillock and exclaimed, "What is that, a hotel?" Indeed, it looked like one with its three stories, great chimneys at either end of the mansard roof, a striped awning on each window, the wrap-around covered porch, and, on the drive, a grand entrance-way through which horse-drawn carriages once delivered guests to the front door.

Clifford Wolfe Smith met them on the top stair of the porch. His face was drawn with sorrow.

"Gwen, I have something terrible to tell you."

She stopped in her tracks, as did the boys, stunned by the heavy grief in his words. They somehow knew what was coming next.

"We've lost Dudley. He's gone."

The boys stood and watched as their mother and their Uncle Clifford embraced and quietly wept on the porch for what seemed like hours, although it was only a few minutes. Then, Gwen turned and took young Dudley's hand and led him up to what was still considered her room in the vast house.

"Please, sit with me, would you?" she asked her eldest son and her brother's namesake. She adored Clifford and had loved the dashing Grafton, but it was her brother Dudley whom she had cherished most. She felt his loss like a physical blow.

Dudley Rochester sat with his mother, not quite knowing what to do or say in the face of this new aspect of her: grieving sister. He was only eleven years old and he remembered his uncle more as a myth than as a man. His mother had always talked about her brother in terms of great adventure and daring exploits. But he loved what he remembered, and, like his mother, he already missed Dudley. He had last seen him the summer before, when his uncle had arrived out of the blue in his two-seater roadster for a visit at their farm in Arlington, Vermont. It had been a fine visit, but all too short; as the larger-than-life man headed back down the driveway the next day, young Dudley stood on the porch wishing he had stayed longer. Beside him, the boy's father said something which struck the ten-year-old as very strange:

"I don't know why, but I think that is the last time we'll ever see him."

It was not like his straightforward father to use such melodramatic words, and the boy never forgot them. He turned back to look down the drive and saw his Uncle Dudley's car disappear around the last bend in a cloud of dust.

Later that month, Gwen and Clifford greeted scores of Dudley's friends, sailing crews, and college classmates at a memorial service in Camden. Without a body to bury, they sat looking at a formal portrait of Dudley draped in black velvet on the altar, remembering the shy smile and gentle power of the man they all loved.

WITHIN THE WEEK, Clifford began his assault. Not knowing what to do with his grief and anger, he turned to the only action he could think of: he started an investigation into why his brother had been left for dead halfway around the world. How did Dudley die? Why was he abandoned on the mountain? Who was with him? Did they die also? Who was in charge and where was he when Dudley was left at the high camp? And why were they not able to bring his body home?

While he waited for the team to return from India, Clifford did his research. He reread every letter the team had written from base camp back to the American Alpine Club, and every one that Dudley had written to him, Gwen, Alice, and his secretary, Henry Meyer. He had the American Alpine Club investigated and its financing and lease in lower Manhattan looked into. He examined Dudley's last will and testament, looking for anything out of kilter. And he learned more about the world of high-altitude mountaineering than he had ever cared to.

Once the expedition members started arriving home, Clifford began scheduling depositions, starting with George Sheldon and Chappell Cranmer, who were the first to return to the States in late September.

After Chap and George had left base camp, they relished every step taken away from the mountain and promised each other that their future climbing would be kept to Wyoming, Colorado, and Canada. After hearing that Dudley had been left sick and weak at Camp VII to await rescue, they both shook their heads, fearing he would never be able to make it down alive. "It's fine to be back," George wrote in Srinagar, "but it's not too good having those other blokes still left out to the mercy of Herr Wiessner." As he and Chap left Bombay for Genoa at the end of August, they received a telegram confirming their worst fears: Dudley and three Sherpas had died. Days later they received another from Jack and Fritz: "WITHHOLD ALL EXPEDITION COMMENT," it warned. Trouble lay ahead for all of them. The firestorm had begun.

On the crossing from Genoa to New York, they struck up a conversation with a handsome, well-dressed woman who lived in both Austria and New York. She asked what they had been up to in Europe, with America on the brink of war. As they began to tell her of the expedition, her face froze. The woman was Alice Wolfe. After she and the men recovered from the shocking coincidence of their meeting, she bought them all a bottle of champagne to share and asked, begged them for every detail they could remember of Dudley and the expedition. George was pleased, and a bit surprised, at how nice she was to them.

Once George was back at Dartmouth, his frostbitten feet completely healed—except for "feeling the cold," as all frostbite victims do—but Chap ended up in the hospital, weak from persistent diarrhea. Given his recent exposure to the remote reaches of the Himalayas, the doctors treated him for dysentery and looked no further. It would be years and many more illnesses before Chap's celiac disease was finally diagnosed.

In early October, Clifford Smith, his attorney, Herbert Connell, and a stenographer traveled to Dartmouth, where they formally deposed George and Chap. Chap arrived forty-five minutes late for the meeting, having been detained in a "Rec"—or Recreation—class. Insulted by what he saw as Chap's rudeness at keeping him waiting for a game of squash, Clifford was brusque with the two young men. For their part, George and Chap "did a good job of saying nothing," as they later reported to Fritz. Apparently unaware that Clifford Smith was in fact Dudley Wolfe's brother, they offered no condolences. Instead, the young men detailed their own climbing resumés and how much climbing they had done without guides, insinuating that Dudley had died because of his inexperience. Clifford wasn't impressed with them, particularly as he knew that both had spent most of the expedition at base camp. Nonetheless, he questioned them about the expedition, its leadership and planning, the trek, the organization, and the team's movement up the mountain. Given that the men had left base camp before the crisis, they could offer little as to what had happened to Dudley and the Sherpas. In closing, Clifford asked them about the ownership of the films, showing them Dudley's letter written from Urdukas about not allowing any member of the expedition access under any circumstances. Chap and George looked at each other and then at Clifford as they handed the letter back to him. Both agreed that until the matter of the ownership was cleared up, they wanted nothing to do with Dudley's remaining films, and Clifford needn't bother to send them copies of the film and negatives.

Clifford returned to New York and deposed Joel Fisher, the treasurer of the American Alpine Club, several days later. He began by asking if the AAC had sponsored the expedition. Perhaps fearing a lawsuit, Fisher lied, telling him that each member had paid his own way and bought his own supplies and that the club was not involved in any of the financing or resulting debt of the expedition. Clifford never learned that the club had advanced the expedition $1,715, most of it to cover Jack's fees, and that the money had been drawn directly from the AAC ledger.

Fritz finally returned to the United States on October 28, only to be met with a letter from his old friend Bill House, urging temperance in his reaction to what was surely going to be a barrage of questions. Having already read Cromwell's letter charging Fritz with murder as well as the early reports out of Srinagar, including Fritz's, House warned his "good friend" to be "exceedingly careful and patient in your explanations of the . . . accident. I think it quite likely that you have rationalized everything that happened and are convinced that everything that was done within your power was right. I don't question this, but an appearance of righteousness is sometimes dangerous . . . No matter how thoroughly convinced you are that your judgments were right please realize that you may have to convince other people and that to convince them you must be patient and understanding."

News of the K2 tragedy was two months old by the time Wiessner disembarked in New York, and many of his enemies had already come out of the woodwork. One man from the Alpine Club of Canada, whom Henry Hall refused to name when he told Fritz of the charge, accused Wiessner of having abandoned a frostbitten

Christine Reid and Elizabeth Knowlton on Mount Robson, the highest mountain in British Columbia, during his descent from the summit the year before. This, like many mountaineering rumors, was unsubstantiated; if anyone had bothered to contact either of the women, they would have learned that Reid in fact blamed herself for gambling with her previously frostbitten feet, and that she considered Wiessner a friend and thought his leadership on Mount Robson had been brilliant.* But no one contacted Reid or Knowlton, so in the midst of the ugly K2 aftermath, the mud stuck.

With his back causing him great pain, and physically and emotionally exhausted by his ordeal, Fritz checked himself into the New York Orthopaedic Hospital on East 58th Street soon after he returned to the city. While he may have considered taking House's advice to remain patient and calm in the coming storm, he barely had time to take even one measured breath before the onslaught began. Within days of his hospital stay, Clifford Smith arrived at Fritz's bedside with Herb Connell and the court stenographer, and for the next several hours they "interrogated the witness," which is exactly how Clifford felt about Wiessner—he was a suspect in a crime, his brother Dudley's abandonment and death.

In the style of courtroom testimony, Connell grilled Fritz on his name, birthright, citizenship, travels to and from Germany, his credentials as a climber, the team, the climb, and finally, the details of his choice to continue down the mountain without Dudley. At one point in the grilling, Connell presented Fritz with a copy of his own expedition report and demanded that he initial each page, "in green ink," so as to confirm that he had read it in their presence. Nearby, Clifford sat taking notes. Fritz was then handed Tony Cromwell's expedition report, a report which the American

---

* Personal correspondence from Reid to Weissner, 1938.

Alpine Club was distributing as the official version, and asked to read it quickly. In quoting Tony's report, Connell asked why Fritz had never mentioned that Dudley was ill at Camp VII. Fritz said that Cromwell had been "depressed" and "that he told several stories which were not correct. Not in a bad way but he just made wrong guesses." Fritz laid the entire blame on Tendrup as being "very bad in his heart, lazy" for telling the rest of the team the summit party was dead so that he could descend the mountain. When asked why Dudley had refused to descend with the Sherpas, Fritz speculated that Dudley had had a "mental breakdown" because of the altitude.

For a German American who had been a citizen less than a year in a country soon to be at war with his homeland, it must have been a frightening two hours. In addition, between Fritz's debt to Dudley and the team's to the AAC for its advances and supplementation of Jack's fees, the expedition and Fritz as its leader owed $3,000 ($45,000 today): a staggering sum, particularly given that Fritz and Jack, the primary figures in the fallout, already lived hand-to-mouth. Achieving the summit of K2 had been Wiessner's one plan for a solvent future.

From Fritz's bedside, Clifford Smith took his entourage immediately to Tony Cromwell's office on Fifth Avenue. As Connell set about his interrogation, Clifford gazed out the window at St. Patrick's Cathedral across the street and listened to Cromwell's version of events. He expected to hear the same volatile anger and accusation which was in the letter Cromwell had written to Fisher at the AAC three months before. But it was as if the plug had been pulled on his rage.*

---

* These and other depositions taken by Clifford Smith and Herbert Connell between October 1939 and February 1940 are quoted verbatim.

Herbert Connell: Do you know of any friction which existed between the members of the expedition?

Tony Cromwell: Exceptionally little.

Q: Was there any between the white members of the expedition and the native guides?

A: None whatsoever.

Q: Any jealousy existing?

A: Not that I noticed; no.

Clifford sat up straight and indicated to Henry he'd like to ask a few questions.

Clifford Smith: This report I have just shown you states that Dudley was sick. How do you know he was sick or otherwise incapacitated?

Cromwell: I have no personal knowledge of that. When I last saw him he was in very good shape.

It was an odd statement, given that Clifford was quoting from Cromwell's own (but unsigned) report, which had been furnished by Joel Fisher at the American Alpine Club. But because Clifford didn't know that Cromwell had written the report, he didn't press the matter. Instead, he wanted to know why Cromwell had left base camp while Dudley was still on the mountain awaiting rescue. It was an excellent question but, like so many others, it was sidestepped and never answered. Instead, Cromwell spoke at length about how the "coolies" had arrived to take the team out on July 22 and he had had to accompany them back down the glacier. What was left unasked was why Cromwell had accused Fritz of murder in August, but now in November was calling him a "first rate mountaineer."

Clifford didn't press Cromwell further, but he returned to Fritz's bedside the next day to ask again about his decision to leave Dudley at Camp VII, particularly given Fritz's stated suspicions that things had gone terribly wrong below him on the mountain.

> *Clifford Smith:* Then, when your suspicions were aroused at Camp 7, if Dudley had insisted on remaining at Camp 7, as leader of the expedition why, on account of these conditions, didn't you forcibly make him descend with you?

No one else, in the entirety of the investigation, asked Fritz this simple question. Like Cromwell when asked why he abandoned base camp, Fritz danced around the question but never answered it.

> *Fritz Wiessner:* When we left Camp 7 we naturally expected food to be at Camp 6,[*] especially as we had left Durrance and the Sherpas there. The whole plan of the thing was to push toward the summit and when a party comes down from the summit they would be in a very tired and bad condition and they would find these camps and would not have to carry anything between camps. And naturally when we were at Camp 7 we expected everything to be at Camp 6.

Still Clifford persisted:

> *Q:* But you say your suspicions were aroused at Camp 7 when you left Dudley?
> *A:* When we came to Camp 7 we just didn't know what was. . . .
> We were distraught.

---

[*] It was another peculiar statement, given that food was not the reason for descending nor did it have any bearing on why he left Dudley at Camp VII. But Smith had no way of knowing the intricacies of the expedition or of Wiessner's fateful descent.

And finally Clifford asked the question that was at the root of the disaster:

> *Q:* Knowing the dangers on the mountain, then why didn't you force Dudley to go down with you even if he wanted to stay at Camp 7?
>
> *A:* We didn't think Camp 6 would be cleared out. We had no explanation for Camp 7.

Although Fritz contradicted himself and didn't address his own concerns about Camp VI being stripped in the face of Camp VII's abandonment, Clifford concluded his questioning. As he and Connell were packing up their papers, Clifford asked Fritz about his $1,300 debt to Dudley, and in what manner he intended to pay it back to the estate. Fritz asked if he could have a year to repay it in $50 monthly installments, and Clifford agreed.

FOR THE NEXT several months Clifford fumed and fussed and busied himself executing Dudley's estate while Fritz, still in his hospital bed, began his own crisis control. With unknown but nonetheless curious reasoning, Fritz decided Dudley's estate should pay the expedition's debt to the American Alpine Club of $1,700 ($25,500 today). He wrote to Tony Cromwell asking that he, as the expedition's treasurer, approach Clifford Smith for the money. Cromwell shot back saying he doubted whether Smith would "feel himself under any obligation to assist in reducing" the debt and that the best bet was to go to the surviving members "pro rata" for the money. But, except for Cranmer and Cromwell, no one had anywhere near that kind of money (for his part, George Sheldon said he agreed that Smith should be asked to pay). Undaunted, Fritz next approached Joel Fisher to ask Smith for the money on behalf of the AAC. Fisher responded that asking for the entire $1,700 was not reasonable, but that he would approach Smith and request that the estate reimburse the $423 ($6,345 today) compensation the club had paid to the families of the deceased Sherpas. Clifford agreed and sent a check for $474, which included the costs of the memorial services, telegrams, and holding the porters at base camp an additional week.

FRITZ HAD ONLY just begun. With Jack still out of the country, he contacted George and Chap at Dartmouth, inquiring as to what they had said and to whom on their trek out, in Srinagar, and since they'd been home. In one phone conversation Fritz became particularly angry and "sounded off" at George for talking to the press when he had still been in India, even though Fritz and Jack had warned him to keep quiet about the expedition. First, George had told the *Times* of India that it had been Fritz who had taken the fall on the icy slope above Camp VII, pulling Pasang and Dudley after him, and, that the fall was stopped by the rope catching on a serac, not by Fritz digging his axe into the ice. George also flippantly described Dudley to the *New York Times* as a "skier, climber and two hundred pounds of love for loud song and great heights." In typical fashion, George shrugged off the scolding, even telling Fritz that the reprimand had been "good for me, you'd be surprised."

After Fritz's exasperated phone call, George began writing an article for the *Saturday Evening Post*, an article which would pay him and the expedition needed dollars to help erase their remaining debt to the American Alpine Club. While wanting to be "clear and accurate," he knew that the expedition, and Fritz in particular, had taken a "terrific shrubbing" and he didn't want to add any fuel to the fire. The article appeared in March 1940 and was clever, detailed, and without a hint of the controversy underlying the disaster; it merely spoke of how their "brave" friend had perished in the pursuit of his dream to climb K2.

In late December, three months after he and Fritz had parted, Jack Durrance finally returned to the United States. Clifford immediately wrote and telegraphed him at Dartmouth, trying to schedule a meeting. Jack also found a stack of messages from Fritz, which he ignored. After a month of avoiding the whole mess, he finally telegraphed Clifford and set up a meeting. On February 7, 1940, Clifford and his attorney again traveled to Hanover. Jack called Chap for support, and the four men met at the Hanover Inn.

From the first moments of the nearly three-hour deposition, Jack indicated that he refused to share what he called his "personal feelings"—about Fritz, his leadership, or the quality of the team as a whole. What he did share was a defiant defensiveness. Clifford watched the young man and couldn't help but feel that he was "excitable" and nervous, and that the tragedy had affected him deeply. But mostly, what Clifford walked away with was a sense that Jack thought more about Jack than anybody else, and that on the expedition, when he was in charge at base camp, he had thought about his own safety and comfort more than either Dudley's or Wiessner's high on the mountain.

While Jack's testimony was guarded and defensive, it is clear that he had not been coached by Fritz before speaking to Clifford and his lawyer. In detailing the expedition he openly blamed the failures, and by implication Dudley's death, on a lack of leadership and communication, both elements clearly in Fritz's domain. Clifford likewise was convinced that a lack of sahibs on the mountain properly instructing the Sherpas led to the severing of the lifeline of supplies between the high camps. He repeatedly asked

Jack why there were not more "white men" in charge on the mountain, and wouldn't it have been better if there were? Jack agreed, but said that it simply wasn't possible.

> *Jack Durrance:* Circumstances had it different. There was no one able. We had been on the mountain too long. No one [at base camp] knew anything about how far they [the summit team] had gone, how they were going to run a summit attempt, because there were no communications.

Clifford then started to ask him what the general plan of the expedition had been, but Jack interrupted, impatient and short.

> *Jack:* I do not know anything about the plans. I didn't know I was going until a Friday and left the next Tuesday, and I never did get the plans.

When Clifford pressed him on Dudley's fitness as a climber, Jack admitted that Dudley was stronger and more suited to altitude than he, but he asserted his belief that Dudley had no business being on the mountain:

> *Jack:* I know he knew he couldn't go alone and depended always on someone to take him on a rope which the rest of the people were able to do themselves . . . I think Dudley's ambitions got away from him.

And finally:

> *Jack:* He was always taken up and Wiessner did it. I think it was a frightful mistake that he went up.

Clifford: You feel that Dudley made up his mind to climb the mountain, come what may?

Jack: I think that exactly.

No matter what did or did not happen on the mountain to cause the tragedy, Jack was Clifford's only witness who actually spoke his truth. George, Chap, and Cromwell all skirted the issue and swallowed their anger and blame, evidently to protect Fritz, and possibly themselves, from a lawsuit. In writing his thoughts on the tragedy to George Trench, Clifford got as close to a reasonable explanation of what happened high on the mountain as anyone ever would: "It might have been that Wiessner came down the mountain for help [with Dudley] rather than to look for further supplies."

In the end, Clifford walked away dissatisfied from his months-long investigation. While he entirely blamed Fritz for the gross negligence that had led to Dudley's abandonment and death, he was without recourse, learning the hard way that Himalayan expeditions are lawless societies because they are totally without objective witnesses. Neither the men nor the altitude allow for rational, clear thought, to say nothing of memory failings weeks and months after the fact. Unless someone is found with a smoking gun or a dripping knife, there are no rules, and while someone's reputation may suffer, no one is ultimately accountable. The only bottom line is the loss of life, but even that is often shrouded in mystery, shame, and, always, a lot of blame.

After the immediate crisis passed, the American Alpine Club had hoped the matter would fade away, but once the conflicting and accusatory reports started coming out of Srinagar from Groth, Wiessner, and Cromwell, and then with Clifford Smith gathering legal testimonies, they realized they too had better pay it some

official attention. In late December the club formed its own committee of inquiry into the "K2 matter." They enlisted five club
stalwarts, including two of Fritz's would-be teammates, Bestor
Robinson and Bill House, who reported that the committee gathered fat folders of oral and written reports from each expedition
member. Oddly, both Jack Durrance and Fritz Wiessner later told
interviewers they had never been contacted by the committee. The
committee also gathered information from the 1938 teammates
and several club members who had climbed with Fritz and could
attest to his personal character. Chief among them was Charlie
Houston, who, upon hearing of his "dear friend" Kikuli's death
and of Fritz's comment about "expecting casualties" on expeditions, immediately and for the rest of his life blamed Fritz personally for the deaths. Houston's implacable censure cast a pall
over the club and began dividing it into factions, pro- and anti-
Fritz. The fact that the country was on the verge of entering its
second world war against Germany was never far from anyone's
mind and it didn't help that rumors persisted that Wiessner was a
Nazi spy. Furthermore, the club was critically aware of Clifford's
looming threat of a wrongful death lawsuit and did everything in
its power to avoid naming names or finding fault. Instead, their
eight-page final analysis, much like Fritz's original report written
in Srinagar, detailed the team's progress up and down the mountain rather than analyzing why it lost four of its members. Citing
Dudley's illness at Camp VII as his reason for not descending,
the report points no fingers of blame or recrimination; rather, it
opaquely suggests that a "weak administration" led to a failure in
communication so that those at base were unaware of the peril
of the summit team above. Years later, Bill House revealed that
the committee focused on two causes for the tragedy: first, that
Wiessner continued his assault on the mountain even after the

team was critically weakened by the loss of Chap, George, and Jack as climbing members, and second, that it considered Jack's stripping of the camps inconceivable and devastating to the safety of the members above him. However, they decided to "back off" publicly blaming Durrance because they considered him to have been mentally compromised by the altitude and not totally responsible for his actions. Above all else, the committee and the club wanted to avoid any dissent which the investigation and growing controversy could start.

Remarkably, in the midst of the club's investigation of what at least one of the team members was calling a murder, the club saw fit to charge the so-called "murdered" man's family his unpaid $15 membership dues for 1939. Clifford Smith once again wrote a check.

Even as "whitewashed" as some club members later claimed the report to be, Fritz immediately filed an objection, writing a sheaf of letters to the committee members, his friends in the club, and renowned climbers all over the world arguing his case—that Dudley was *not* ill when Fritz left him, that he in fact had "insisted" on staying on the mountain for another try at the summit, that Fritz's leadership of the team had been strong, clear, and direct, and that the team failed because the camps had been stripped.

While he previously had been content to place the blame on Tendrup for "fabricating" the story of the summit team's death and taking it upon himself to strip the upper camps, Fritz evidently now decided to take Tony's tack and began blaming Jack for what he called the most egregious error of the entire expedition: the stripping and abandonment of the camps. Fritz even said he had found a note which Jack had left at Camp II stating his goal to clean the mountain of gear (a note which has never been found). What's odd is that it was clearly and inarguably Tony Cromwell who gave the directive to clear the lower camps, not Jack. Why Fritz targeted Jack and not Tony for blame is unknown. But the blame stuck, mostly because Jack Durrance refused to defend himself in the wake of the attack; instead, he withdrew to the mountains of Colorado where he finished medical school, worked, and raised his family for sixty-three years.

On row after row of dusty shelves in a narrow file room at the American Alpine Club reminiscent of the last scene in *Raiders of the Lost Ark*, boxes contain table assignments for the club's annual dinners from the 1920s and 1930s and every letter sent or received by the club president at the time. Yet the entire K2 Committee of Inquiry investigation materials—scores of oral and written accounts, letters, interview notes, phone conversations, everything—are missing from the archives. The official eight-page report remains, but the documentation concerning how the committee reached those conclusions has been lost or destroyed.

IN THE MONTHS after the expedition, while Fritz repeatedly urged others to approach Clifford Smith to pay the expedition's debt, he ignored his own oral agreement with Smith to settle his personal $1,300 debt to Dudley. Finally, in October 1940, Clifford sent Wiessner a letter asking for payment in full. While the money was insignificant to Clifford, he couldn't let Fritz just walk away, neither from Dudley on the mountain nor from his financial debt. Collecting it, however, wouldn't be easy.

After several more months of delays, Fritz sent his first $50 in July 1941. Further months passed with no payments. In responding to Smith's reminders, Wiessner bemoaned his failing business and the poor financial climate, yet at the same time he was writing to Roger Whitney that he would be able to pay his stockholders dividends because of his "very heavy" season. Ironically, given Fritz's ugly speculation that Jack had wanted to have the sleeping bags from the high camps so he could "use them with women," it was Fritz who ended up selling the expedition's bags to those who inquired, one of them to a Miss Selma Jones.

With each of the few sporadic payments he made, Fritz asked Clifford for Dudley's original films and photos, particularly those taken on the mountain.* Incredibly, given his growing hatred of the man, Clifford gave him copies of the negatives and film footage.

In March 1942, the two met in New York, where Fritz asked Clifford if he could settle his remaining $950 bill for just $300, arguing that he had been delayed at great expense for several weeks getting out of India and that Clifford should take that into account. Clifford couldn't quite believe his ears. Hadn't Wiessner's lack of judgment led to Dudley's being left on the mountain in the first place? But after consulting with Gwen, who also wanted to be rid of "this Wiessner person," the family agreed to settle the remaining debt for $500. Another six months later, Fritz paid the estate $250. It was the last payment Clifford Smith received. In two years of monthly letters and reminders from Clifford, Fritz ultimately paid less than half of the $1,300 he owed Dudley.

At the same time Fritz was bemoaning his penury to Clifford, he was actually becoming financially successful for the first time in his life. He was working for the large firm Ultra Chemical— one contract with Sears, Roebuck and Company was reportedly worth $1 million (or $15 million today)—and, in 1942, his ski wax business received an enormous order from the US Army: 600,000 tubes for its 87th Mountain Infantry Battalion, which

---

* While the last rolls of film that Dudley shot disappeared, several shot previously at the lower camps had been taken down the mountain and sent home with the mail runners.

in 1944 became known as the 10th Mountain Division. Not only was the order huge but it was "rush," enabling Fritz to charge the army even more. Fritz later told his biographers that although he was thrilled at the size of the order, he was "shocked" at its size and thought it typical of the wasteful US military because the battalion's 30,000 troops would never be able to use that many tubes.* That year he reported his combined income from the chemical firm and his wax business between $500 and $800 a month ($7,500–$12,000 today).

Unaware of Fritz's windfall, and, thinking that he was trying in vain to get blood from a stone, Clifford ended his vendetta and walked away, hoping never to hear of Fritz Wiessner again.

In closing out Dudley's estate and notifying his beneficiaries, Clifford received many letters of condolence, shock, and thanks. One, from Dudley's Harvard classmate Albert Gould, expressed the emotions of many:

> But how sad it is that he had to leave us! Yet he was doing the thing he liked when the end came, and was filled with the spirit of high adventure. I like to recall the many happy hours I have spent with Dudley ashore and afloat and to think that in his death as in his life he was engaged in manly pursuits which required courage, endurance, and imagination, as well as the ability to endure hardships with a cheerful spirit.

Dudley's friend and sailing colleague John G. Alden wrote, "If there were others more like him, the world would be better off."

———————

* In addition to the wax, the army ordered those same 30,000 troops 150,000 pairs of skis and 200,000 pairs of boots.

THROUGH SETTLING Dudley's estate Clifford came to know his brother more deeply in death than he had in life, and learned of Dudley's remarkable friendships and generosity. In his will, Dudley bequeathed $75,000 to endow a new wing at the Knox County Hospital, $150,000 to Bowdoin College to establish a Smith Fund in his grandfather and great-uncles' names, $25,000 to Harvard, $100,000 and his sloop, the *Highland Light*, to the US Naval Academy, even $25,000 to the Old Sailors' Home in Boston. He also remembered his favorite mountain guides and sea captains, a handful of college buddies, his secretary Henry Meyer, each of his three nephews, and finally his Wolf cousins in London. In the end, even with his share of B. F. Smith's trust left untouched, he gave away most of his personal estate, close to $500,000 ($7.5 million today).

YEARS LATER, in 1983, Wiessner sold Dudley's expedition film footage—the same footage that Dudley had tried to protect forty-four years before—to National Geographic for $440. On the contract, Fritz Wiessner claimed he was the sole owner and rights holder of the film.*

After the firestorm finally died down, Fritz returned to his life: running his business, having his family, and climbing challenging rock walls well into his eighties. During the fifty years after the

---

* Clifford Smith died in 1964 and so he never learned that Wiessner assumed ownership of Dudley's prized films. In addition, there are several expedition photographs which have Wiessner credited as the photographer, many of them high on the mountain. While he may indeed have taken the images, there is no record of his ever having operated a camera during the expedition or, in fact, in his entire life. Further, there seems to have been an agreement among the surviving team members to share the expedition's best photos—including Dudley's—because each of the Cromwell, Durrance, Sheldon, and Cranmer collections all contain photos in which the owner/photographer appears in one of "his" own photos, indicating that someone else took the image. Several of these include photos in which Sheldon, Durrance, and Cranmer all appear; these were most probably taken by Dudley Wolfe, including the one on the cover of this book.

expedition he thought not of Dudley's death and his own part in it but of his lost victory on the summit. While he would admit to his children and some of his climbing partners that he had been physically unable to get the incapacitated Dudley off the mountain, he nonetheless publicly continued to blame others in the disaster, and specifically Jack (but not Tony) for stripping the camps and breaking the lifeline. In 1953 he wrote, "I lost the summit (which was a setup for me) in 1939, through no mistake of mine but through the phantastic [sic] errors made by others . . ."

Chapter 13

The Reckoning

*Whenever found, [Dudley and the Sherpas] will be buried
at the foot of the mountain. [If they are never found] K2 still
remains a greater monument than man could ever build to four
such brave and courageous men.*

—CLIFFORD WARREN SMITH, Dudley Wolfe's brother

Dudley Wolfe standing on the glacier below Broad Peak, K2's
8,000-meter neighbor, on the last day of the 330-mile march into
base camp. *(Courtesy of the George C. Sheldon Family)*

For over sixty years, the puzzle of why Fritz left Dudley and in what condition and why Wolfe and the Sherpas died on K2 developed into one of Himalayan climbing's greatest mysteries. Did the Sherpas reach Dudley and then all four die on their descent? Did the Sherpas regain Camp VII only to find Dudley already dead? Or were the Sherpas killed by an avalanche before they regained Camp VII, leaving Dudley waiting hours, then days, until his body gave out?

While we will never know exactly how long Dudley survived, we know he most likely died alone in his tent, which was eventually brought down to the glacier by a massive avalanche and found sixty-three years later. Because Dudley's skeletal remains were found lying in the debris of a canvas tent and scattered vintage climbing equipment, it is all but certain that he came down in the tent. Otherwise he and his equipment would have been long since separated by the wind, weather, scavenging birds and snow foxes which prowl the area, and the violent freezing, thawing, and churning movement of the glacier. We also know he refused or was unable to descend by the time the three Sherpas reached him. But given his love of solitude and the quiet joy he found in nature, both on the ocean and in the mountains, we can hope that he died at peace. He was where he wanted to be, and from high-altitude experts we know that he gently slipped into a coma as the last of his life forces slowly left his body.

When he finally made it off the mountain, days, weeks, maybe even years later, he was in his tent, surrounded not by the trappings of wealth but by the barest essentials—a Sherpa's thin, filthy sleeping bag several sizes too small for his frame, a cooking pot, and a Primus stove rendered useless by his lack of matches and the strength to get it lit.

K2 REMAINED unvisited for the next fourteen years, as war and then the turbulent partition of India and Pakistan in 1947 closed the area. The first team onto the mountain after 1939 was the third American expedition in 1953, once again led by Charlie Houston. When Houston reached 23,400 feet on the mountain, he found the ruins of the 1939 team's Camp VI, where Tsering had waited in vain for two days for Kikuli, Kitar, and Phinsoo to return: two destroyed tents, sleeping bags rolled into one corner awaiting the three Sherpas who had gone to rescue Dudley, a stove, gasoline, and a small packet of Darjeeling tea wrapped in a handkerchief and tucked under the stove. Another of Houston's 1953 expedition members, Bob Craig, found several letters and rolls of film Dudley had left at Camp V on his ascent. It's unknown if those letters or film ever made it back to his family in Maine. The only remnants of Camp VII ever found were found at the base of the mountain in 2002.

DUDLEY WOLFE's teammates descended from the mountain and came home to their lives and families, but each was marked by that tragic summer.

Jack Durrance never engaged in the dispute over the stripped camps. While Fritz first privately blamed Jack in letters and conversations with the American Alpine Club members and officers, it was not until 1956 that he did so publicly, in an account in *Appalachia* magazine (where his friend Miriam Underhill was the editor). While furious, Durrance never defended himself. And even though he didn't consider himself responsible for the four deaths, he never said so because he "never felt anyone would listen" to him. It was only after Tony Cromwell's death in 1987 and Fritz Wiessner's in 1988 that Jack finally allowed his diary to be released, revealing for the first time that Tony had sent the order to him at Camp II to strip the low camps.

Why Fritz fingered Jack and not Tony, and why Jack accepted the blame, is unknown, but many have speculated that Tony's wealth and standing in the American Alpine Club were the root causes.

Fritz's dogged determination and lobbying of club officials to have his expedition report seen as the official one, as well as Jack's absence from the debate, allowed the blame to rest squarely on Jack's shoulders. While many observers continued to question Fritz's abandonment of Dudley and his oppressive leadership style, his reputation as a gifted climber gathered him a growing fan base within the American Alpine Club, an admiration which persists to this day.

JACK STRUGGLED with demons most of his life, ones that only became more pronounced after the expedition. His girlfriend, Maria, became engaged to another man while Jack was on K2. Heartbroken, he married his climbing buddy's sister somewhat on the rebound, and it was a troubled marriage during which the cultivation of irises became his passion. Several months after his return, he went to see Charlie Houston and for two hours talked nonstop about the expedition. It was perhaps the only time he spoke at such length and detail about the trip. What Charlie remembered most about the evening was how tormented Jack appeared, sitting hunched over, talking hour after hour in a rambling monotone. Always a heavy drinker, after the expedition he became a functioning alcoholic, making it through medical school* and able to maintain a practice, but barely. As a teaching physician at the University of Colorado in Denver, he frequently would take his medical students drinking on what he called the "Red Tour," beginning with red beer at a college pub near the campus, then another at the Red Ram in nearby Georgetown, concluding with a call to their wives from the Red Onion in Aspen. He was a difficult, roving husband and a wildly eccentric father who nicknamed his five children Worm, Bird, Ant, Dee Dee, and Yum Yum, names that they maintain in their middle age. A lover of fast cars, he had a stable of them and well into his eighties he would boast that no one could beat him to the Eisenhower Tunnel, a particularly treacherous section of Interstate 70 west of Denver. When the family drove to Wyoming on vacations, a trip that normally took eight hours would take Jack only four because he drove 100 miles per hour the entire way, thrilling his children and terrifying his wife. Always hating confrontation of any kind, if the children in the back seat began to squabble, Jack would offer them money to stop fighting. He also had a rare Mercedes 300SL gull-wing. When the children were small he would drive them to school and because it had only two seats, the older children would sit on the pontoon fenders wearing goggles to protect their eyes as they navigated through the streets of Denver. He eventually totaled the car, as he did most of his cars. One daughter remembers him driving his Cadillac off the road at full speed to chase rabbits across a field. When he was sixty-five he had a particularly bad automobile accident involving a train and was threatened with forever losing both his driver's and his medical licenses. He quit

---

* Chap Cranmer's family, grateful to Jack for having saved their son's life, paid for his medical education at the Waring Institute at the University of Colorado in Denver.

drinking cold turkey, but it did little to tame his acid tongue and biting wit. Even his closest relatives considered him a "crusty old soul," and his relationship with his children was so complicated and fraught with emotion that none of them wanted to speak at his memorial service.

K2 haunted Jack Durrance, yet he deliberately surrounded himself with its ghosts. His inadequate ski boots, which caused him so much anxiety and pain on the expedition, were tacked to his kitchen wall until the day he died in 2003 of Alzheimer's disease.

CHAPPELL CRANMER, always a quiet man, came home from the mountain and retreated inward, becoming a laconic country minister who never discussed the expedition with his family. In the years that followed, Jack and Chap remained close friends and their children grew up together. But more often than not, Jack would needle Chap about his and George Sheldon's early quitting of base camp, because he had felt abandoned and left alone to deal with Wiessner, the rescue, and the mess that followed. As Jack's harrying of Chap became painful for those who watched, the taciturn pastor would merely sit there, his face growing redder and redder, but he would never respond. Even the Durrance children, who witnessed many incidents of their father's cruel goading of Chap, wondered if Chap didn't secretly hate Jack. Perhaps Chap simply felt he had to take it because in fact he had abandoned his friend and the expedition just when Jack needed him most.

At some point in the years after he returned from the mountain, Chap wrote a telling yet cryptic postscript in his diary:

Someday I must write the whole story as Jack told it to me—the parting above [Camp] VI, Fritz out of his head, etc. Fritz's "diary,"

Tony's departure, Jack's talk with Pasang [Lama], and all the other details Fritz will always deny . . .

He hadn't done so by the time he died in 2000, so his explanation and story died with him. On his memorial is written what his family called his motto: "Preach the gospel always. Use words where necessary."

GEORGE SHELDON, a gifted writer and the team's official chronicler, sold his expedition story to the *Saturday Evening Post* and was working for the *Kansas City Star* when he was drafted into the army during World War II, where he became an espionage expert. He never wrote professionally again. He too never discussed the trip with his children, but both his son and daughter felt a heavy darkness around him whenever the subject came up. He died of lung cancer at his home in Thetford, Vermont, in 1989. He was seventy-one years old.

OLIVER EATON "Tony" Cromwell threatened to resign in protest from the American Alpine Club if it didn't expel Fritz Wiessner for what Tony considered his near-criminal mistakes as the team's leader. The club refused, so Cromwell resigned in 1940 and lived much of the rest of his life in Europe. Years after Cromwell's death in 1987, when asked the whereabouts of the journal he had kept on K2, his grandson replied that "he probably burned it." John E. Cromwell said his grandfather never spoke to him of the expedition, but he said that there was always a sense of "infamy" around his grandfather having decided it was time to "pull up stakes" and order the camps stripped. While Tony Cromwell never faced charges publicly, there remained in his family an impression of shame and possibly guilt for his part in the ill-fated expedition.

PASANG LAMA, the only other witness to Fritz's summit assault and the decision to leave Dudley at Camp VII, was also affected long after the expedition. While he had an obvious wealth of information that could have clarified the story, sadly, few asked him to tell his version. One who did, Sir Edmund Hillary, later remarked to Durrance, "I know more about your expedition to K2 than you do," but the circumstances just then didn't allow him to elaborate and Durrance never followed up.

In a rare interview with Kurt Maix, co-author of *The White Spider* with Heinrich Harrer, Pasang called Wiessner "completely crazy! He want we climb whole night. Climb, climb, climb, and he say 'when dark we at summit.' I never see someone climb like he. I no see nothing—it night. But Wiessner say 'it very bright.' Maybe he see with fingertips. I say 'I go no further.' Crazy. No one climb like he." Maix noted that while Pasang's words were said with real fear of Wiessner's ruthless climbing ethic, they were also said with real admiration for Wiessner's strength and talent. In 1982 and in failing health, Pasang wrote Fritz asking for financial help; Fritz sent him $100.

As FOR Fritz Hannes Wiessner, the brilliant climber but bullheaded leader who had abandoned his last man on the mountain and then pointed a finger of blame at every other person on the team, he came home to a sea of criticism. Like Cromwell, he resigned from the American Alpine Club shortly after its report was released, but after an ardent campaign in 1966 by two club members he was reinstated as an honorary member.

While Wiessner was able to return from K2 and live a productive, active life into his late eighties (he died of a series of strokes in 1988), many closest to him felt he was forever obsessed, not by the tragedy but by his lost chance at the summit—how close he had gotten, and how if he had been given just one more chance, he could have made history. Ironically, given all that we now know about physical and mental deterioration at high altitude and Wiessner's own account of his confusion and exhaustion, if he had found the crampons at Camps VIII or VII that he needed for another stab at the summit, the chances of his dying on descent would have been very high. The lost crampons and the stripping of the camps became his excuse to descend and to do so without the burden of an incapacitated Dudley Wolfe. That chain of events—so disappointing at the time—probably saved his life.

It's doubtful that Wiessner ever had that thought, as he remained forever bitter about his lost summit bid. Of Dudley Wolfe, he almost never spoke again.

The World's Highest Graveyard

Dudley Wolfe's plaque on the Gilkey Memorial. (*Jennifer Jordan / Jeff Rhoads*)

Sixty-three years after he was left to die on the mountain, Dudley Francis Wolfe was finally put to rest at its base. It was a far cry from his beloved rocky coast of Maine or the mountains above Zermatt, but at least he had finally made it down off the mountain.

After our discovery of his skeletal remains, Jeff and I all but ran back to base camp, pulled out the satellite phone, and called Charlie Houston in Vermont.

"Jennifer! Tell me, how is my beautiful K2?"

"Well, it's a different place than when you were here, Charlie. Now it's littered with a lot of expedition garbage, and with those who have died."

I chose my words carefully, painfully aware that the body of Art Gilkey, his 1953 teammate, had only recently been found.*

"Yes, I suppose you're right," he said after a pause, his voice thick with emotion. "I hate to think of K2 that way; when we were there it was pristine and spectacular."

"It's still spectacular, it's just rather depressing. That's why I called," I said, eager to tell him my news. "Charlie, we found Dudley Wolfe. Well, we found his remains."

---

* Gilkey, a handsome, fun-loving member of Charlie's 1953 K2 team, had suddenly been stricken with phlebitis, or blood clots, high on the mountain. A potentially fatal diagnosis at sea level, at 26,000 feet they are a death sentence. Still, Charlie and the team rallied to carry Gilkey down on an improvised stretcher. As they navigated a steep, icy slope below Camp VIII (very close to where Dudley, Fritz, and Pasang had fallen), one of the men slipped, pulling the entire party off their feet. In one of Himalayan climbing's most heroic and miraculous moments, Pete Schoening saw what was happening below him and was able to dig his ice axe into a rock before the weight of five men and a gurney came onto the rope at his waist. Incredibly, he held on, and the rope didn't break. Each man survived, although some, including Charlie, were severely injured. As they picked themselves up, Gilkey in the stretcher was left anchored on the slope while the other men quickly put up a couple of tents to tend to the injured. When they went back to the slope for Gilkey, he was gone, most likely swept off the slope by an avalanche. As the men descended the mountain in the morning, they climbed down through a bloodstained trail—so horrific a scene many had no memory of it until years later. Before they left base camp, they erected a stone monument to Art. The Gilkey Memorial stands to this day and now bears the names of seventy-eight other fallen climbers.

Silence greeted my announcement. I allowed my dear friend time to absorb the news.

"Dudley Wolfe. My God, I haven't thought of him in decades. Where did you find him?"

"On the glacier, about a mile southwest of base camp, almost all the way across the glacier toward Broad Peak."

"It's good he can finally be put to rest." I could hear tears in his voice.

IN THE TRADITION of mountain burials, we hammered a plaque from a tin dinner plate we found in Dudley's wreckage and fastened it to the memorial that, in 2002, held the names of fifty-two lost climbers.* On it we put the words: "Dudley Wolfe—The first man to die on K2, but not the last."

IN RESEARCHING this book, I spent years gathering Dudley's letters, photos, and memorabilia. During this time I had many pleasant conversations and emails with his nephew, Dudley F. Rochester, a retired pulmonary specialist living in Virginia. In one of our exchanges he told me that he had attended an American Lung Association conference in Estes Park, Colorado. At dinner, the conversation turned to high-altitude medicine, given that most of the doctors at the table were struggling with the elevation, having flown in from sea level to the meeting at 7,600 feet. Someone brought up K2, and that it was becoming the deadliest Himalayan peak, and Dr. Dudley Rochester offered, "My uncle died on K2 in 1939."

---

* As of the end of the 2009 climbing season in mid-August, the number of climbers who lost their lives on K2 stood at seventy-eight.

The man to his right slowly turned to face him.

"You're Dudley Wolfe's nephew?"

"Yes, I'm Dudley Rochester," he said, offering the man his hand.

The man looked as if he'd been hit by a hammer. After several moments he took Rochester's hand.

"I'm Jack Durrance," he said.

Rochester, knowing very little of the particulars of the expedition, smiled and told Jack he knew who he was and that it was an honor to meet him.

"I barely knew my uncle," Rochester went on, "but he was always something of a mythical figure in our family, a real adventurer type who just pushed the envelope too far on his last journey."

Durrance seemed to bristle.

"Your uncle died because he was fat and clumsy," Jack said sharply. "He had no business being up there."

Rochester thought the comment was a bit odd, but he had no reason to doubt a man who had been there, so he believed it, and years later repeated it to me as his understanding of how his Uncle Dudley had died on K2.

I told him, gently but firmly, that Dudley Wolfe did not die on K2 because he was fat and clumsy, that in fact no one gets to where Dudley did on that mountain without incredible strength, determination, and skill. Did he need help on the ascent? Yes, many climbers do. Did he find the route difficult, demanding, and in parts terrifying? Yes, many climbers do. Was he, at the end of the day, unable to make it down without help? Yes, many climbers are.

No, I told him, Dudley Wolfe died on K2 because he climbed beyond his ability to get back down, and after two months at those extreme altitudes, he needed someone else to help get him down safely. And those who were there were either beyond their capacity or chose not to try.

Either way, Dudley Wolfe died on K2 because he was left there.

If we deserve nothing else, we deserve to be remembered fairly, for our gifts as well as our faults. But Dudley's written epitaph has been a cartoon of a millionaire out to put his foot on the summit, regardless of the risks. According to his teammates and the expedition's various chroniclers through the years, he was overconfident, clumsy, fat, slow—the adjectives describe a stereotype, not a man. What is most unfair is that they are almost without exception untrue and unearned.

Dudley Wolfe was a kind, gentle, quiet, unassuming, generous, adventurous soul. His family adored him. His women fell in love with him fast and hard. A loner by nature, he didn't surround himself with scores of friends and associates, but those he had were close and real. His hard-as-nails ex-wife begged him for reconciliation, writing him the plaintive love letters of a teenage girl. His army buddies wrote fond reminiscences of their wartime adventures in Rome and Paris; his long-lost uncle sent holiday cards and gifts; and his siblings signed their letters "with love, always."

It was this Dudley Wolfe whom I want history to remember as the first man lost on K2.

Special Thanks

I list the following people in no particular order as each was invaluable as I gathered information about people I had never met, altitudes on K2 I had never reached, prep schools I had never attended, armies in which I had never fought, ski areas I had never schussed, and boats I had never built nor sailed. Writing is indeed a collaborative endeavor and I am indebted to each of the following for making this book as comprehensive and accurate as possible.

THE FAMILIES

Dudley F. Rochester, Cynthia Seefahrt, Joanna Durrance, Charis Durrance, John Durrance, Ada Durrance, Stella Durrance, Polly Wiessner, Andy Wiessner, Jeanie Cranmer Clark, Bruce Cranmer, Betty Cranmer, Allen Cranmer, Forrest Cranmer, Holbrook Mahn Cranmer, George M. Sheldon, Susan Sheldon Cercone, John E. Cromwell, Alisa Storrow, Sidney Howard Urquhart, Maggie Howard, Janice Vaughan Smith Snow, Crocker Snow, Jr., and Zaidee Parkinson

THE MOUNTAINEERS

Charlie Houston, Nazir Sabir, Jeff Rhoads, Jed Williamson, Henry Barber, Steve Roper, Ed Webster, Paul Sibley, Conrad Anker, Hector Ponce de Leon, Ted Wilson, Dee Molenaar, Charley Mace, Annie Whitehouse, Sandy Hill, Charlotte Fox, and Paula Quenemoen Bowman.

THE SAILORS

Tom Kiley and Rye Kiley, Jonathan Webber, John Keyes, George Keyes, Ann Montgomery, and the staff of the Camden Yacht Club.

THE FELLOW RESEARCHERS

Dr. Hans Joachim Maitre, Hannah Townsend, and Kasey Morrison.

And those glorious friends and family who provided a warm bed and delicious meal while on the research trail and those who listened patiently to my theories, stories, updates, and frustrations, on the hiking trail, over endless emails and at the kitchen counter: Alice Webber, Muffy Ferro, Geralyn White Dreyfous, Jenny Mackenzie, Ronna Cohen, Becky Hall and Charley Mace, Chub and Nicole Whitten, Marcie Saganov and Susan McClure, Charlotte Fox, Laura and Paul Bruck, Nancy and Charlie Gear, my editor Star Lawrence, my copyeditor Allegra Huston, my agent Jill Kneerim, and always, patiently, and "with love in his heart," Jeff Rhoads.

Source Materials

UNPUBLISHED DIARIES (each from the family's private collection)

Fritz Hannes Wiessner, Jack Durrance, George C. Sheldon, Chappell Cranmer, and Alice Damrosch Wolfe.

UNPUBLISHED LETTERS

Dudley Francis Wolfe, Alice Damrosch Wolfe, Clifford Wolfe Smith, Gwendolen Wolfe Sharpe, Mabel Smith Wolfe, Marion Smith, Lucien Wolf, Arthur Wolf, Janice Smith Snow, Fritz Hannes Wiessner, Jack Durrance, George C. Sheldon, Chappell Cranmer, Lt. George Trench, Oliver Eaton Cromwell, Henry Hall, Joel Fisher, Walter Wood, Lawrence Coveney, Robert Underhill, Charles Houston, Robert Bates, William House, Bestor Robinson, Al Lindley, Lincoln O'Brien, Lincoln Washburn, Bradford Washburn, Adams Carter, Dr. Hans Kraus, Dr. Hjalmar Schacht, Paul Petzoldt, Major Kenneth Hadow, Roger Whitney, Betty Woolsey, Christine Reid, Rosi Briscoe, Dorothy Dunn, Capt. R.N.D. Frier, E. L. Shute, Percy Olton, Lowell Thomas, Pete Schoening, Galen Rowell, Dee Molenaar, Sterling Hendricks, Yvon Chouinard, Nick Clinch, Hank Coulter, Dr. Karl Maria Herrligkoffer, Dick Burdsall, and Hassler Whitney.

LEGAL DEPOSITIONS

Fritz Hannes Wiessner, Jack Durrance, Oliver Eaton Cromwell, Pasang Lama Sherpa, Dawa Sherpa, George C. Sheldon, Chappell Cranmer, and Joel Fisher.

INTERVIEWS AND CORRESPONDENCE

Charles S. Houston, Gail Bates, Andy Wiessner, Polly Wiessner, Joanna Durrance, Charis Durrance, John Durrance, Jeanie Cranmer Clark, Bruce Cranmer, Forrest Cranmer, Allen Cranmer, Betty Cranmer, Holbrook Mahn, George Sheldon, Susan Sheldon, John E. Cromwell, Bob Craig, Dee Molenaar, Charley Mace, Thomas Hornbein, William Putnam, Bernadette McDonald, Alisa Storrow, Sidney Howard Urquhart, Maggie Howard, Janice Vaughan Smith Snow, Crocker Snow Jr., Zaidee Parkinson, Jed Williamson, Henry Barber, Steve Roper, Ed Webster, Paul Sibley, Conrad Anker, Michael Brown, Ted Wilson, Dr. Peter Hackett, Dr. Colin Grissom Dr. Paul Rock, Dr. Louis Reichardt, Dr. Lorna Moore, Dr. Erik Swenson, and the high altitude research team at NASA.

AMERICAN ALPINE CLUB ARCHIVES

Andrew Kauffman Files, Henry Hall files, the 1938, 1939, and 1953 American K2 Expedition files and with the invaluable assistance of the AAC Library's Beth Heller and Gary Landek.

ALUMNI, HISTORICAL, AND PROFESSIONAL SOURCES

Robert Glatz, Harvard Varsity Club
Barry Kane and Pat Dyer, Faculty of Arts and Sciences, Harvard University
Andrea Bartelstein, Dartmouth College
Suzy Akin, Hackley School, New York
Charlene Swanson, Pomfret Academy, Connecticut
Ruth Quattelbaum and Tim Sprattler, Phillips (Andover) Academy, Massachusetts
Jennifer Neuner, Manlius Pebble Hill School (formerly St. John's School at Manlius)
Todd Knowles, Family History Library, Church of Jesus Christ of Latter-Day Saints, Salt Lake City
Jack Driscoll and Bob Dunn, New England Ski Museum, Franconia, New Hampshire
Gunnar Berg, Institute for Jewish Research, New York

Flora Rodriguez, New York Junior League
Michael Kennedy, *Alpinist* magazine
Matt Samat, *Climbing* magazine
Niels Helleberg, Alden Boat Designs
Dave Graham, Corinthian Yacht Club, Marblehead, Massachusetts
Morten Lund, *Ski* magazine
Ted Hennes, Knollwood Country Club, Elmsford, New York
Union Boat Club, New York
Cannell, Payne and Page, Yacht Builders, Camden, Maine
Diane Shoutis, National Outdoor Leadership School
David Little, historian, 10th Mountain Division Resource Center, Denver
Adriane Hanson, Princeton University Archives

Selected Bibliography

BOOKS

Auerbach, Paul, ed. *Wilderness Medicine*. St. Louis: Mosby Publications, 2001.

Bell, Helen G. *Winning the King's Cup*. New York: G. P. Putnam's Sons, 1928.

Child, Greg. *Thin Air: Encounters in the Himalayas*. Salt Lake City: Peregrine Smith Books, 1988.

Conefrey, Mick, and Tim Jordan. *Mountain Men: Tall Tales and High Adventure*. London: Boxtree, 2002.

Curran, Jim. *K2: The Story of the Savage Mountain*. Seattle: Mountaineers Books, 1995.

Curran, Jim. *K2: Triumph and Tragedy*. Boston: Houghton Mifflin, 1989.

Finletter, Gretchen Damrosch. *From the Top of the Stairs*. Boston: Little, Brown and Company, 1946.

Fuess, Claude M. *Phillips Academy, Andover, in the Great War*. New Haven: Yale University Press, 1919.

Hall, Lincoln. *Dead Lucky: Life after Death on Mount Everest*. Adelaide: Random House, 2007.

Hornbein, Thomas F., and Robert B. Schoene, eds. *High Altitude: An Exploration of Human Adaptation*. New York: Marcel Dekker, 2001.

Houston, Charles S. *Going Higher: The Story of Man and Altitude*. 4th edn. Boston: Little, Brown and Company, 1987.

Houston, Charles S. *Going Higher*. 5th edn. Boston: Little, Brown and Company, 2005.

Houston, Charles S. *High Altitude, Illness and Wellness: The Prevention of a Killer.* Guilford, CT: Globe Pequot Press, 1998.

Houston, Charles, Robert Bates, et al. *Five Miles High.* New York: Dodd, Mead and Company, 1939.

Houston, Charles S., MD, Robert Bates, et al. *K2: The Savage Mountain.* New York: McGraw-Hill Book Company, 1954.

Houston, Charles S., John R. Sutton, and Geoffrey Coates, eds. *Hypoxia and Mountain Medicine: Proceedings of the 7th International Hypoxia Symposium Held at Lake Louise, Canada, 1991.* Oxford: Pergamon Press, 1992.

Isserman, Maurice, and Stewart Weaver. *Fallen Giants: A History of Himalayan Mountaineering from the Age of Empire to the Age of Extremes.* New Haven: Yale University Press, 2008.

Kauffman, Andrew, and William Putnam. *K2: The 1939 Tragedy.* Seattle: Mountaineers Books, 1992.

King, John, and Bradley Mayhew. *Karakoram Highway.* Hawthorn, Australia: Lonely Planet Books, 1989.

Knowlton, Elizabeth. *The Naked Mountain.* New York: G. P. Putnam's Sons, 1933.

Lawrence, Ruth. *Genealogical History of the Smith Family.* New York: National Americana Society, 1932.

Mason, Kenneth. *Abode of Snow.* New York: E. P. Dutton, 1955.

McDonald, Bernadette. *Brotherhood of the Rope: The Biography of Charles Houston.* Seattle: Mountaineers Books, 2007.

Neale, Jonathan. *Tigers of the Snow: How One Fateful Climb Made the Sherpas Mountaineering Legends.* New York: Thomas Dunne Books (St. Martin's Press), 2002.

O'Connell, Nicholas. *Beyond Risk: Conversations with Climbers.* Seattle: Mountaineers Books, 1993.

Potterfield, Peter. *In the Zone: Epic Survival Stories from the Mountaineering World.* Seattle: Mountaineers Books, 1996.

Ridgeway, Rick. *The Last Step: The American Ascent of K2.* Seattle: Mountaineers Books, 1980.

Rowell, Galen. *In the Throne Room of the Mountain Gods.* San Francisco: Sierra Club Books, 1986.

Shipton, Eric. *Blank on the Map.* London: Hodder and Stoughton Limited, 1938.

Smith, Benjamin Franklin. *A Maine Family of Smiths.* Glen Cove, ME: privately published, 1922.

Styles, Showell. *On Top of the World: An Illustrated History of Mountaineering and Mountaineers.* New York: The MacMillan Company, 1967.

Viesturs, Ed, and David Roberts. *K2: Life and Death on the World's Most Dangerous Mountain.* New York: Broadway Books, 2009.

Webster, Edward. *Snow in the Kingdom: My Storm Years on Everest.* Eldorado Springs, CO: Mountain Imagery, 2000.

Whittaker, Jim. *A Life on the Edge: Memoirs of Everest and Beyond.* Seattle: Mountaineers Books, 1999.

Wickwire, Jim, and Dorothy Bullitt. *Addicted to Danger.* New York: Pocket Books, 1998.

Willis, Clint, ed. *High: Stories of Survival from Everest and K2.* New York: Balliett and Fitzgerald, 1999.

ARTICLES, PAMPHLETS, AND PAPERS

"Interview with Fritz Wiessner." *Ascent* 1, no. 3 (May 1969): 15–19.

Cranmer, Chappell, and Fritz Wiessner. "The Second American Expedition to K2." *American Alpine Journal* 4 (1940–42).

Cromwell, Eaton. "Spring Skiing in the Vale of Kashmir." *Appalachia* 23, no. 2 (1940).

Dietz, Thomas. "Altitude Tutorial." International Society for Mountain Medicine, 2001. www.ismmed.org/np_altitude_tutorial.htm.

Dill, D. B., E. H. Christensen, and H. T. Edwards. "Gas Equilibria in the Lungs at High Altitudes." *American Journal of Physiology* 115 (April 1936): 538–8.

Edwards, H. T. "Lactic Acid in Rest and Work at High Altitude." *American Journal of Physiology* 116 (1936).

Grocott, M., et al. "Arterial Blood Gases and Oxygen Content in Climbers on Mount Everest." *New England Journal of Medicine* 360:140 (2009).

Houston, Charles S. "The Effect of Pulmonary Ventilation on Anoxemia." *American Journal of Physiology* 146 (1946): 613–21.

Houston, Charles S., and Richard Riley. "Respiratory and Circulatory Changes During Acclimatization to High Altitude." *American Journal of Physiology* 149 (1947): 563–88.

Pugh, L. G. "Physiological and Medical Aspects of the Himalayan Scientific and Mountaineering Expedition, 1960–1961." *British Medical Journal* 2 (September 8, 1962): 621–7.

Roberts, David. "The K2 Mystery." *Outside* IX, no. 9 (October 1984).

Sheldon, George C. "Lost Behind the Ranges." *Saturday Evening Post* 212, no. 38 (March 16, 1940).

Wiessner, Fritz. "The K2 Expedition of 1939." Translated from the original German. *Appalachia* 31, no. 1 (June 1956).

Zimmerman, Mark D., et al. "Survival." *Annals of Internal Medicine* 127, no. 5 (September 1997).

Index

Note: Page numbers in *italics* refer to illustrations.